ACTION RESEARCH FOR MANAGEMENT

*A Case Report on Research and Action
in Industry*

THE IRWIN-DORSEY SERIES IN
BEHAVIORAL SCIENCE IN BUSINESS

EDITORIAL COMMITTEE

ACTION RESEARCH
FOR MANAGEMENT

A Case Report on

Research and Action in Industry

By WILLIAM FOOTE WHYTE

New York State School of Industrial and Labor Relations
Cornell University

and EDITH LENTZ HAMILTON

Associate Professor, Program in Hospital Administration
School of Public Health, University of Minnesota

With the collaboration of

MEREDITH C. WILEY

Associate Program Specialist, Institute of Industrial Relations
University of California at Los Angeles

1964 • HOMEWOOD, ILLINOIS

RICHARD D. IRWIN, INC., and THE DORSEY PRESS

First Printing, January, 1965

Library of Congress Catalog Card No. 65–12421

ACKNOWLEDGEMENTS

The project here reported was originally part of the research program of the Committee on Human Relations in Industry at the University of Chicago. W. Lloyd Warner was Chairman of the Committee, Burleigh G. Gardner Executive Secretary. Other members of the Committee, in addition to myself, were George Brown, Allison Davis, Frederick Harbison, Robert J. Havighurst, Everett C. Hughes, and Neil Jacoby. I am indebted to the Committee for its sponsorship of and interest in my research activities at the University of Chicago.

A grant from the Foundation for Research in Human Behavior made it possible, after a lapse of years, for Edith Lentz Hamilton and Meredith Wiley to meet with me to plan the book and get it written.

We are indebted to my colleagues at Cornell's New York State School of Industrial and Labor Relations, Leopold Gruenfeld and William Wasmuth, for reading a draft of the book and giving us valuable suggestions.

It was Warren Bennis who urged putting the case into theoretical perspective, and this suggestion led to a substantial revision and expansion of the final chapter. Leopold Gruenfeld was particularly helpful in this theoretical statement.

WILLIAM FOOTE WHYTE
*New York State School of
Industrial and Labor Relations*

CORNELL UNIVERSITY
Ithaca, New York

TABLE OF CONTENTS

INTRODUCTION [1]

In March of 1960, I was a speaker at a meeting of the National Industrial Conference Board under the title of "Latest Developments in Human Relations Research." Before the meeting began, I was approached by a reporter from a national magazine who requested some background regarding the "latest developments" I was about to reveal.

Having secured my consent for the interview, she sat down, opened her notebook and, with pencil poised, asked me what I was going to talk about.

I told her that I was going to report on a project carried out in the years 1945–46. That was all I had a chance to say. At the mention of the date, she unpoised her pencil, closed the notebook, thanked me very much, and walked away.

Her reaction was natural enough. How could a project carried out a decade and a half earlier qualify as a "latest development in human relations research"? Nevertheless, while I did not select the title for the meeting, I could justify the subject of my talk under that general title then as well as now. So far as I know, nothing quite like our "Tremont Hotel Project" had ever been attempted before or since.

What was the project? This was an action-research program for management. We developed a process for applying human relations research findings to the changing of organizational behavior. The word *process* is important, for this was not a one-shot affair. The project involved a continuous gathering and

---

[1] W. F. W.* Initials in first footnote of each chapter indicate the chief chapter author: W. F. W. (William F. Whyte); E. L. H. (Edith Lentz Hamilton); and M. W. (Meredith Wiley).

1

analysis of human relations research data and the feeding of the findings into the organization in such a manner as to change behavior.

o The project also involved development of a new role for the personnel man. He became a specialist in human relations, with the primary responsibility for the application of research findings. o

The project appeared to be successful, in some ways that were measurable and in other ways that may have been equally important but were not subject to measurement.

If the project was both unique and successful, why has it not been reported long before this? There are two main answers to that question, and their relevance changes with time.

Edith Lentz, the field research worker on the project, did write a monograph on *The Tremont Hotel Study* as early as 1947. Had that monograph not been written at that time, the present book could not have been written.

With minor revisions, the Lentz monograph seemed to me—and to others who read it—eminently publishable, and yet we made no effort to publish it. Why not?

As the readers of this book will see, an adequate report of the Tremont project is necessarily an intimate document and not completely disguisable. The Tremont is a fictitious name, but the project was carried out in a hotel, and we could not change the nature of the work setting without taking leave of reality altogether. Had these studies been published shortly after completion of the project, the hotel could have been identified by many people within the hotel industry, and even some of our chief characters could have been so identified. More important still, the members of the Tremont organization could have identified themselves and their associates in the book, and this seemed to us a violation of the pledge of confidentiality we had given them.

We therefore put the monograph aside temporarily—and "temporarily" turned out to be much longer than we had planned.

I should point out that this was a voluntary decision. The contract the University of Chicago held with the Tremont Hotel gave me the right to publish as I saw fit. This was a painful decision to make, but I could see no alternative. Edith Lentz, who had much more at stake than I, did not question that decision.

✓As we put the manuscript aside, we assumed that the passage of time would bring such changes that we could one day publish our report without the risk of serious embarrassment to the individuals involved in it.

How much time had to pass? In effect, that question answered itself as all three of us involved in the project went on to other work so that we had neither the time nor the live interest any more to put the report in publishable form.

The rebirth of the project occurred at the University of California at Los Angeles in early 1960. I had been invited there to speak at their annual conference on personnel research. One of my talks was to deal with problems of applying human relations research to industry. I had prepared some general remarks on this topic.

Before I took off for Los Angeles, I received a telegram from Meredith Wiley, who had been the personnel man in the Tremont project. I had lost track of him in the intervening years, but now he was a management consultant in that city, and he wondered whether we could get together for dinner.

At dinner we talked over old times at the Tremont, reviewing some of the things that had happened when we had worked together and also some of the developments that had taken place during the two years following the termination of research, as Wiley remained at the Tremont as personnel director.

That evening served to rekindle my enthusiasm for the Tremont project. I decided to scrap the general talk I had prepared and instead make the Tremont story the case on which to build all I had to say about applying human relations research to organizations. I invited Wiley to join me at the meeting and to share the platform during the question period.

It is always difficult for a speaker to judge how well his talk is going over, but I had the feeling then that I had never had an audience more absorbed in what I had to say, and the questions thrown at Wiley and me later seemed to justify that impression.

This was essentially the same talk that I gave later at the NICB meeting, where the response seemed equally warm—except for the magazine reporter.

Having brought the Tremont story back to life before these audiences, I could not let it die. I felt now that enough time had passed to cover our obligations to the people involved. In the 15 years since the end of our project, a number of the main characters in our story have either died, retired, or gone on to work elsewhere. The risk of damaging an individual now seems small and the possibilities of contributing to knowledge regarding the research application process look as bright as they did when we finished work at the Tremont.

The Lentz 1947 monograph, now considerably revised by her, has provided the major part of this book. I have added introductory and concluding chapters. Meredith Wiley has reported on developments at the hotel in the period after the research project.

When three people work on a book together, there are bound to be some differences in style and point of view. Rather than try to homogenize the product, I felt it might be helpful to readers to be able to identify the chief author in each chapter and thus have a better understanding of the point of view from which it was written. It is for this reason that identifying initials are placed in a footnote at the beginning of each chapter.

Chapter I

HOW WE BEGAN [1]

The Tremont Hotel project had its inception, fittingly enough, in the Hotel Tremont. It occurred toward the end of my year-long study of human relations in the restaurant industry, financed and sponsored by the National Restaurant Association. As part of the process of letting Association members know that something was going on, I was invited to give talks at regional meetings in several cities. One such talk I gave at the Hotel Tremont, and Mr. Smith, vice-president and general manager of that hotel, was present in the audience.

He told me later that the notion that relations among people could be subjected to study was a completely new idea to him; apparently he was fascinated with it. He persuaded me to stay over an additional day in the city to present my talk to a meeting of the hotel management organization.

Mr. Smith then consulted me about the position of Tremont personnel manager, which was then vacant. Could I recommend a man, trained along the lines of my own work, who would become his next personnel manager? I inquired regarding his recent experiences with men in that position and learned that he had had three men on the job in little more than a year. Apparently it was a rather hazardous job. I told Mr. Smith that I could not in good conscience recommend the job to any student of mine, but I was prepared to make a counterproposal. If

---
[1] W. F. W.

he would accept—and finance—an action-research program under my general direction, I thought I would be able to recommend to him a good potential personnel manager and also to
provide a field research worker. He thought it over, and, in a
subsequent meeting, we worked out the arrangements.

It was in this way that Meredith Wiley came to be personnel
manager of the Tremont Hotel. Edith Lentz assumed the role of
field research worker. Miss Lentz was to be responsible only to
me, but we arranged that she work closely with Wiley and that
he have access to all her notes on interviews and observations,
just as I did. No one else in the hotel was to see these notes, no
matter how curious or how important he might be.

I was to spend one day a month at the Tremont discussing
progress with Miss Lentz and Mr. Wiley, consulting with Mr.
Smith, and talking with other management people either in
meetings or individually. Miss Lentz was to spend two days a
month at the University of Chicago going over progress and
plans with me.

Though the Tremont Hotel put up the money, Miss Lentz
received her paycheck from the University of Chicago. Wiley
was directly on the payroll of the hotel, responsible to Mr.
Smith, with a mandate to develop a new approach to the Tremont personnel program. While I had no direct control over
Wiley and had to take care that Mr. Smith and I did not find
ourselves pulling in opposite directions, Wiley, Miss Lentz, and
I firmly intended to work as closely together as we could in developing this action research program. In fact, we recognized
that unless we could so work together no such program would
develop.

As I look back upon this beginning, I am rather awed by the
nerve we had in undertaking the project at all. Now that I am
a good deal older and perhaps a little wiser, I wonder whether
I would dare to take on an enterprise so uncertain in outcome
when I was equally uncertain in advance as to how I should proceed.

Consider this picture for the three main participants: At the
beginning of the project, I was 31 years old and had had field

research experience in only two industrial settings, the petroleum industry and the restaurant industry. I knew nothing about hotels—except that they had restaurants in them. I had never applied human relations research findings to anything. In my short experience, I had seen no more than one personnel man in action.

Meredith Wiley was then 25, and he was moving into a position where he would outrank many men much older than he. He had studied personnel administration—among other things— but he had had no experience in personnel work, let alone as a director of personnel. Nor did he know anything about hotels.

Edith Lentz came to the project with a background of a number of years of factory experience obtained before she resumed work for her college degree. She had worked with me on the restaurant industry study, beginning as a part-time waitress who kept a work diary and later moving on to a regular research position. While she was then far from the professional she has since become, her experience in field research was probably closer to the responsibilities of her new job than was the case for either Wiley or me.

From the standpoint of Wiley, Lentz, and Whyte, the Tremont Hotel project was in part an adventure story. We began with only a vague idea of what we were doing and learned as we went along. Uncertain as we were, particularly in the early stages, we had to give the hotel staff the impression that we knew what we were doing. While we were trying to find out for ourselves what we were doing, we had to keep up our own spirits on the many occasions when we were puzzled and discouraged.

I have stressed our lack of previous experience in the type of project we were now about to undertake. However, it should not be assumed that we went in completely unarmed, hoping to make our way on a catch-as-catch-can basis. We were armed with certain skills, and we went in with certain reasonably well-founded assumptions as to the problems with which we would have to deal and with certain general strategies of action.

For the purposes of this report, I should present a memorandum, written *before* the project began, telling in general what we might expect to find and, at least in very general terms, what we proposed to do about these problems. Unfortunately, no such memorandum was ever written. We are thus faced with the task of reconstructing our beginning state of mind and trying to keep it from being contaminated by what we learned in the course of the project and in the succeeding years.

While the accuracy of such a retrospective statement cannot be guaranteed, by examining some of the things we learned in the restaurant study which immediately preceded the Tremont project [2] (together with the literature of research familiar to us at the time) we can make some reasonable assumptions as to what we knew in 1945 (before Tremont) and as to the skills we possessed.

The restaurant experience was particularly relevant, since the hotel contained three large restaurants and a soda fountain, and two thirds of the hotel's income was then coming from food and drinks. We could then begin in familiar restaurant territory, without feeling that we were ducking important problem areas.

Judging from our restaurant experiences, and from what we had heard about Mr. Smith, we assumed that the hotel would be managed by rather high-pressure, top-down supervision, with little effective communication coming from the bottom up. Since we had been impressed with the importance of work-flow relations in the restaurant (customer-waitress-service pantry-kitchen, for example), we assumed that the hotel would have an even more complex and sensitive network of lateral relationships and that this area would provide many severe friction points. Our project would involve examining the hierarchy of authority and the networks of lateral relationships and devising a strategy for working on both sets of relationships together in some systematic way.

We assumed that executives at high levels in the organization would have inadequate knowledge and distorted ideas regarding problems existing at the work level. This would come about partly because demands on the executive's time would make it

---

[2] William F. Whyte, *Human Relations in the Restaurant Industry* (New York: McGraw-Hill Book Co., Inc., 1948).

difficult for him to give much attention to any single problem at the work level. Another prime source of distortion we expected to find was in the pattern of communication up and down the hierarchy. Given the existing top-down pressures, we could expect each man to tailor his reports to his boss in terms of his perception of what the boss wanted to hear and in terms of what the subordinate thought would be useful to himself to say. In earlier research, I had found some really fantastic notions about work level problems lodged in the heads of presumably able and certainly well-paid executives. These notions seemed a natural product of the refraction that took place as a story moved up step by step from the bottom to the higher levels.

With direct access to the lower levels of the organization, I had no doubt that concerning human problems, we could gather information that was otherwise inaccessible to men at higher levels. I did not expect that this information would come easily to us. As had been the case in other studies in my experience, I expected that our activities would be met by widespread suspicion and anxiety and that few people would be willing to talk freely with Miss Lentz or Mr. Wiley in the early stages. I believed that they could accept resistance and even hostility as a normal response to strange people and strange new activities and live with those reactions until they were able to work their way through them.

This is, in fact, what happens when a skilled interviewer enters an organization for research purposes. At first people respond to him with superficial generalities, and he takes care not to press them with questions that would require them to commit themselves on sensitive issues. He may tell people that his first task is to understand the jobs in a department and how they fit together. His first questions can be answered entirely in technical terms, but the informant may go on, if he wishes, to volunteer comments about the supervisor, the union, and other sensitive matters. The interviewer counts on building up a certain frequency of interaction with potential informants so that, as they get used to having him around, they begin to test him out with feelings they want to express but hesitate to discuss freely.

If relations in the organization are reasonably harmonious and little tension is felt, informants are likely to open up with little hesitation. If the level of tension and conflict is high, the resistance to the interviewer will at first be high also. On the other hand, the higher the tension, the more important it will be to organization members to be able to talk to someone about their problems. If we played our parts correctly, eventually the dam would break and people would begin to confide in us.

I was therefore confident that we could get the data that were out of reach of the executives. I was also confident that we could analyze the data to better effect than could someone who had not been trained in our field of study. In part, I was counting on a theoretical framework, which, rudimentary though it was, helped us to know what to look for and how to analyze what we found. This is not the place to present that framework,[2] but it may be helpful to point out three of the major ways in which we expected that our approach would differ from that of the executives and supervisors in the hotel.

1. *Moral judgment or explanation?* Based on our experience with other management people, we expected the hotelmen to look at human problems in moral terms. If something went wrong, their question would be: who is to blame? Instead, we would be seeking to explain human events, to discover the pattern in them.

2. *The individual and the group.* In a society which places a great emphasis upon individualism, we expected the hotelmen to seek their explanations of problems through examining the personality and character of particular individuals. While events would sometimes force them to recognize social forces influencing the individual, somehow these forces would be considered illegitimate. They wanted each man to respond to the job situation in terms of his abilities and moral fiber. While we necessarily gathered much of our information through interviewing individuals, we recognized that many of the human problems we would study could more profitably be viewed as group phe-

---

[2] Theoretical ideas are discussed in the final chapter.

nomena. That is, the individuals were not reacting to the job in social isolation. The individuals had their place in a social system. Since we often found individuals occupying the same organizational position reacting similarly, we had a pattern of behavior to observe and explain. Not that it is unimportant to seek to understand individuals. In a concluding chapter, I shall consider the limitations of our emphasis upon group phenomena. Here I am simply noting our initial assumption that a group approach would be more explanatory than would an analysis in terms of individual psychology.

3. *Cause and effect or mutual dependence?* I had noted within management a common tendency to think in rather simple cause-effect terms, at least in the field of human problems. If something went wrong, "the cause" had to be found, and causes tended to be sought right in the immediate situation. As a corollary to this, a given management action was expected to have an effect only in the immediate situation in which the action was taken. We had found management people constantly being surprised at the unintended consequences of their actions. This surprise grew out of their failure to recognize that they were dealing with a social system, made up of mutually dependent parts. Here mutual dependence means that a change introduced at one point in the system will give rise to changes in other parts of the system. The executive will therefore find it useful to abandon search for "the cause," and to broaden his vision so as to see his actions and those of others as fitting into the pattern of a social system of mutually dependent parts.

If we could get the information and make sense out of it, could we transmit it in a useful fashion? If people were to talk freely with us, we had to guarantee them that what they said would be confidential—and we had to keep that promise. This meant that the information we presented had to be general enough to protect our confidences and yet revealing enough to be helpful to management. Here we knew what we were aiming for, but we had to work out the specific techniques in practice.

What actions would we take or recommend in order to solve

the problems we were to find? In detail, that of course depended upon what we found, but we had some general strategies in mind.

To ease downward pressure and to stimulate upward communication, we had great faith in group meetings. We assumed that if the supervisor would call his subordinates together on a regular basis—perhaps once a week—to discuss the problems of the department with them, this could have a constructive effect upon both morale and efficiency. If the meetings were conducted skillfully by the supervisor, the subordinates would have a feeling of catharsis through getting their problems off their chests. While this could be of some importance in itself, particularly in a high tension situation, we recognized that the good effects of opening the upward channel of communication would soon disappear if they were not accompanied by changes in the initiation of activities. We did not believe, as it was then so often said, that good human relations were simply a matter of good communications or of "making the workers feel they are participating." As subordinates participated in these discussions, they would raise complaints and make suggestions. If the supervisor took no action on these complaints and suggestions, the discussions would soon lose their cathartic effects, and the meetings would do management more harm than good. On the other hand, if the supervisor responded to these complaints and suggestions on a reasonably regular basis, changing his own behavior and the organization of activities in his department, then a real change in management would have taken place. Thus the supervisor would be building a problem-solving organization, and the subordinates would feel a real sense of participation in the department.

We knew in a general way how the supervisor should act in order to achieve these results. We were going to have to learn how to get the process started and how to help the supervisor perform in this new leadership role.

We expected also that much of Wiley's efforts toward change would be channeled into consultation with individual supervisors and executives. Here we were not counting on Wiley to tell people what to do. We had great faith—too much faith, as later events disclosed—in the power of the interview. We assumed that if Wiley began by interviewing the supervisor or executive on his problems, this process would have two constructive results. First, the informant would get things off his chest. We felt he would need this catharsis as much as the workers did, and this effect would strengthen his ties with Wiley. Second, the process of being interviewed would help him to clarify his ideas about the human problems of his department. Here Wiley would not be simply a passive listener. His questions would point to aspects of the problem the supervisor might have overlooked.

We did not rule out advice giving altogether. At times we expected that such action would be necessary and desirable. But our aim was to strengthen people in solving their own problems, so Mr. Wiley was to try to help people work through to their own solutions rather than give them his solution.

How would we exercise our power in the organization? We never fully answered that question in advance. We recognized that we necessarily carried great potential influence. Our aim was to change the organization through having people voluntarily decide that the new ways were better. We were not at all sure how this would work out in practice.

As to our relations with the structure of the organization, we had our strategy worked out in these general terms: I would be primarily responsible at first for interpreting the project to Smith and for consulting with him and the other key executives. Wiley would, we hoped, develop relationships such that he could work on problems at all levels of the organization. When the problem in question occurred at a low level, Wiley would try to help the immediate supervisor to solve it instead of reporting the problem to the top. Smith would only receive reports on problems when lower level officials had begun to make progress on them. We expected that this strategy would help us to win the cooperation of the first-line supervisors and of middle managers. But would it satisfy Smith, who was inclined to want to know everything and to get quick results?

Chapter II

THE TREMONT AS WE FOUND IT [1]

What was the setting within which we launched the action-research program?

Some of the problems we faced were typical of the hotel industry at the time. Others were more specific to the Hotel Tremont. We shall begin with the general picture and then describe the specific situation we faced.

LIFE IN THE HOTEL INDUSTRY

Hotels differ from other forms of business organization in several important ways. Production organizations have an impersonal market. Their business success is achieved by standardizing their product, producing efficiently, and selling aggressively. The problems of the market and the problems of production are usually quite distinct.

In a hotel, a different situation prevails. The main product for sale is not a material good but human service and this is very difficult to standardize. One guest who tips well and who knows how to handle people will get top performance while another guest who lacks finesse and cash will get the irreducible minimum.

Any efficiency-minded guest can roam around needling the employees and threatening their job security unless they do things as he requires. Just as one employee can ruin a guest's

[1] E. L. H. and W. F. W.

14

stay with the organization and counteract the most expensive public relations program, so one irritable guest can ruin a good employee's morale by undue criticism or brash treatment.

Favoritism is built into hotel operations. When the house is running close to capacity, it is customary for the top executives to keep some rooms in reserve for last-minute demands from VIPs—or from personal friends. When ordinary mortals are being turned away, the VIPs are accommodated. With such a pattern being set at the top, employees at lower levels, who have personal contacts with the guests, are naturally inclined to give out special favors—in hopes of getting favors in return. The supervisor who seeks to standardize performance finds his department enmeshed in this exchange of favors with guests.

If guests occasionally play the role of supervisor, the reverse is also true. When a supervisor eats in the hotel dining room or attends a civic function in its meeting halls, he cannot relax and enjoy himself as he would in another location. He tends to look around uneasily, notice mistakes, make public criticisms. He is too conscious of the mechanics of things and his awareness makes the employees nervous. We found that the Tremont waitresses would rather wait on almost anyone else than a Tremont "officer."

The hotel industry differs from many others in the interdependence of its departments. While interdependence is commonly found in other industries, there are many cases in which coordination need be achieved only over relatively long time intervals. Between some hotel departments the time requirements for coordination may be measured in minutes or even seconds. For instance, the dining rooms are at a loss without smooth cooperation from the kitchen and even the laundry. If they run out of fresh linens during a busy time of the day, it is just too bad for the service. Similarly, a room clerk cannot house an incoming guest if the maids have been negligent about putting vacated rooms back into order. Yet a maid and a room clerk never meet. Neither do laundry workers meet restaurant workers except in rare instances. Service to the guest is utterly dependent upon coordination among departments.

Hotels also suffer from irregularities in work loads. The restaurants fluctuate between leisurely periods and rush hours. Check-out hour brings lines of guests waiting at the cashiers. Checking in may sometimes be fairly evenly spaced through the day, whereas at other times everyone seems to come in at once. The maid may be delayed in starting her work by a number of late sleeping guests and then be under pressure to have rooms ready for incoming guests. And so it goes. To some extent these fluctuations are predictable and can be planned for, yet some rush hours are more intense than others. Even the best planning cannot entirely relieve the nervous tensions involved in these work fluctuations.

Hotel People

While there are sharp distinctions made by the employees themselves between what are termed the "uniformed" workers and the white-collar ones, we found that they have much in common.

Both "sides of the house" confess to a fondness for moving around. It is a good industry for those who enjoy travel. They can move with that portion of the public which goes south every winter and north each summer. They can visit resorts all over the world and have a considerable chance of finding work anywhere, since the low wage scale causes a perpetual shortage of help. This ease of mobility is a major reason why hotel people lack roots in their community.

Another reason is the 24 hour a day, every day in the week nature of the industry. One front-of-the-house employee emphasized this in discussing the effects of his job.

> In the first place, consider the hours a man works. He doesn't work like normal people; he works nights, mornings, all hours. He works Sundays, holidays. When real people are resting or playing, he has to work. What does that do to a man's personal life? Not only that, it doesn't do a man any good morally. Say he gets out at eleven o'clock at night, he doesn't want to go home and to bed any more than a normal man who quits at five wants to go to bed then. So he goes out to find some fun and where can he

find it at that hour? Another thing, the people he associates with aren't good for him. Ninety percent of the people who come to a hotel come for a good time, and that's the truth. They don't want to work, they want to play. He sees them playing and he wants to play too. So he goes out and what does he do? He drinks! He sees them drinking so he wants to drink too. No wonder hotel people are like they are. They are notoriously unstable, how can they help it? It's the hours and the company they keep.

Other people have acquired fixed ideas about what a hotelman is like. He is one who doesn't show up in church on Sundays. (They don't realize that he has to work Sunday mornings too.) He is one who drinks more than is good for him. He goes about with flashily dressed people. Whole groups of hotel employees are discriminated against when it comes to getting insurance on their lives (bartenders, bellmen, etc.). They can't get financial credit except at exorbitant rates of interest. One bellman remarked:

It's what people think. Now understand, I think the bellmen here are as fine a bunch of men as you can find any place. In any business you can find some bums, naturally, but these fellows are good guys. They are respectable and steady and good guys. They are, but who believes it? A bellman is a bellman to most people. And they take it for granted that he is mixed up with liquor and women. It is silly, but there it is.

We found that the front-of-the-house people frequently enjoyed the glamour and excitement of a big hotel. They would comment that "once you get into this business, nothing else satisfies you." Certainly the ordinary office would seem dull in comparison to the constant show of a big hotel lobby. The association with rich and notable citizens is an attraction for some. And for a bellman, for instance, after being on the right end of the tipping system for a number of years, it would be extremely difficult to adjust to unskilled work in another industry where tips are unknown.

Since hotel jobs seem to set the employees apart from "real people," they are frequently taken by people who already have low social status. This is most true, of course, of those back of the house. There are many such employees who come from the more disparaged race and nationality groups. Some can't speak English well enough to get other work. Others lack the educational background or training necessary for skilled trades. There are many with psychological adjustment problems and physical handicaps. We are speaking now of the unskilled workers, not of the relatively few highly trained ones such as master bakers or engineers.

The majority of employees at the Tremont acted as one might expect such an unstable group to act. A large portion of their income was spent on "status goods." For example, the waitresses were beautifully dressed when in their street clothes. The bellmen bought the most expensive cars. This desire to raise themselves socially by material possessions also kept them in debt to loan sharks and one of the daily griefs of the accounting office was handling garnishments. One might expect hotel people to drink, and drink they did. If you were a front-of-the-house man you might drink Scotch at the beginning of the pay period, cheaper whiskey at the end. At the other end of the hotel social scale you poured into one pitcher the remnants of the customers' drinks and as the evening grew long you drank that. Some snitched canned heat from the hotel storeroom and ate it with a spoon. Nobody drank wine. We never heard of anyone who actually preferred beer. Relaxation wasn't the thing; what was desired was total blackout.

If this sounds lurid, remember that it did not apply to all hotel workers. Some of them were exceptionally hardworking and sober citizens. They worked long hours and under constant tensions, the nature of which will become clearer as this report gets under way. During World War II, these tensions were particularly acute. The constant undersupply of help threw a heavy burden of work upon the employees who were faithful to their jobs.

WHAT WERE THE PROBLEMS?

When we put together the nature of the hotel and the nature of the employees in it, we find

1. A highly personal view of work and relationships, which made the introduction of impersonal, systematic procedures exceptionally difficult.
2. A high level of nervous tensions.

More specifically, the main problems of the Hotel Tremont at the time of the launching of our study can be summed up under five headings:

1. *Labor turnover*. During the preceding 12 months, labor turnover in the hotel had been 250 percent, or slightly over 20 percent per month. There was, of course, a wide range of variation from department to department. In some groups, such as telephone operators, there was hardly any turnover. In other groups, such as dishwashers and miscellaneous kitchen help, the hotel was hard pressed to keep anyone on the job for more than a few days. However the figures might have been explained, it was evident the working force was too unstable to make for efficient operation. The higher turnover was symptomatic of a low level of employee satisfaction. Absenteeism was also a serious problem.

2. *Factional strife*. When Mr. Smith came in to take over as top operating manager of the hotel, he brought with him a number of executives who had served under him in the hotel that he left. These people were widely referred to as "the Sheridan crowd," and those who were not a part of it assumed that this "crowd" had the inside track with Mr. Smith. As we have already pointed out, the hotel is a sensitive organism involving complex interdepartmental relations. We found serious frictions at many points, whether connected or not with "the Sheridan crowd" problem.

3. *Autocratic supervision*. Management's direction was autocratic at the higher levels. Some of this autocratic approach was

observed at lower levels in the organization, but we also found many lower level supervisors who were weak and indecisive, apparently feeling caught between pressures from the top and resistance from the workers. Organizational channels were not observed—at least on the way down.

4. *Unclear lines of authority.* Many people did not know to whom they were responsible. In some cases, two or more people were giving orders—sometimes conflicting—to the same individual.

5. *Union grievances.* It was not so much existence of grievances as the lack of any adequate means of handling them that presented a problem. Stewards in the various departments felt powerless to take action, and therefore the grievances all went to business agents who had responsibilities all over the large city. These men in turn had difficulty in handling problems with hotel personnel, so that often a grievance, after a long delay, would reach the office of the hotel association, where a man who knew very little about the Tremont itself would try to handle it.

Top Management

So far we have described the Tremont and its problems with only incidental reference to top management. As we might expect, the top men had important impacts upon the functioning of the organization, and the success of our project depended in large measure upon our ability to change their behavior. Let us see what it was we had to change.

The Vice-President and General Manager. Mr. Smith, the vice-president and general manager and the top operating executive of the hotel, was a self-made man along the heroic lines of American tradition. He went to work in a hotel as a dishwasher at the age of 14. When we met him, he was in his late thirties and well on the way to the first of the many millions he eventually accumulated.

Smith was a man of vision, but at the time his imagination was devoted largely to schemes for renovating the hotel physically and introducing the most modern equipment. While he had no well-developed personnel ideas of his own at the time we came in, he had been looking for such ideas. In fact, sometime earlier, he had bought a program designed to improve morale. For $100 a month, the hotel received each month a number of copies of a new inspirational poster, accompanied by a little booklet indicating what management might say to employees on the theme of the month. We will never forget one of these posters. It carried a slogan regarding the values of neatness and was addressed particularly to the hotel maids. The model was a beautiful Hollywood star, dressed in a maid's costume, shown in the act of pulling up a silk stocking—way up. (How many maids have you seen who resemble Hollywood stars?)

By the time we came on the scene, Smith had become skeptical of the value of his poster program. Profits continued to be high and personnel problems acute, so he was looking for another new idea. Nor were we to be his last new idea in the personnel field, as we shall see.

We found that in general the managers and supervisors had a tremendous admiration for Smith's ability and enjoyed the feeling of being part of an organization that was so obviously going places, and yet, at the same time, they experienced great difficulties in working under Smith. We later analyzed these problems under the following headings:

1. *Consulting subordinates.* Smith often failed to consult his executives regarding changes affecting them and their work.

2. *Keeping subordinates informed.* Smith often failed to inform his subordinates in advance of important decisions affecting them and their work.

3. *Delegation of authority.* At times Smith stepped in to give orders directly to subordinates two or more levels below him instead of channeling the orders to his immediate subordinate. He also responded freely to members of the so-called Sheridan clique who bypassed their superiors and went directly to him.

4. *Giving personal recognition.* Smith seemed to expect perfection of his subordinates and rarely complimented anybody for anything. A subordinate might at times say to himself that Smith probably thought he was doing a good job because Smith

had not given him hell recently, but this clearly was not an encouraging way of looking at the situation.

5. *Recognition of suggestions.* When he was contemplating changes, Smith sometimes thought to call for suggestions from those immediately involved. However, by the time he decided what to do he appeared to have forgotten all about the suggestions he had been given. He gave no recognition for suggestions accepted and no explanation for suggestions rejected.

6. *Planning for meetings.* Smith had no regular program of meetings with his executives. He might call them into his conference room at any time without advance warning or without any indication of what was to be discussed. If there had been a regular pattern of meetings, it would have become clear to subordinates what matters were likely to be discussed without any advance announcements. As it was, the call for a meeting stirred great apprehension among subordinates, and they went into the conference room neither emotionally nor mentally prepared for whatever Smith wished to discuss.

7. *Protection for the standing of subordinates.* Subordinates had come to expect to be raked over the coals in private and to consider this more or less part of the job. They found it more difficult to face the situation when Smith jumped on them in the presence of other executives. These open reprimands did not happen often, but they seemed to be a constant threat, and it was partly this which made the management meetings an unpleasant experience for the executives.

8. *Handling of group meetings.* Smith acknowledged to us that in his management meetings he had had no success in getting other executives to express their opinions and ideas freely. In addition to the points already covered, we found him expressing his own opinions so strongly that others hesitated to venture any opinions at all.

9. *Communication of orders and ideas.* Sometimes Smith criticized subordinates for failure to follow instructions when the subordinates seemed sincerely convinced that they had not received any such instructions. We interpreted the situation in this way. Smith did not talk over his plans with his subordinates,

and he was often thinking months and even years ahead in the development of his hotel. When he planned steps 2, 3, and 4, he sometimes neglected to issue the order for the first step and was later surprised to find that action had not been taken on it.

10. *The timing of action.* Smith criticized his subordinates for failure to plan ahead, and yet he seemed to us to contribute to this failure. He never really brought them in on the master plan he was developing. He often ordered changes that seemed to conflict with orders he had given earlier, so that his subordinates found it difficult to get any sense of direction. If he had taken them into his confidence on the major plan, perhaps they might have seen some of these apparently conflicting orders fitting into a pattern and so have felt that they had the general guidance necessary to their own planning.

The Resident Manager.   Resident Manager Kraus was a former officer in a European army and a former member of a firm of hotel auditors. With that firm, his job had required him to go around the country, stopping for a week or two at each hotel to go over the financial records and to tell management which people should be fired and what other changes should be made. He had never had the responsibility for carrying through changes. A more inappropriate background for a high management position would be hard to imagine. Furthermore, Kraus was then in his mid-fifties, so we could expect that he would find it difficult to change his approach to organizations.

We found that he spent approximately half of each working day—and he worked a long day—patrolling the hotel. He would issue orders directly to employees right down to the work level. For example, while the chef cursed under his breath in the background, Kraus would taste the soup and tell the cook, "Put more salt in it." We learned also of occasions when he had fired a worker without any consultation with, or notice to, the worker's supervisor. It might sometimes take the supervisor two to three hours to discover whether the worker in question was absent or had been fired.

Kraus believed that unless you read the riot act every now and then to your subordinates, they would not be on their toes doing a good job. He was quite conscientious about reading the riot act.

This description may make Kraus seem like a tough man, and so he did appear to many people, yet others reported that he was a softhearted sentimentalist. This seemed to come out in him particularly in the case of women employees. If a girl who had been fired would come into his office, cry, and tell him about the terrible family responsibilities she was facing, and ask his forgiveness, more than likely he would take her back. But note that this response only followed an open expression of personal dependence on Kraus.

THE DILEMMA WE FACED

While it was apparent to us from the beginning that any substantial changes in human relations in the hotel would necessarily involve important changes in the behavior of Smith and Kraus, at the same time we were in no position to move in on these two top men right at the beginning. We felt that our problem was to get a foothold in some department and begin to show improvements there, with the hope that this would give us the strength to effect improvements at higher levels also. Still, we recognized that it might be difficult or impossible to get things moving constructively at the department level without effecting changes higher up. This was the dilemma we faced as we began our work.

Chapter III

LAUNCHING THE PROJECT[1]

Before we could settle down to work, our project had to be introduced to those with whom we would be working. The introduction process took up much of our time during the first two weeks.

Our first meeting was with top city officials of the hotel and restaurant unions. Since we had worked closely with Chicago union officials on one phase of the restaurant research project, we were able to secure from them a letter of introduction.

After Mr. Whyte had described our project, the president of the Joint Board laughed and made this comment:

> Speaking of human relations reminds me of a guy I knew back in 1925. He was a champion strikebreaker, and he had cards made out for himself that called him a "Human Engineer."

We laughed with him, and, having got this off his chest, he talked with us freely and in a friendly fashion. He and his associates painted a picture of autocratic management at the Tremont and of exceptionally high labor turnover even for a hotel. But one of them tempered his remarks in this way:

> Don't misunderstand us, Smith isn't a bad guy. He's a good businessman, but he could be more successful if he paid more attention to his human relations problem. Maybe you can fix him.

---

[1] E. L. H.

We left with mutual pledges of good will. In the future we would have occasion to wish that other introductions could go as well as this.

Our general introduction to the hotel management was to take place at a meeting conducted by Smith. When we arrived in town, we learned that Smith would not be present at the scheduled meeting time. He was out of town, seeing about buying another hotel; he had left word with Kraus that we should go ahead without him.

This was a serious blow to our morale. It indicated that our project was not nearly so important to Mr. Smith as we had assumed it would be. We would have to compete for his attention with other and sometimes more pressing concerns.

Should we go ahead, or should we wait a day for Smith's return? Mr. Whyte decided—probably unwisely—to go ahead.

Mr. Kraus, who, as we later discovered, had been told next to nothing about our project, now took over the responsibility for launching us. He called together all management people down to first-line supervisor, and we found, to our horror, that we were to meet in the grand ballroom. We were seated on a raised dais, backed by crossed flags, and in front of us sat the department heads and supervisors in row upon row of stiff chairs. Mr. Kraus introduced Mr. Wiley as the new personnel manager and Mr. Whyte tried to explain how Mr. Wiley's position differed from that of most personnel men in that he would be circulating about the organization getting to know people and their problems whereas the usual personnel officer is bogged down with office details. He explained that our main purpose was to see whether we could develop a new type of approach to organizational problems. We had hoped to avoid the term "personnel manager" because we realized the confusion it would cause, and Mr. Whyte explained carefully that since Mr. Wiley would be depending upon the confidence of the entire staff, he would not be in a position to perform such routine personnel duties as arranging transfers, dropping people from the payroll, or any similar task connected with rewards or punishments. If he were to act as judge of people's work, obviously they would not feel free to confide in him concerning their difficulties.

We talked about growth being slow and of our desire to know the people and problems before taking action. Our first problem was how to acquire the essential knowledge in the quickest and most accurate fashion.

Our remarks didn't seem to register. The supervisors seemed to feel that this was something new and big and they waited for spectacular things to start happening. We did our best to convey the idea that our work would be carried on openly and that we welcomed their participation in it, but when they saw no actual changes occurring during those first weeks, they became alarmed and wondered what was going on behind the scenes.

Mr. Kraus also chaired the meetings held for our introduction to the employees, a department at a time. Usually Mr. Wiley would make a short speech on this order:

> It seems to us that if we want to understand your job and to get ideas about how to improve it, the best way to get the information we need is to talk to you. That's what we plan to do. We want to talk to each of you separately and find out what your ideas are concerning the problems you meet in your work and your ideas for any changes which would make it possible for you to do a better job. These conversations with us will be absolutely confidential. We will never mention anyone's name in connection with such matters. What we will do, after talking to the whole group of you, is to pool all of your ideas and then pass along the gist of them to your supervisor and to Mr. Kraus and Mr. Smith in a way which seems most likely to benefit everyone concerned, both management and employees. We will come around and talk to you on the job and we hope you will feel free to drop into our office anytime you feel you want to talk something over with us.

Having made this introduction he would ask for discussion. The employees would look at us, sitting there up front with their supervisor on one side of us and Mr. Kraus on the other, and no one would volunteer a word. Then Mr. Kraus would say gruffly:

> I know you have problems, we all have them, so here is your chance to get them off your chest. All right, don't just sit there! Let's hear somebody say something!

They would grin and we would grin back and say that it was all right, we would talk with individuals later on in a more confidential way. Then several of the employees would speak up on noncommittal topics and the meeting would be over.

If the formal introductions did nothing else, at least they served to acquaint people with our names and faces. We were free to walk about and talk to people at their work and the rank and file employees seemed pleased to see us actually coming around to visit them. We limited these early contacts to noncontroversial discussion about the work they were doing and they would show us around their departments.

CLARIFYING MR. WILEY'S ROLE

A good bit of the first few weeks Mr. Wiley and Miss Lentz spent in the personnel office studying employment records. Each department was analyzed to determine what percentage of new employees it had, what type of background its people came from, and so forth.

It was in the personnel office that our first real difficulties began to appear. Miss Dickson, the secretary, had taken it gracefully when Mr. Smith ordered her out of an inner room (which had higher prestige) and had her things removed to the outer office where applicants waited for interviews. She helped us move into the inner room with every show of good humor. But as time went by and she continued to get all the headaches of the office while we went roaming around visiting people, she was irked and asked, reasonably enough, what we were hired for. Everyone called Mr. Wiley the personnel manager. It didn't make any difference what name we called ourselves. There was no niche for our kind of work, so they used an old one. Even Miss Dickson was embarrassed not to be able to figure out how our work was to fit into her own. Employees, assuming that Mr. Wiley was there for that purpose, were coming to him with problems of vacation pay, grievances, requests for advances on their wages. Supervisors brought him discipline problems. If they came when he was out of the office Miss Dickson didn't know whether to have them come back to see him or to take care of them herself. She finally announced firmly her intention to resign, and Mr. Wiley persuaded her to sit down and explain the nature of her difficulties. In the course of the interview she said, among other things:

> Things are in such a mess around here. I've tried to do the best I could to fix it up, but I'm not a personnel person anyhow. This is the first time I've ever had a job in personnel work. They don't cooperate, Mr. Wiley. I can't do my work. A dozen people stick their noses in here. An applicant will come in and say she filled out an application and left it with "that man." Now how am I supposed to know which of a half dozen people "that man" is? I feel like such a fool!
>
> WILEY: You say things are in a mess?
>
> DICKSON: Yes, everyone does things differently. It depends on the department head. And they don't pay any attention to me, they go around me. I can't get my reports in because I can't get the information from the department heads.

After the long conversation, Miss Dickson felt relieved and returned to work amiably, but it was clear that her problems were real and deep-rooted ones.

When Mr. Whyte came to the hotel just one month after the inauguration of our project, we went over our findings with him, explaining the organization and human relation problems as we had found them. Mr. Smith had just handed Mr. Wiley a list of functions he wanted to see handled by the personnel office, and the list included such things as a magazine for the employees, a recreation program, insurance plans, health and safety campaigns, and so forth. Even he expected a personnel manager! As long as there was no one qualified to carry out necessary personnel functions, it became evident that Mr. Wiley could not escape them.

We decided that the best and simplest thing we could do was to give Mr. Wiley the title of personnel manager and all the traditional responsibility that went with it. In that capacity he could do something positive about straightening out the tangled policies of the office. He could begin to work on organizational problems. There were wage realignments which had to be made if any degree of harmony was to be brought about. Departments would have to be brought into some workable agreement on such matters as vacation policies, overtime pay, etc. This position would not only make such things possible but it would give Mr. Wiley the sort of function that the hotel could understand and respect. He would be working daily with the supervisors and thus could get a realistic knowledge of their habits and techniques of supervision.

It also meant, however, filling Mr. Wiley's day with routine personnel affairs and it will be apparent throughout this report how serious a complication this became. In the first place, it took time he needed for human relations work. Also, it became impossible to keep his human relations functions separate from his official capacity as personnel manager. For example, he would become involved in settling a grievance for an individual employee in a department, and perhaps have to determine policy on leaves of absence from that department. By the time he began work as human relations consultant with the department's supervisor, he might already have prejudiced his claim to impartiality in the eyes of some of the people in this group. At every step, therefore, he had to stop to consider both of his functions.

Time being such an important factor, it was decided that Mr. Wiley would restrict his human relations work to contacts with top management until personnel matters were better under control. This left the rank and file employees to the care of Miss Lentz. She was to study the departments one at a time and report to Mr. Wiley and to Mr. Whyte her analysis of problems and possibilities.

The next day, at a general supervisor's meeting, Mr. Smith announced our decision that Mr. Wiley was to be officially in charge of the personnel office with Miss Dickson reporting to him. Everyone seemed to breathe a sigh of relief. Mr. Whyte, according to our plans drawn up the evening before, led a lively discussion on ways to handle new employees, and this served further to relax the supervisors. The topic was one of general interest, yet it did not cast reflections on any individual among them since it was recognized that all departments could be expected to have trouble in this respect during wartime. Mr. Whyte asked them how the project was going and they reported that there was talk of

"Gestapos." It seemed to us that in relating how a few of their employees were reacting they were working off some of their own latent antagonisms. The project was explained again and Mr. Smith, who had been absent from the meeting at which we were introduced, gave it his hearty backing.

After the meeting, Mr. Kane, the head housekeeper, came to us and said proudly:

> Been taking up my ideas, haven't you? Why my ideas were behind that whole meeting up there, far as I could see. You got the whole thing from what I've been trying to tell you.

While we could not recall just what ideas he was referring to, we welcomed his feeling of participation in the project. From that time on he was friendly. The other supervisors also seemed to warm up after this meeting. At last we were really started.

REORGANIZING PERSONNEL ACTIVITIES

Mr. Wiley was now free to reorganize personnel activities. From the first, Miss Dickson talked freely to us concerning her experiences in the office and her relations with other departments. Our sympathetic audience probably helped somewhat to win her confidence, but what did most to win her loyalty, probably, was Mr. Wiley's defense of her before a supervisors' meeting. Mr. Kraus, typically, jumped on Miss Dickson before the whole group because the overtime payroll was running too heavy and because too many people were employed. She remarked to Miss Lentz later:

> All that talk about overtime, what has that got to do with me? He ought to know by now that I don't handle that. And telling me we have too many people employed here! You know I only hire people when the department heads tell me to. How on earth should I know how many people are needed? (*pause*) Mr. Wiley was awfully nice. He put himself in just enough to hold Kraus back. None of the other managers ever did that for me. Mr. Wiley spoke up a couple of times. I appreciated that. It was just enough to show them that he knew what was going on and I felt he was on my side.

After Mr. Wiley was made the personnel manager, he was able to shield her still more, but since he wanted to be as free as possible from routine personnel duties, he was anxious to build up not only the morale but also the status of his secretary. Obviously she could not handle the office so long as the department heads felt they could push her around. He outlined carefully to Mr. Smith the work he saw immediately ahead for the office and indicated just how much responsibility he planned to delegate to Miss Dickson. He spoke of her potentialities and pointed out her difficulty of handling people of higher status so long as she was classified as a secretary. It took several sessions with him and a careful cultivation of the idea before Mr. Smith consented to give her a slight raise in salary, the title of assistant personnel manager, and one meal a day at the expense of the hotel. The meal was an important feature. All executives had this privilege and it symbolized publicly her new equality with them.

As her status was raised, we began to draw her into our project. She listened sympathetically to our plans. In time she began to interview employees herself, encouraging them to express their ideas about their work. She had always been sympathetic toward their personal problems but like her supervisors she had unconsciously adopted the pattern of autocratic authority when it came to work relationships. Now she typed out her first attempts at employee interviewing and forwarded them to Mr. Whyte in Chicago who was able to compliment her on their quality. She sat in on some of our discussion and planning sessions and continued to lend valuable insight into people and situations.

The personnel records, we found, were in fairly good shape. The big thing was to get policy matters straightened out. Along with working on human relations within the office, Mr. Wiley began an effort to get uniform solutions accepted for such issues as vacation pay, overtime pay, and a multitude of similar matters which had always plagued the office. It was trying work. On vacation pay, for example, varying views were expressed by the resident and general managers and the Hotel Association. Through persistent discussion, Mr. Wiley would get them to come to a decision on one case which was more or less acceptable to all of them.

Then the next case he would argue on the basis of this precedent. It became understood that the Tremont would no longer decide one way in one case and the opposite in the next.

Relations with Top Management

For the most part, the attitude of top management was one of watchful waiting. Mr. Smith, as the initiator of our project, was inclined to favor us. During these early months he had little to say to us directly but we were conscious of his moral support.

Our main problem with Mr. Smith at this stage was his impatience and his tendency to push Mr. Wiley toward personnel activities he had read about in a book. If Wiley had indeed responded to Mr. Smith's suggestions regarding an employee magazine, a recreation program, and all the rest, he would have had no time for the human relations functions that were the heart of our project. It was one of Mr. Whyte's most important contributions that he was able to curb Mr. Smith's impatience, assure him that progress was being made even before it showed, and sidetrack his demands for more and better personnel programs. Mr. Whyte agreed that the functions Mr. Smith had proposed were all "good things," but he argued that they could not be carried out until our project was at a much more advanced stage of development.

Mr. Kraus was inclined to view us with suspicion. Mr. Wiley tried to win his good will by drawing him out in nondirective interview fashion, but it didn't work. He wouldn't talk. He not only wouldn't talk to us on business matters, he wouldn't talk on anything. When he wanted something done in our office he would phone Miss Dickson and have her come up to his office.

Grievance Handling

Mr. Wiley found himself listening to grievance after grievance. The first ones were called forcibly to his attention by the supervisors. Their attitude was, "Well, you're personnel manager, what are you going to do about it?" Mr. Wiley would listen to each case and try to establish clearly just where his jurisdiction stopped and the supervisor's started. Wherever possible, his technique was to bring the most important elements out into the open and then

to sit back and let the two opposing parties reach their own conclusions, often sitting in his office and arguing it out in front of
him as before an impartial witness.

For example, there was the case of the fired elevator girl. The
first we knew of her trouble was when she came crying into our
office.

> It's about my job. I was sick last night and I guess Pete thought
> I had walked out on him, but I hadn't. I was upstairs in the dressing
> room until ten o'clock. Then I went to go home and found my card
> wasn't in the rack anymore. Has he fired me or what?

It was the custom around the Tremont at that time to pull a
person's card out of the rack as a sign to him that his services
weren't wanted. Since timecards were also missing occasionally
due to negligence on the part of the payroll clerk, it wasn't a very
good signal. Employees were frequently coming up to our office,
their faces white, to inquire whether or not they were still working for the hotel. Mr. Wiley invited her to sit down and tell her
story.

> You see, I've been getting my divorce and this was the last day
> of the trial. I didn't know how long it would take, you know how
> these things can be. The judge takes his own time, you can't very
> well hurry him. So I asked Pete if I could be off today and he said
> no I couldn't. He said it so short—I know he didn't mean it, but he
> can be so short sometimes. I don't know whether he understood the
> circumstances, but it didn't seem fair. . . . Gee, here I got my di-
> vorce and I got seven dollars a week for my little girl and now I
> haven't got a job!

The interview suggested that Pete may have been in complete
ignorance of the true situation. She hadn't told him she was leaving the post but simply told the other girls. Pete was brought into
the office separately and the situation explained to him. He agreed
to sit down with the elevator girl in Mr. Wiley's office and talk
it over. The story, when both sides were told, appeared in a new
light. It happened that several days earlier he had been in sore need
of an elevator girl but Lillian had refused to work overtime to help
him out. When she came around asking for a day off, he didn't

give her a chance to explain why she needed one but curtly refused her and walked away. She became so upset by this that after an hour or so she was unable to operate her car and so retreated to the dressing room. Pete, still not knowing the reasons behind her behavior, had assumed this was an act of petulance and had "pulled" her timecard. The session in Mr. Wiley's office wasn't long. There was time enough to say the necessary things; for the supervisor to "save face" by scolding Lillian for not cooperating with him and pointing out how noncooperation breeds noncooperation on the part of others. Then he said, "Well, I'll tell you, I'll take you back." After she had gone, he turned to Mr. Wiley and said, "I think that was the thing to do, don't you?" He repeated the remark three or four times later that day, each time he met one of us in the lobby.

Mr. Wiley had tried not to give Pete the feeling that he was being pushed into anything, that the decision was his own. However, a few days later he came into our office apologizing for letting another employee go before we even knew that trouble was brewing there. It turned out that Pete had every reason to dismiss this particular man. We had to reassure some supervisors that we weren't necessarily pro-employee, that the personnel office wasn't a court before which they had to plead. As in other aspects of the project, we found that what we said here didn't have much effect. It took a long acquaintance with us and our ways before they came to feel secure with us.

As for the rank and file employees, their initial timidity toward us wore off gradually as people like Lillian went back to them with stories of Mr. Wiley's helpfulness. Where at first it was mainly the supervisors who came to us with problems, before long the initiative seemed to change hands and it was the employees who came bringing the tales of woe.

With people coming up with problems, it wasn't long before the question of union grievances came to a head. The union steward in the hotel laundry was the first to bring the matter up.

Why can't we come to you when we have a grievance for little things like a girl not paying her dues or something; I think little problems we could solve ourselves. I'm the shop steward but I can't see this running to the union all the time.

It wasn't so strange that this girl felt the need of some backing closer than the union hall. Her supervisor was openly antiunion, and, when workers refused to fulfill their union obligations, the steward was placed in an embarrassing position until the business agent found the time to take the case over.

Shortly after the above conversation took place, the laundry union's business agent came in about another case. Mr. Wiley had the man talk to Mr. Whyte who happened to be in town on one of his periodic visits. In a short time, the agent was explaining the basic problems of union–management relations at the Tremont:

Mr. Wiley seems to be a very fine type man, but I want to ask you, professor, what is the use of a personnel manager if he don't handle grievances? Now take this case that I've been working on. We've got a man sixty-five years old working in the laundry here. The supervisor takes him off the wringer job [a highly skilled task and hence one with prestige] and puts him to work cleaning up. Well, this man has worked here for two years and we got seniority provisions and all that in the contract. It isn't right for her to change him around like that without giving him consideration. The man wouldn't stand for it so he quits his job and he comes to the union. Either we should put him back to work on the wringer job or get him a week's pay.

I go back to the supervisor and she says he ain't entitled to nothing because he quit without notice. But I say that the man was a wringerman and she had no right to change his job like that. Now I don't know just what we should do in a case like this. If they come to us and tell us that a man isn't capable of doing the work, he's too old or something like that, then we're willing to go along with them and try to persuade the man to change or take a week's notice. But in this case we didn't get the opportunity to do that so now I have to push the case.

I told it to Mr. Wiley, not that I thought he could do anything about it. Then I went up to Smith and he said he didn't know anything about it so he refers me to O'Brien. He's the man who handles labor relations for the Hotel Association, you know, but that man has hundreds of places he has to take care of and a lot of them are out of town. The stuff piles up on his desk and it may be weeks before he gets to a grievance. When it finally gets to O'Brien he comes down and talks to the supervisor. Well, naturally he represents the hotel so he doesn't get a fair picture of it. It's not just the decision, it's the delays of these things. You know, when you have little grievances accumulating over a period of weeks, it's bad. It's bad for management, it's bad for the workers, and it's bad for the union. They begin to get disgusted with the union when they don't get action, so we have to go around threatening. In this case I'm about ready to give a ten-day strike notice and throw it into government conciliation. Now why shouldn't we settle it on the spot? These things should be settled right inside the hotel, but in this place, we can't seem to do that.

Shortly after this episode, the Laundry Workers' Union appealed to Mr. Wiley to put pressure on several laundry employees who weren't paying their dues. Under the contract, the hotel was required to drop anybody from the payroll who didn't fulfill his union obligations, so Mr. Wiley asked the laundry supervisor to remind her workers of this fact, only to find that, a bitterly anti-union woman, she flatly refused to cooperate. She was obviously in the wrong and Mr. Wiley could have forced her compliance, but to what end? As human relations man he didn't want to incur her wrath at such an early point in the project. It ended with his doing the work himself. We had never envisioned dues collection as part of the job of a human relations man, but there we were. In the course of time the Hotel and Restaurant Workers Union, the biggest one to have a contract with us, fell into the habit of sending their official dues collector around to our office. She took care of the work herself but used the personnel office as the base of her operations. It seemed as sensible a place as any and preferable to having her chase after the employees through the crowded hotel as she had done previously. We developed friendly relations with her and all went smoothly.

When grievances arose Mr. Wiley would try to settle them within the hotel, but wherever there was a question as to whether the union should be notified or not, he would always advise the employee to keep them informed of events. The union men got into the habit of taking matters up with him first. He would usually recommend that they contact the supervisors directly but it seemed to reassure them that he knew about the case and was following developments.

This is not to say that everything always ran smoothly. Mr. Kraus continued to take unilateral action, and the personnel office would suddenly find itself on the firing line before it knew a battle was brewing. This happened, for example, when Mr. Kraus decided to remove all the waitresses from the hotel's finest dining room, the Zebra Room, and replace them with waiters. Nobody was consulted ahead of time, neither the dining room supervisor nor the personnel office nor the union. As soon as the change was announced to the waitresses, they complained to the union leaders. Mr. Kraus then decided to transfer the girls to a second dining room, the King Cole Room, but the union refused to allow him to hire new waiters to take their places, the King Cole room resisted his efforts to "borrow" waiters from it, and the waiters in question revealed their sentiments when, transferred against their will to the Zebra Room, they took two days off and called it sick leave. It was Mr. Wiley who had to move in and soothe waiters, waitresses, and union officials to avoid a strike. It was months before the two dining rooms concerned recovered from this blow.

Upsetting as it was, even such a crisis could be turned to the advantage of the project. As we shall see in a later chapter, Mr. Wiley used it to clarify responsibilities regarding organizational changes and to reshape his relations with Mr. Kraus.

Chapter IV

BEGINNING IN THE COFFEE SHOP [1]

When a total organization is to be studied, where does one begin? We decided to select one department, a part of the institution small enough to be relatively manageable and to show relatively good prospects for improvement. Our hope was that by working creatively within one area of the hotel, we might win the confidence of people throughout the organization.

There were several reasons for selecting the Coffee Shop as the starting place. We ate there at noon every day, hence already had a superficial knowledge of it. The supervisor appeared to be an intelligent and competent person and seemed to be harmoniously related to her staff. We were particularly anxious to begin our work with a "good" supervisor. Furthermore, the Committee on Human Relations in Industry had already done some work within the restaurant industry elsewhere. If we were largely ignorant about hotels, here was one area in which we felt somewhat secure.

A study of records in the Tremont Personnel Office revealed that the Coffee Shop had the highest turnover rate of any department except Housekeeping. In August, when our intensive study of it began, this rate was 32 percent per month. Seventeen of its twenty-three employees had worked for the hotel less than six months. This was in a department where business was in-

[1] E. L. H.

39

creasing rapidly. Along with the accelerating need for efficiency there obviously was a decreasing amount of time for training and supervision. If we could help matters here, surely this would be a good demonstration for management and employees.

It was decided that Miss Lentz would conduct the intensive study of this department. This was to include observations at various hours of the day, the rush periods and the recovery ones, and also interviews with all personnel beginning with the supervisor.

This work had no sooner begun than Mr. Kraus dropped a bomb on us. He decided to "crack down" on inefficiency in the hotel dining rooms just when we most needed a period of calm. He called a special meeting of supervisors and told them that he was ashamed of the way their rooms were operating. The Coffee Shop, he informed Miss Paris, its supervisor, was the worst of the lot. The trouble was, they were all too soft. They should demand more of their employees or it wouldn't go well with them. And he would appreciate it if Miss Paris would call her waitresses together for a meeting that afternoon so that he could speak to them himself!

Miss Paris and her assistant talked in troubled tones to Miss Lentz just before this meeting.

> Mr. Kraus thinks we are too soft on them. He said that again today. So I guess we will have to bear down on them at the meeting. That's the only way I can think of to impress him with the fact that we aren't such softies as he thinks we are.

She was quiet a minute, then added:

> What do you think about driving people? Don't you think that you get just as far by trying to win their good will and cooperation?

Her relief hostess nodded her head vigorously and said:

> That's what I think too. I don't believe in this driving all the time. It doesn't work with me, so why should I expect it to work with the girls? The thing is, I know how the girls feel because I've been a waitress myself. I don't see where that shows I'm soft.

The meeting was called for three o'clock but it was 20 minutes after three when Mr. Kraus arrived. The girls hadn't eaten since before they went on duty at eleven. Mr. Kraus came in without a smile, his face red from some exertion. He began to speak before he sat down.

> Well, let's get this thing going. I have another meeting after this one. (*He sat down.*) We're spending a lot of money to make this place over and to improve the service to the customers. So far as I can see, our efforts have been positively wasted. We ask for your cooperation and what do we get? Nothing! This has got to stop. All of you are making good money here and you seem to think, "Why should I worry about the customers?" Things have got to change around here. This hotel is not going to be run for the employees' benefit any more. It is a place of business and it is going to be run that way. If any of you don't like it you can get out! We don't want you here! [etc., etc., etc.]

He went on to warn them of specific sins, such as swearing in the kitchen and forgetting to present customers with their checks. With each recital of wrongs he would repeat that they must do better or be fired.

After Mr. Kraus had unburdened himself, he called upon Miss Paris to speak. She did her best to imitate his behavior. She said, in bullying tones:

> I have a set up here on the table. Please study it. Goodness knows you ought to know by now how to set a table but evidently some of you must be reminded. Another thing, I want you to cooperate with each other more. Why can't you work together? You should help each other without being urged.

Mr. Kraus interrupted:

> Don't make that a request, it's an absolute command. No cooperation, out you go! Is that clear? And don't think I don't mean it, because I do.

After this meeting, the Coffee Shop employees were understandably jumpy. In addition to the scolding received from their superiors, they had the additional burden of a still strange person,

Miss Lentz, sitting around observing them and their work. The person who seemed most agitated was Miss Paris. She took to heart every word Mr. Kraus had spoken. Instead of being her usually calm self, she became highly nervous and demanding. Several days later she commented:

> I know Mr. Kraus was right the other day. We don't do as good a job as we should. I don't know what to do. I keep telling them over and over but they never seem to change. Mr. Kraus said we must keep pounding till the girls finally learn right from wrong. I have tried to be nice to the girls. I don't know, I just don't know. They have been so upset since the meeting the other day, yet they had it coming. They don't do as well as they could. Mr. Kraus thinks I'm too soft and I believe I am too, but what are you going to do?

What she did was to "pound" on the girls at every possible occasion. She jumped them for lateness, for untidy appearance, for slow service. The girls in turn became jittery and began to make more mistakes than ever. All of the things Mr. Kraus specifically warned them about began recurring—for instance, swearing at the cooks. He had been adamant about that and had pointed his finger at one culprit, roaring "And I mean you!" Three days later this girl broke down in the kitchen again, fought with the cooks, and ended up by screaming at the chef himself. Another waitress had wondered (tears in her eyes) why Mr. Kraus had stared at her the whole time during the meeting. (If he had, we had not observed it.) This girl simply failed to show up for work several days later, and didn't even telephone in. One of her closest friends commented:

> That isn't like Helen. It just isn't Helenish. I was out with her last night and she seemed all right then. The only thing she said was just that there was so much tension this week . . . . It's been worse in the kitchen too.

One of the other waitresses began going to the doctor.

> It's that throat of mine again; it was better, I thought, but I've been so nervous all week and I couldn't imagine what ailed me.

Then I talked to my doctor and he said it was probably my throat so I'm going over to see him again today.

The next day this girl tripped and fell with a heavy tray of dishes. All the girls complained of tension and it was a week before anything resembling equilibrium was restored.

THE WAITRESSES SPEAK

Meanwhile, interviews proceeded but stayed on relatively superficial levels. The waitresses talked about physical equipment and other safe topics. They said that the hotel had not been replacing worn-out equipment. They had to struggle along with malevolent toasters, egg cookers, and so on. But what bothered them most of all, they said, was water. There was no running water in the dining room. The main rival hotel in town had running water right in the dining room, but at the Tremont the waitresses had to go clear to the far side of the kitchen for it and tote pitchers enough to satisfy from 300 to 500 customers a day. All they got were customer complaints about keeping the water glasses full. Why couldn't the Tremont run a pipe through the dining room wall? There was running water right behind this wall for the dishwashing equipment. It would be simple enough to run a pipe, but no, management was totally indifferent to employee welfare. They were indifferent even to their own welfare, when it came to acting upon employee suggestions.

When the waitress slipped with the tray of dishes, the girls added to their catalog of woes the absence of rubber mats on the steps leading to the kitchen. Directly across from these steps were identical ones used by customers as they walked from the cashier's desk to the lobby. The customers' steps were neatly covered with rubber mats. Why did the waitresses not have any? Obviously because management couldn't care less. Employees were expendable.

As the excitement of Mr. Kraus's visit subsided, the waitresses relaxed in their interviews and talked more freely about themselves and their problems. These were younger women than those in the other dining rooms. They came from rural areas, were high

school graduates without specific occupational training. When
time came for them to earn a living they drifted to the city and
took the kind of work which seemed to require the shortest ap-
prenticeship and gave most promise of adequate return. The
Coffee Shop would accept relatively inexperienced waitresses.
Most of these girls had few friends in the city. They usually lived
in small apartments with two or three other waitresses and developed passionate loyalty to one or two people in their new environment and to their families at home. They spoke wistfully
of home, and the good times they had in high school, and how
when they returned now they found all the young people gone
and no one to greet them.

The reputation of waitresses apparently isn't very high in the
American community. The girls revealed that they found themselves prejudged as unprincipled and unstable. They were extremely sensitive on the point of social acceptability. One of them
remarked on their chagrin at Mr. Kraus's attitude.

> The girls don't like him and everything he says they resent. It
> wouldn't make any difference how nice he tried to be, they resent
> him. You know some people think waitresses are beneath them.
> Mr. Kraus thinks they aren't in his class and his attitude shows it.
> Well maybe they aren't in his class, but he oughtn't to show it
> the way he does. It makes them resent everything he has to say.
> His attitude isn't right. Now Miss Paris is different. They like her.
> They would do anything for her, really they would, and they
> should, too. She is very nice to them.

Miss Paris, on the other hand, was fond of saying publicly:

> We have such a nice group of girls here, don't you think so?
> There is really a fine spirit among them, not like what you find
> in most other restaurants.

Encouraged by their superior to think well of one another, to
take pride in belonging to a group of "nice girls," the waitresses
showed signs of a group spirit which seemed to us to be one
promising feature in the human relations situation. It was by no
means a uniform one. We heard stories of bickering among the

girls. One pair in particular was especially troublesome to Miss Paris. She begged Miss Lentz to help with this situation.

Miss Lentz called both girls in and gave them freedom to talk without censure. Each spent a large part of the interview time talking about the other. Their early comments were extremely vindictive. As the interview wore on, the vindictiveness slackened. By the end of it each girl was saying somewhat sheepishly that of course maybe she herself was not perfect either.

One of the satisfactions of the interviewing process was that after a few days of it the overt hostility of waitresses toward each other dropped off noticeably. Miss Paris asked in gratitude, "What in the world did you say to those girls?" It was hard for her to believe that it wasn't necessary to say anything. The bickering among the waitresses was one way to work off the tensions they found within their work situation. The interviews acted as a safety valve, siphoning off these tensions harmlessly, if temporarily.

Other stresses and strains were more difficult to relieve. Everybody bossed them, the waitresses said. They could take it from the customers; they could take it from Miss Paris and her relief hostess; but it was unbearable when the food checker, the cooks, the chef, and Mr. Kraus also "poured on heat." Why couldn't all orders be channeled through their supervisor? They could accept her leadership, particularly because she seemed to know when to correct them and when to offer support. Over and over they repeated this. She was a tower of strength when the rush hour was upon them. When she scolded them it was during the slack periods and when they needed correction.

They asked also for instruction. They would say wistfully that they knew they weren't "good waitresses." They wished they knew the refinements of their trade. If only they could have meetings, not with Mr. Kraus present, but "just us girls," with Miss Paris there to teach them and freedom to talk things over.

Interviews and observation of Miss Paris supported the waitresses' assessment of the situation. Hardly a day passed without Mr. Kraus coming into the Coffee Shop to issue an order, correct a waitress, criticize the service. It wasn't that he was always cross.

Sometimes he was in a jovial mood, but they were always nervous in his presence. They knew how quickly his moods could change.

On one occasion the Coffee Shop was very busy indeed. Two busboys were supposed to be on duty, a third had quit a day or two earlier. One of the remaining pair failed to show up for work. The one who came in was half sick from taking typhoid shots earlier that day. He was just a youngster anyway, but he worked hard trying to do the work of two. In the midst of the noontime crush of work he retired to the men's room for a few minutes, to be discovered there by Mr. Kraus. The Resident Manager inquired brusquely what the boy was doing off duty. The boy said he wasn't well, whereupon Mr. Kraus promptly ordered him to leave.

About half an hour later, Miss Paris reported to the personnel office, very upset. What should she do? She had noticed the dirty dishes piling up all over the Coffee Shop and, upon inquiring for her busboy, was told that Mr. Kraus had sent him home. She said distractedly:

> I just hope Jerry isn't fired. If only I knew whether he was coming back or not, that would help. It is so difficult to plan ahead. Now I can't even make out tomorrow's schedule.

On top of her other problems, Miss Paris remarked with some bitterness that her pretty relief hostess had been brought in to help her, and Mr. Kraus started right off paying her 5¢ an hour more than Miss Paris received. True, Miss Paris took home more money, but she worked overtime to earn it and even with this additional money her wages were painfully inadequate. She realized this, but what hurt most was that nickel difference between her and her assistant.

We heard a lot about the old days, before Miss Paris was hired. One of the older and most competent waitresses told us:

> When I came here there were two old girls who really ran the department. Between them they divided all the good customers. We would come on duty and the hostess would be up-

stairs primping. There wouldn't be any schedule made and no-body would know what to do.

Now Miss Paris is manager and the schedule is always made out ahead of time so that we know exactly what station we will have the next day. Believe me, she runs this department! No old girl has any more to say than a new one. Miss Paris is boss. And that's the way it should be, don't you think so?

WHAT WE DID

Action on the Coffee Shop situation began long before the interviewing ended. We would take a step, try to assess the re-actions to it, and, in the light of this, take another step.

Our first move occurred during Mr. Whyte's visit to the hotel, two months following the launching of the project. Whyte, Wiley, and Lentz discussed the Coffee Shop situation at great length. While we already felt confident of our diagnosis of the departmental problems, Mr. Wiley had not yet begun to work on them with the supervisor, Miss Paris, and we did not want to make a higher level report until she had been able to show some progress. On the other hand, unless we could somehow restrain Mr. Kraus, little progress was to be expected.

We found our way out of this dilemma through a manage-ment meeting at which Mr. Smith had asked Mr. Whyte to speak. Our solution was for Mr. Whyte to talk about the Coffee Shop without appearing to talk about it. He began by saying that it was too early to report on the Tremont research, but perhaps the group might be interested in some aspects of the restaurant study we had recently concluded. The aspects selected, of course, were those we knew to be particularly relevant to the Coffee Shop situation. (This meeting is reported in full in Appendix B.)

Whyte drew a diagram for the group, illustrating the typical pressures experienced by waiters and waitresses (see p. 48).

Besides the "line authority," there were others trying to initi-ate action for waiters and waitresses, such as food checkers who examined customers' trays and sent the waiter back if they weren't properly garnished. There were the cooks who criticized the way orders were placed, and to whom the waiter would have

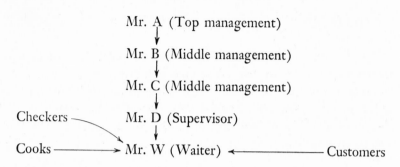

to return food which customers rejected as not hot enough or poorly prepared. There were the cashiers who examined sales-checks and there were, of course, the customers, who could not only be unpleasant upon occasion but who could threaten a waiter's job. When combined pressures were too great to be tolerated, where could a typical Mr. W blow off steam? The traditional place was in the kitchen. He could scream at the cooks and pantry girls. If this didn't suffice, the chances were that he would begin to vent his frustrations in the dining room.

Mr. Whyte explained that a wise management tried to relieve these tensions by such devices as personal interviewing and by creating group meetings. He stressed the importance of sending management suggestions "down the line" through the front-line supervisor, rather than having Mr. A, B, or C leaping over others and speaking directly to the Mr. W's. Not only that, the same line organization which carried orders down to the work level should be carrying communications back up. It was their responsibility to encourage the Mr. W's to express their needs and ideas. If one of the officers failed to respond, this link between top and bottom of the organization would snap and disunity would result. Mr. W would become hopelessly frustrated, difficult to handle, and would finally lose interest in his job altogether and quit. The hotel couldn't afford its present turnover rate. Something must be done. This didn't mean passing along each and every suggestion or criticism, but it did mean giving a courteous hearing to ideas from all levels of the organization, enabling people at each level to express themselves freely and to feel that they were being represented to Mr. A and Mr. B by their supervisors.

Mr. Kraus spoke up, asking what Mr. B could do if he lacked confidence in Mr. D. Mr. Whyte stressed the need for all employees, regardless of their level of authority, to work in an atmosphere of approval. Even if a man wasn't doing the best job in the world, he explained, if he was worth keeping at all he deserved an opportunity to grow and develop. In order to do so he needed the security that came from feeling his superior believed in him, had confidence in his eventual ability to do an acceptable job.

This elementary lesson appeared to go over surprisingly well. The supervisors seemed to take to heart what Mr. Whyte said about methods for encouraging upward communications. A few days later Miss Paris remarked to Mr. Wiley:

> You know, Mr. Wiley, I was just thinking. Maybe we should have meetings in the Coffee Shop like those you had for supervisors. I could have one once a week and we could get the girls to bring suggestions and we could talk them over. I think they would learn a lot, don't you? Maybe we should try it.

Mr. Wiley nodded.

> I think you have something there. Not only would the girls get training that way, but they would probably appreciate your bringing them in. It wouldn't surprise me if you'd get a lot of cooperation.

Miss Paris was at first enthusiastic about the idea of weekly meetings, democratic style. She remarked to Miss Lentz, "That supervisors' meeting was the best ever, don't you think so?" But in a few days, she began to have doubts.

> Mr. Kraus wouldn't like it, I know. He's always telling me, "Don't ask them, tell them!" I can't picture him allowing anybody to make suggestions, can you? Asking the girls for their ideas? He's always telling me, "Don't put it that way, tell them, lay down the law!" What do you think of that? Can we do it one way when he wants it another?

The effect of the supervisors' meeting was quite as striking with respect to Mr. Kraus as it was with the supervisors. Someone had asked at that meeting whether Mr. A or Mr. B should be present at group meetings. Maybe it would be better if the Personnel Office ran them? Mr. Whyte didn't encourage that idea. He thought representatives from the Personnel Office might occasionally sit in on a meeting, and also that Mr. A and Mr. B might sit in sometimes, but felt that ordinarily department meetings should be run by the department head or his assistant. Mr. Whyte added that managers should leave the direction of the employees to their immediate supervisors. If Mr. A or Mr. B had criticisms to make, they should be made directly to the supervisor, not to his subordinates.

Mr. Kraus took this to mean that he wasn't wanted at meetings. For a while he didn't come to any of them, then gradually he began to attend some but would sit on the sidelines and talk from there, doing his best to avoid taking over.

Other management people drew their own conclusions as to what the meeting meant for Mr. Kraus, in some cases going a good deal farther than we had intended. As the meeting broke up, Mr. Kane, head of the Housekeeping Department, stepped up and shook Mr. Kraus's hand, saying "Well, so long, Kraus. It's been nice knowing you."

With Mr. Wiley's reassurances, Miss Paris now went ahead and experimented with her new-style meetings. At first weekly, and then about once every two weeks, the girls came together and discussed their problems. Soon they were remarking about how much better things were going. Pressed to explain, they said,

> Oh I don't know, we get along so well together now. And I think those meetings help a lot too.

They also liked being presented with a spigot! At first they couldn't quite believe it. It wasn't the best spigot in the world, but it represented to them a change in management's attitude toward them and their ideas. When Mr. Wiley reported to Mr. Smith the need for such a spigot, he found that Smith knew nothing about that situation. Mr. Kraus, knowing of plans to renovate the Coffee Shop, had just pigeonholed the suggestion each time Miss Paris had brought it to him. Upon a suggestion from Mr. Wiley, Mr. Smith also ordered rubber mats for the steps from the Coffee Shop to the kitchen and there was no more occasion for the waitresses to fall with laden trays at that particular spot.

Meanwhile tensions continued between the waitresses and the kitchen staff. When they mounted over one weekend, Miss Paris mentioned to Mr. Wiley that she was considering inviting the chef to sit in on a Coffee Shop meeting. Did this seem to be a good idea? Mr. Wiley, of course, was delighted. He talked privately to the chef and found him highly skeptical. He had been to Coffee Shop meetings before, in the past, he said, and why should he open himself to that kind of punishment? Wiley had to stress the possibility of constructive action arising from it before the chef agreed to come, somewhat reluctantly. When the day came and the chef failed to show up for the meeting, it was Mr. Wiley who went down and coaxed him, agreeing to sit in on the meeting to offer moral support.

It was quite a meeting. At first the waitresses, politely but plainly, told the chef of the troubles they were having. For one thing, they had trouble getting fruit juices. The pantry girls didn't want to be bothered pouring it out glass by glass. For another thing, the cooks played favorites and that got everyone upset, and so forth. The chef answered them calmly, asking for suggestions on such things as the fruit juice crisis. The waitresses suggested that the juices be poured into pitchers so they could pour out glassfuls themselves as needed, and he agreed to so order it. There was remarkable give-and-take at this meeting, and by the time it came to a close the chef had the girls asking him for advice where at first they had had only criticisms. They had agreed on a number of minor changes and where he felt change was impossible the chef patiently explained the reasons why.

The meeting over, Mr. Wiley complimented both department heads on the skillful way they had handled this situation. He did it at the time and then later told each one privately. The waitresses told Miss Lentz how much better they felt after getting their complaints off their chests.

Several days later Miss Paris came to Mr. Wiley and volunteered:

> You know they even got the fruit juices in a pitcher now, so they can get it easily. And the cooks are repeating orders, even Sam. Of course last Sunday was still bad, but he is trying to do something about it. The girls have been coming to me saying how much things have improved.

One of the complaining waitresses said to Miss Lentz:

> I guess we can't expect everything to improve at once, but it *is* better in the pantry, I'll have to say that. Most of our trouble has been in the pantry, you know.

A day or so later another waitress commented:

> Honest, it's like a miracle. That kitchen's a different place. It's almost a pleasure to go out there, no fooling.

Eventually, as the wave of reform swept slowly through the hotel, Miss Paris got her raise and this helped to ease the strain between her and her relief hostess. Not having Mr. Kraus pop up unexpectedly was a relief, too. Turnover dropped each month from the 32 percent at the time the study began in August, to 8 percent by the end of the year. As the girls were now working with a steady group, they began to make friends among themselves and their social adjustment improved. When Christmas came and the management gave them a party, everybody came and joined in the fun. One of the supervisors said to us,

> You'll never know how much things have changed since you people came in here. I think the main difference is in Mr. Kraus. He doesn't bawl us out any more. Of course he doesn't come in and kid with us either. I kind of miss that, but I guess if I had to make a choice, there's no question which I'd take.

CONCLUSIONS TO COFFEE SHOP STUDY

In the course of three months, several changes had taken place in the Coffee Shop. There were the new spigot and the rubber mats, symbolic of a new relationship between top management and the employees. Some of the pressure coming from Mr. Kraus's direct interference in the department had been reduced. The supervisors and waitresses had been encouraged to think through their own problems and to take action on them. They had been talking about the need for a spigot for months, for instance. When Mr. Wiley got them one, they could feel it had been due to their suggestion. They weren't so timid about asking for improvements after that.

Miss Paris had been holding occasional group meetings for the waitresses before the study began, although they had been management-dominated ones. Their character changed following the supervisors' meeting, but it was at her own initiative, Mr. Wiley providing the needed encouragement. Since these meetings were directly in line with what the waitresses had asked for in their interviews with Miss Lentz, they could also feel a sense of partnership in them.

Even the idea of having the chef sit in with them originated with the group. The girls complained to Miss Paris about worsening conditions in the kitchen, she spoke to Mr. Wiley, and he worked behind the scenes to help bring it to pass. After the meeting, he congratulated the two supervisors, thus helping to lay groundwork for future cooperation. Mr. Whyte used this incident as an example of ways to improve interdepartmental relations when he next addressed the general supervisors' meeting and this also helped to cement a new and good development.

In other words, a situation had been created in which it became possible for people to work and grow harmoniously. The achievements of this period were obviously not all due to the human relations project. We picked a relatively good bet to start with, and Miss Paris, the chef, and Mr. Smith were intelligent and willing co-workers. Even Mr. Kraus went docilely along with Mr. Smith's plans, up to this point.

The Coffee Shop study also proved an important milestone in our progress in the hotel as a whole. By the time of Mr. Whyte's third monthly visit to the Tremont, we felt that we were ready to present our Coffee Shop study to Mr. Smith and to a general management meeting.

We now had a success story to tell, and Mr. Whyte sought to tell it in such a way that the key management people involved could get the maximum public credit from it. Most time was spent upon Miss Paris's skillful leadership, especially her handling of the group meetings. The chef received special recognition for the way he handled a most difficult interdepartmental situation and won the waitresses over to a better understanding of the problems of the kitchen. Mr. Smith got credit for the water spigot and the rubber mats, and he was told that these changes served to convince the waitresses that top management was really interested in the employees after all. Since Mr. Kraus's contribution had been to get out of the way, it was hard to give him credit directly, but Mr. Whyte tried to suggest that Kraus as well as Smith had been right behind the program at every step. Mr. Whyte also quoted several waitress comments indicating a constructive change in the social atmosphere of the Coffee Shop. Mr. Smith responded by commenting that he himself had noticed this improved atmosphere, and he was sure that it meant improved efficiency as well as greater employee satisfaction.

After this point, we had the feeling that the anxiety toward us on the part of the supervisors had markedly declined. No longer did we seem to be such threatening figures. Perhaps we might even be able to help them. Now we were even asked, "When are you coming in to study my department?"

Chapter V

THE HOUSEKEEPING DEPARTMENT [1]

We decided to make the Housekeeping Department our second study. It was the largest department of the hotel, with maids and housemen being responsible for the guest rooms and public rooms and areas. We already knew that the department was torn with internal dissension, but by now we felt we should be ready to handle such problems.

KANE VS. GRELLIS

It was here that we encountered most directly the "Sheridan clique" problem. Mr. Kane, the department head, had been brought in when Smith took over and had been placed in charge, over Mrs. Grellis, and the two did not get along. This split carried right through to the bottom of the organization.

Mrs. Grellis looked upon us as potential allies right from the start and unburdened herself in this way:

> I was head of the Housekeeping Department for nine years and never had a bit of trouble. I had two girls die on me and outside of that I didn't lose a girl. But they don't think that's the way to do things. They must not, for Mr. Smith brought Mr. Kane in and gave him my job. Now I'm under Kane. He's just what they want because he's good and tough. I don't know what to do, and I can't be like that. It isn't my nature. It actually gives me a

_____
[1] E. L. H.

complex . . . . I think that you have to understand human nature, treat other people like you'd like to be treated yourself. The maids don't like to be pushed around, they tell me that.

Mr. Kane was a cheerful, blustery individual in private life. He lived very quietly with his wife and his one form of recreation was hunting. He had known Mrs. Smith since childhood and had worked for Mr. Smith for over 17 years. There was no questioning his intense loyalty to his boss, and we suspected that he tried his best to copy Smith's ways. He would pound on his desk, issue orders in loud tones, tell employees if they didn't like the way he ran things they could get out. Mr. Kane would give an order to the maids demanding that they do better work and then Mrs. Grellis would fly to the protection of "her girls." There were two supervisors in the department. One was a partisan in Mr. Kane's camp, the other in Mrs. Grellis's. Not only the two housekeepers but their supervisors gave conflicting orders, and none of this was lost on the maids and other employees.

It took Mr. Kane quite a while to warm up to us. He told us, later in the year:

> You know you people came in here and my idea was, get her in and get her out and get it over with. I couldn't understand it when you didn't tell me right off the bat what's wrong with my department. Now I realize your work isn't like that. This human relations business is something that goes on all the time, long as we live, is that right?

Once Mr. Kane came to feel that we respected him as a person and welcomed his participation in our project, he invited us to work with him. We were careful to let him structure our work for us as far as that was possible, telling us just how he would go about it, whom to contact first, and so forth. It was important that he sense our respect for his authority.

ORIENTING NEW MAIDS

When Mr. Whyte talked to him just as we were getting under way, Mr. Kane confessed that there was something he was at a loss to understand.

Well, I do have one problem. Old employees don't want to help break in the new ones. I don't know what they're afraid of. Maybe they think that the new ones are going to take their jobs, but anyway they don't want to teach them. And that starts at the top. One of my supervisors doesn't want to help to teach and she sides in with the older employees on that. Says it takes too much time! Now you know damn well that that's a lie because if you take a girl around to do a room with you and you show her the work, why certainly she's going to be some help to you.

When a situation is full of tension, it isn't always easy to win the confidence of employees. People tend to stand off and wonder which "side" you will be on. But as Miss Lentz trailed along after the supervisors on their daily rounds, worked the sewing machines in the linen room, and helped the maids make beds, they became used to seeing her around and it became easier to talk to her. The problem of training newcomers came up for discussion quite often.

The overworked supervisors would try to get the old employees to train the new ones for them. After working with an older maid for two or three rooms, learning the routines and details expected of her, the new maid would be put on a corridor of her own and be left to get along as best she could. The supervisor would make a special effort to get back to see the girl and lend her a hand, if possible, in order that she could get her quota of 16 rooms finished for the day but, with the shortage of help, the supervisor often was somewhere else in the building doing maid's work herself. The older maids were bitter on the subject. It seems that Mr. Kane misunderstood the amount of "help" a new girl gave an older one. Actually if the two worked on four rooms together, the new girl was credited with two of them toward her quota of sixteen, while the older girl was credited with the other two. The time she took to instruct the girl wasn't counted. One of them cried indignantly:

Lorraine brings the girls to me for their training and I think that's wrong. How can I train them and do my work too? They should have somebody special to train the girls. Now take yester-

day, that new girl was turned over to me. Well, I worked with
her for an hour or more, two hours altogether, at least. It takes
time! I have to show her where the linen closet is, where the
soiled linen chute is, where she can get supplies, how she is to
do this and that. It takes time to do that and do it right! Then I
still have my 16 rooms to do; they don't make any provision for
that at all. I'm just as responsible that day as any other for my
own work. I don't mind training the girls. In fact I'd like it if
they made some arrangement that would take care of my rooms
that day. But I can't do both jobs without getting behind in my
own work.

Another maid found the high turnover extremely discouraging.

Yesterday that girl worked with me for four rooms. They
counted that as two for her and two for me. I still had 14 other
rooms to do by myself. They didn't give me any credit for the
time I spent showing her around and I was way behind. That
girl looked like a fine maid to me. I put a lot of pains into training her and now I hear she quit already. It is so discouraging,
they all quit after a day or so. What use is it for me to take
pains? After a while you get disgusted. You don't want to show
them around, you just want to give them the most important
things and then turn them loose. That isn't right either, they
should be given every help at the beginning . . . .

The department stores have a regular training room for new
girls where they learn how to take care of customers. Why don't
they have something like that for new girls here? Just one room
for them to practice in . . . . After all, a maid is important. She
meets the customers and when they talk to her she should talk
back politely. Well new girls should be told about that, don't
you think so? We don't have time to do that, either. New girls
are lucky if they get shown the important things. If we had one
girl responsible for training them, I think she should tell them
how to talk to people, too. Maybe if the new girls felt that the
job of maid was important, they would stay on better than they
do. Nobody wants to be just a maid!

Mr. Wiley decided to use this problem to help solve the problems of Mrs. Grellis. Here was a woman of considerable experi-

ence and executive ability who was burning out her energies in futile griping. We recognized the loyalty existing between Mr. Smith and Mr. Kane and had no desire to change the situation by removing Kane. He had a very difficult job, working with an assistant who was much shrewder than he and who could outtalk him on any occasion. For all his blustery manner, he was genial and kind, and we had no reason to criticize him for wanting the efficiency of his department increased. The thing to do was to find satisfactory work for Mrs. Grellis which would relieve the tension between the two and at the same time utilize her gifts.

RECOGNITION FOR MRS. GRELLIS

When we came to study Mrs. Grellis, we found her problem to be deeper than it seemed at first. She complained bitterly about Mr. Kane and his "interference" in her work. Why she had had the department running like clockwork before he arrived, and now look at it. But it wasn't just resentment of him, we felt.

She would say over and over that she had learned nothing from "this regime," meaning Mr. Smith's management. "These men" didn't know how to organize the work, they did it backward. Mr. Smith, she would say, was clever but he couldn't handle people. What finally helped us to understand her difficulty was an incident which occurred after she had prepared a parlor for a guest. An assistant manager had requested her to do this and she had worked overtime to do a beautiful job. She took Miss Lentz up to see the room when it was completed, and it did look attractive. The following day Mr. Smith asked Mr. Kane what happened to a certain set of furniture which he had wanted sent to his summer cottage. When it was discovered that Mrs. Grellis had innocently used it for this parlor, he was indignant and, without ever seeing the room, gave orders that she was never to set up a parlor again unless he specifically ordered her to do so. Mrs. Grellis was completely crushed. Right after this, a run-in with Mr. Kraus sent her off into hysterical tears.

> I've worked here ten years, ten years. Nobody ever talked to me like these men do. Ten years and what do I have to show for it? They talk to me as though I was a stable cleaner.

It was so unlike what we had come to expect of her, that it helped us to realize how badly she lacked recognition. She respected Mr. Smith but rarely had any contact with him. He carried out his work through Mr. Kane and had no way of knowing what caliber of service she was rendering. What was the sense of putting forth special effort if it was never noticed? Perhaps if her work were recognized she would take greater satisfaction in it.

When in the course of a conference with Mr. Smith the subject of the Housekeeping Department came up, Mr. Wiley explained how the two executives didn't seem to know what their respective jobs were. There was overlapping at many points, and it was here that friction was occurring. As in other parts of the hotel, the organization might be made clearer and responsibilities defined.

Mr. Wiley also called Mr. Smith's attention to the turnover statistics for that department. Of the maids who quit the preceding year, we found 51 percent had done so within one week of being hired. Thirty-seven percent had quit within their first three days on the job. The maids were telling Miss Lentz that the training was inadequate and they were becoming discouraged at breaking new people in. Perhaps we could cut down turnover and improve the efficiency of the department by inaugurating a formal training program. Mr. Smith was interested and promptly suggested that Mrs. Grellis run it—which was just what Mr. Wiley was aiming for. Mr. Kane was called into the discussion, the facts presented to him concerning the expensive turnover, and he too was interested in the idea of a training program. So it was arranged.

Mr. Smith questioned Mr. Wiley concerning Mr. Kane's attitudes.

> He's too loyal to me. He follows everything I do and when I give him an order, he carries it out to the letter without any criticism at all. That isn't always good either.

It was true that Mr. Kane was devoted to his superior. We were wondering how we could convince him not to bluster when

Mr. Smith blustered all the time, but this problem was solved by Mr. Smith. He called Mr. Kane up to his office shortly after Mr. Wiley's visit and ordered him to stop shouting at his people. "You've got to treat the employees better, Kane," he shouted. What else was said during this lecture, we don't know, but things began to change, for the most part in the direction Mr. Wiley was encouraging Smith to move. It wasn't long after this that both housekeepers got a raise in pay. There was a Christmas party for executives, and Mr. Smith and Mrs. Grellis got into conversation and discovered they had a common dislike for a former hotel manager at the Tremont. Mr. Wiley had been encouraging Mr. Smith to be more friendly with the employees and to speak to them when he met them in the corridors, and shortly after this he stopped on several occasions to speak to Mrs. Grellis in a most cordial way.

The difference in her was little short of amazing. She told us with genuine amusement how Mr. Smith had kidded her for saying she was tired and said, "You couldn't be working as hard as all that, why you're getting more gorgeous all the time." It amused her but it warmed her heart, too. Now she began to remark on how much she had learned from this regime, why she was learning all kinds of things. She went on to list them, showing how much thought she had been giving to this. She added,

> Things have been so much better lately, Miss Lentz. Mr. Kane has been altogether different. I don't know why it is, maybe Mr. Smith talked to him. He's been like a different person.

She told how Mr. Kane had been dividing the duties, taking over the management of the public rooms and leaving her in charge of housecleaning the guests' bedrooms. She enjoyed planning the work herself and seeing it carried through to completion. When the work was done, she could say it was her own.

> He's got lots of nice ways, he really has. I'm lucky to have such a fine person to work with, I know that. I've always liked Mr. Kane. Oh, I get provoked with him, I don't mean that, but just the same I like him, he's a good man. And he's fond of me.

GROUP MEETINGS

Another problem that came up in Miss Lentz's interviews was the desire for group meetings. During the Smith management the maids didn't have a common lunchroom but each ate by herself in her linen locker. Since they also worked separately, they got lonesome.

> You know [one oldtimer said] Mrs. Sheetz used to have meetings for us. Get togethers, they were, and we would make suggestions and she would say how she wanted things done . . . . I don't know how the other girls felt but I thought it was a good idea. People should have a chance to speak up and give their viewpoint. I thought those get togethers were a fine idea. Since Mr. Smith came in, we haven't had anything like that . . .

Another thought a lunchroom would help.

> Of course we used to have the lunchroom too. That's where we could meet our friends easiest. We could sit around and talk things over. A lot of things that came up we could figure out there, like little disagreements we could straighten out over the table. I don't know, it was different.

We tried to get them their lunchroom back but were unsuccessful. The hotel was to be renovated and Mr. Smith promised that the new wing would have an employees' cafeteria in it, but that was a postwar project. Meanwhile we had to be patient. The group meetings they did get. Mr. Smith suggested that Mrs. Grellis run them, too! They turned out to be better than any of us had expected. Problems came up for discussion and were fully aired.

One such matter was the linen problem, for example. During one meeting it was reported that there was "linen trouble" all over the house again. The maids cried, "We can't make the beds with no linen." They were getting complaints from the guests and from the front office because they couldn't put rooms in order quickly enough. Aspersions were cast on the linen truck man for being slow in carting fresh linens around to the girls, but he said it wasn't his fault, the stuff didn't come from the laundry until late in the day. Mr. Kane agreed to look into the matter. The following week the subject came up again and he took the time to explain just what the situation was.

> There is a very bad shortage of pillowcases and I get reports that some of you girls have a lot of pillowcases in your linen closets while others don't have any. Now Tom you go with George [the linen man] and help him get that straightened out today, will you? See that they are distributed as much as possible. The only way we can get along is if you share what there is and if you bring down your dirty linen and put it in the chute just as fast as you can. Get that, girls? Don't keep the linen in your bins, get it down the chute. I talked with Mrs. Daly today [head of laundry]; we had a long talk. She said if we got the pillowcases down promptly, she'd have them sorted out and she'd see to it that they got washed first. That way we will have fresh ones to put back on the beds.

> So do like I say, share what we have and work together. Now if it comes time for you to go home and you still have a couple of rooms without pillowcases, please report them and we will see to it that the night girl puts them on as soon as she can get them. Everybody straight on that?

We had heard complaints about linen shortages ever since we first talked with the maids, but following this meeting they abruptly fell off. Once the employees were shown the reason for such a difficulty and understood that management was facing the problem and making progress on it, they were content.

Miss Lentz sat in on these meetings and took notes both for the benefit of the project and as a record for the Housekeeping Department, so we were able to watch their development closely. After several months had passed and the meetings had assumed a stable pattern, she again interviewed the employees, asking in a casual way how they felt the meetings were coming along. There were scattered complaints.

> The only complaint I have is they take too much time. Now last week wasn't so bad but the week before that the meeting ran over an hour. That means we get home too late. I had six check-outs

waiting for me that week and had to hustle like the dickens to get out of here.

They are all right, I think they're fine. Of course they cause some hard feelings, though, I'll tell you that. The girls shouldn't make remarks about each other do you think so? Otherwise I like them.

Some of the girls seem real hurt because people hop all over them.

Miss Lentz passed the criticism along to Mr. Wiley, who in turn conveyed them to Mr. Kane, without mentioning any names, of course. The meetings continued to be held once a week but we noticed that Mr. Kane kept them much closer to the half-hour mark than before. Mr. Wiley had advised him and Mrs. Grellis to steer away from personalities. Occasionally one of the maids would make pointed references to another maid, but both Mr. Kane and Mrs. Grellis exerted an impersonal attitude from this time on. When Mr. Wiley talked the matter over with the Housekeeping executives he let them know how immensely popular their meetings had become, on the whole, as indeed they had. Over and over we got the same reaction.

I think they're swell. They give us a chance to get things cleared up. I always did say that we should have meetings once in a while.

I haven't been to one of them, I have Thursdays off. Isn't that a gyp? Don't you think they should give Thursday girls a chance too?

They suit me fine. I learn something every time, like those Venetian blinds, I never did know how to work them. I was glad to learn that. . . .

I think they are the most wonderful things. I believe in that, if you have something on your mind bring it out into the bright. Don't sit around whispering to the other girls, bring it up where everybody can hear it. Then everybody knows what is the right thing, not just one or two, isn't that right? I like that way of doing.

After Mr. Whyte publicly praised the Coffee Shop and the

chef for getting together on common problems, the other department heads followed suit, Mr. Kane among them. Once more interdepartmental tensions lessened for having been brought "into the bright." Compliments on the improved service in the Housekeeping Department began coming in from the front office and the service department and each one served to bolster Mr. Kane's and Mrs. Grellis's pride in their new techniques.

INTRODUCING CHANGE

Physical improvements began to take place as a result of suggestions made in group meetings. One such change seemed quite significant. Management had been trying to encourage the idea of the maids using lightweight trucks to haul about their linen supply. As it was, the women were toting each room's supply of linen separately from linen closet to guest's bedroom. The trucks had always been bitterly opposed by the workers, who felt that something was being put over on them. Now two things happened. One was that *Life* magazine published an article on the Waldorf-Astoria which showed their maids using such trucks. The other was that this time, when the matter was broached, it was put to the Tremont maids as a question to be discussed, not as a command. Mrs. Grellis remarked after the meeting:

> They were always dead against them. They were thinking of those big trucks with laundry bags attached to them and they are too heavy for a girl to push around. What we are talking about is a smaller truck for their sheets and supplies. I really think it would be a big help to them. Well after thinking it over, they decided they would like the truck after all. Imagine, them dead against it for years and threatening to quit if they had to use them! So now the housemen want trucks too. If that isn't a laugh! They think if the maids have trucks, why shouldn't they?

There were many other problems still to be dealt with on which we didn't take action, but, for the most part, Mr. Kane and Mrs. Grellis were aware of the problems which remained and they plainly were enjoying working things out for themselves. Mr. Wiley would be called upon for opinions and he would slip in suggestions or criticisms but it pleased him to see the department heads taking the initiative themselves.

We found that supervisory behavior was undergoing a distinct change. Mr. Kane was evidently passing along his new-found wisdom to his subordinates. Mrs. Grellis told us with pleasure of the improvement in the supervisor who had always been a Kane supporter and imitator. Mrs. Grellis had found it difficult to get along with Lorraine, but here again her attitude was undergoing a remarkable change.

> You know Lorraine is a good supervisor. She's intelligent and she carries out orders. But one thing about her, she gets it in for a person and then just picks and picks at them. I keep telling her, she can't afford to do it. She must learn to put the House first before her own likes and dislikes. Well, she's trying to, like Kane. She says to me every once in a while, "I'm trying to make myself over." That's all you can ask of a person, isn't it? Now Bessie [her old favorite] isn't nearly as good a supervisor as Lorraine is. She's too soft with the girls. That isn't any good either, you have to show more gumption than that.

CONCLUSION

So it seemed to us that the split in the Housekeeping Department between the Kane school of thought and the Grellis one, while not healed, was on its way to being overcome. Mrs. Grellis appeared to be better adjusted now that she had her own work marked out for her and was getting recognition for it. The maids had become accustomed to being interviewed and to having a chance to express their ideas in open meeting. There was less reason for feeling chagrin at being "just maids," especially since Mr. Kane began to pass on compliments to them when other departments remarked how much better the service was. The Housekeeping Department was making progress both in efficiency and in worker satisfaction.

Chapter VI

MIDSTREAM[1]

As the end of the first six months drew near, we could look back and see some landmarks behind us. There were occasional whispers of "Gestapo" during the first month or so. As the Coffee Shop study drew to its close and the Housekeeping one gathered momentum, these whispers died away. People had talked to us and nothing bad had happened to them. In fact, they could point to specific improvements that grew out of the studies. It was said that Mr. Wiley could help you if you got into a jam. Miss Lentz had worked along with the rank and file employees in several departments when a crisis arose due to labor shortage. As we became known to them and our faces familiar, the wariness disappeared. We were beginning to be regarded as possible friends, and in some places our welcome was warm.

MERRY CHRISTMAS

What did more than any other single thing to win employee good will was the Christmas parties. It had been years since any management had remembered the employees at the holiday season, and nobody expected it any more. One waitress remarked, for instance,

> Nobody as much as wished us a merry Christmas! Why there wasn't a wreath, not a sprig of holly around!

---

[1] E. L. H.

We were inclined to think that a series of small parties, one for each department, would serve to unite the work crews, thus cutting down turnover and also uniting the workers with top management. To our gratification Mr. Smith was extremely interested in the idea. He ruled out our timid suggestion of ice cream and cake and ordered full course turkey dinners with presents for each employee, turkeys to be raffled off, etc. He ordered everyone to cooperate with us to the fullest extent in putting the affairs across.

The new chef gave us every encouragement, although his department bore the brunt of the work along with the heavy load of Christmas shopping trade. Mr. Kraus, the resident manager, did not. His latent antagonism toward the personnel office was beginning to express itself openly about this time. He was against the party idea from the first and seemed to throw every possible obstacle in our path. As head of the Banquet Department he effectively barred us from calling upon it for help, informing Mr. Wiley with glee that he had decided to give "the girls" the week off!

In the end, with the volunteer help of employees, we set the tables ourselves, moved the furniture, wrapped the gifts, served the food. It made it painfully clear to everyone in the hotel who was fighting on whose side. And the parties went across! Months later people were still talking about them. One maid said:

> All the girls were talking about it up in the locker room again, and everybody said the same thing. It made us feel so good just to know that they appreciate our hard work. It wasn't just the good time, although it was wonderful food and all, but it was thinking that maybe they did notice us after all and see how hard we try to keep the place looking clean.

The difference in attitude among the workers toward one another and toward management was so striking that Mr. Kraus finally came to Mr. Wiley and before witnesses complimented him on his work, saying that he had been wrong about the parties. He was generous in admitting his error to other executives and that helped our prestige and warmed our hearts.

Holding Christmas parties was certainly no invention of ours. It is considered a tried and true personnel policy in many institutions. We had never anticipated striking results, but what we hadn't fully realized was the great loneliness of the average hotel employee. Many of them came from broken homes, had drifted about the country without accumulating friends. At Christmastime this social isolation was especially obvious and the parties fulfilled a real need. In our ignorance we had hit a bull's-eye.

After that, interviewing was easy. Where before we had had to go to them for interviews, now the employees came flocking up to our office. The problem of winning the employees' confidence had disappeared.

Similarly the union leaders were accepting us as people with whom they could work. Mr. Wiley was being consulted on grievances at various levels by employees and by the union representatives themselves, who got into the habit of dropping by his office whenever they were in the hotel. Mr. Wiley was careful not to overstep his role as middleman and always consulted the union when that seemed in order. The union steward in the Housekeeping Department had escorted Miss Lentz to a union meeting, to the delight of the maids and housemen.

SUPERVISORY RELATIONS

The feeling of having progressed in our relationships didn't extend as far into the supervisory levels as we could have wished. A few people were definitely moving in our direction and these, significantly, were the ones with whom we had worked most closely. Miss Paris, manager of the Coffee Shop, was coming to Mr. Wiley quite regularly to ask his advice or to discuss her newest plans. Mrs. Grellis of the Housekeeping Department talked to us freely about her problems. She had taken Miss Lentz under her wing, was inviting her to meetings of professional housekeepers in the city. Mr. Kane saw a good bit of Mr. Wiley. He would go to lunch with him, talk over departmental matters, ask his advice on the handling of human relations problems.

There was one occasion, for example, where he requested Mr. Wiley to solve the problem of two maids quarreling. Instead of accepting the invitation, Mr. Wiley encouraged Mr. Kane to handle the case himself. Mr. Kane insisted that Wiley sit in on the session while he got the two women together, drew out their conflicting tales, smoothed the trouble away, and let the women go. Mr. Wiley's warm approval of his handling of the case improved the friendship between them and clarified the point to which Mr. Kane's authority extended and at which Mr. Wiley's stopped.

Other supervisors were still bewildered by our actions. Some left us strictly alone, but Larry, head of the King Cole dining room, presented positive opposition. It was Mr. Kraus, oddly enough, who proved to be the key to that situation. Larry came to us complaining that his employees ran to us with their troubles. He demanded an explanation of Mr. Wiley's "interference," and Mr. Wiley wasn't making much progress explaining the function of a personnel manager until he brought forth the following argument:

> I think there are a lot of cases where employees can talk to an outsider about their problems easier than they can talk to their supervisor, Larry. If you remember, you talked to me about Mr. Kraus scolding you in front of your employees. Another time you talked to me about his firing your employees when you didn't know anything about it. Do you remember that? It was much easier for you to talk to me about that than to go to Mr. Kraus.

Larry thought that over for a minute, then replied:

> Yes, yes, that's right. And you did something about it, didn't you? I can see a lot of changes. I can see that you have been doing a lot of things, and it has improved the hotel a whole lot. I guess it's good for them to talk to you. Well, I have always told everyone in my department that I want them to talk to you or Miss Lentz any time they have something on their minds. . . .

So Larry backtracked on his complaint, but his change of heart didn't last very long. He was a problem to us until we went into his department to study it as a whole.

Occasionally we heard such remarks about how "we" had improved Mr. Kraus, but we knew that the change in him wasn't taking place fast enough. Miss Paris had hesitated to try out our type of group meetings because she felt sure Mr. Kraus would object to them. We couldn't expect the supervisory level to come over to our way of thinking until the higher levels of management came over. The workers were moving our way, the union was moving our way, but the supervisors, being closer to top management, were much more cautious. They seemed to sense that between us and Mr. Kraus a psychological tug of war was going on, and they stood on the side lines watching us, placing no bets.

One thing that worked in our favor was the circulation of a pamphlet written by Mr. Whyte and his associate Burleigh Gardner,[2] which showed the predicament of the people who stood between management on the one hand and the workers and unions on the other. We heard a lot of appreciation for the article. Supervisors would remark that it certainly presented their side of the story; then ask, "Are you going to show it to Mr. Smith?" Our whole program made more sense to them, we thought, when they found that we were trying to interpret their difficulties to top management as well as the difficulties of the rank and file. It pleased them to think that we were also "educating" Mr. Smith to consider his administrative staff in the light of good human relations.

Relations with Top Management

Mr. Smith, of course, had been favorably disposed toward the project before he brought us into his hotel, and from the first he had stoutly supported everything Mr. Whyte proposed.

At first it seemed that it was Mr. Smith's personal appreciation for Mr. Whyte and his respect for the University of Chicago that carried the project along. He seemed disappointed that we didn't start right in by making startling changes and he remarked to Mr. Whyte somewhat ruefully:

If you say there is progress being made, I'm satisfied. That's

---

[2] "The Man in the Middle: Position and Problems of the Foreman," *Applied Anthropology*, Vol. 4, No. 2 (Spring, 1945).

good enough for me. After all, it may seem like a long time but it's really been less than two months, hasn't it?

It was during this same conversation that Mr. Smith made another comment which threw light upon the way his mind was working. We found it disturbing at the time and later it became the basis for a turning point in our relations with him.

> Now I'll tell you one thing that I think Wiley might have done if he had been on the job. You know we had a lot of trouble with our chef. We finally had to get rid of him and now we find we are getting along a lot better. He seemed to be a disturbing influence in the kitchen. If Wiley had got on to that in time he could have saved us a lot of trouble. I should know about those things.

Mr. Whyte explained that while Mr. Wiley had been aware of the situation in the kitchen, he didn't feel free to criticize the supervisors to Mr. Smith. Instead he was trying to win their confidence and hoped to change their behavior through consulting them and giving such guidance as he could for the handling of their problems. We didn't want the job of stool pigeon and Mr. Smith wasn't asking for that. What he wanted was objective knowledge of his organization and the tensions which tended to lower morale and undermine efficiency. The problem was, how could we get such information to him in such a way that it violated no confidences and was helpful to the organization instead of being just critical? How could we put light on a trouble spot without increasing the heat on it?

In the course of time a new chef was hired by the Tremont. Mr. Kraus had been running the kitchen during the interim and it was he who had most to do with selecting and hiring the new man, a very well-trained and highly recommended chef. No sooner had the chef gone on the job, however, than he and Mr. Kraus began to have difficulties. The chef told us the story later.

> I've had a lot of trouble with him, I had to balk him every day, the first month I was here. He used to come down and tell the cooks what to do. Maybe he does know something about food; he took special care to tell me he has been 35 years in the food busi-

ness. But I can't run a kitchen under conditions like that. I told him five or six times he would have to keep out of the kitchen or I couldn't run it as it should be. If I was to be chef, I had to be chef!

From the sidelines Mr. Wiley watched this tension develop between the two men. We knew Mr. Kraus well enough by now to recognize his habitual pattern of behavior. His attitude toward the chef was no different from that toward Mr. Wiley, Miss Dickson, or any of his other administrators; he had to feel that he was the boss. As new executives were added to the staff we found that in each case it was the same story. No sooner would a new man come into the organization than Mr. Kraus would commence giving him orders at every turn, interfering in his department until either the man quit, gave in completely, or, more rarely, convinced Mr. Kraus that a compromise had to be effected.

Before our handling of this problem can be understood, other developments must be considered.

While Mr. Kraus sparred with Mr. Wiley and refused any direct offers of cooperation, he was nevertheless changing in his behavior in other parts of the hotel. We heard such comments all over the hotel. Earlier we quoted Larry, the King Cole supervisor. We got a similar report from the Coffee Shop. We got it from the Housekeeping Department. Mr. Kane was telling Miss Lentz about it a month or so later when recounting his difficulties in trying to follow Mr. Whyte's advice.

KANE: Now here's something maybe you can help me understand. That diagram thing the Doctor put on the board about Mr. A and Mr. B and Mr. C, you know what I mean? Well, I understand that the Doctor doesn't think Mr. D should go cutting around Mr. B. Right?

LENTZ: That's right, that's the general idea.

KANE: Well, how can that diagram work when Mr. A knows what Mr. D is talking about and Mr. B doesn't? Then what?

LENTZ: You'd better explain what you mean, I guess.

KANE: Well, take the other day, they decided they wanted a table to seat 13 people put into the Penthouse. Now I knew darn well that Mr. A doesn't want a table up there. I know that little fellow through and through—ought to, been working for him for

17 years! So Mr. Kraus and Mr. Hume both told me to put a table in, now what was I to do?

LENTZ: What happened?

KANE: Well, the old man says I got to get along with Mr. B, see? So I just said, "Yes, sir" to Mr. B and Mr. C and then I went upstairs and sat in my office wondering what to do. Finally I called up Mr. A and I told him. I know that's cutting around Mr. B the way the Doctor said we shouldn't, but what was I to do? So I told Mr. A a table would maybe scrape the paint off the doors on the way in and out and I just asked him, see? I didn't say what I thought but I just asked him, "Do you want a table, because I can put one in in a minute if you do." So he says, "Damn it, Kane, you know I don't want a table in there, why do you ask?" Now what do you think of that? Did I do right?

LENTZ: It puts you in the middle, doesn't it?

KANE: I'm always in the middle. What should I do? That diagram doesn't work.

LENTZ: Well, it seems to me that if you know it isn't working, that's the important part, isn't it? Then you will realize something is wrong and try to straighten it out. I think it's like you were saying a few minutes ago. It is a matter of Mr. A educating Mr. B so that he will know what should be done. In the meantime Mr. D has the job of being patient and tactful so that Mr. B doesn't get the idea that his authority isn't being respected. Eventually the diagram will work, isn't that right?

KANE (*pausing to think*): Yeah, that's right. B gets educated and the thing works itself out. Yes, I can see that. And Mr. B is learning, too. Don't think he isn't, he's a darn smart man. I understand him. We used to fight all the time, but now we get along swell. Remember how he used to come around yelling his head off? Well, he doesn't do that anymore.

LENTZ: Is that right?

KANE: Yes, he says to me, "*Will* you do this or that?" and I say, "Yes, sir." It works fine. Much better than it used to be! He's learning all right.

LENTZ: Since when has it become better, Mr. Kane?

KANE: Oh, the last few months, I'd say. He's a bright fellow all right, he's learning fast.

Reined in by his chief in some areas, Mr. Kraus naturally could be expected to find outlets elsewhere. Just as he was hammering at Mr. Wiley on odd occasions, so he was jumping the new chef. If either situation were to be relieved, new outlets would have to be provided him.

Tension between Mr. Kraus and the chef now began to flare dangerously. We heard rumblings of trouble from the cooks who found themselves with two bosses and didn't know which one to obey. We heard rumors from department heads that Mr. Kraus was making public remarks about what a poor choice he had made to bring the chef in in the first place. An explosion was plainly approaching, and, so far as we knew, Mr. Smith was unaware of the growing seriousness of the situation. What were we to do? It was impossible to discuss the problem with Mr. Kraus and the chef did not hold the initiative.

Mr. Wiley discussed the matter at length with Mr. Whyte. It seemed to them that Mr. Smith had absorbed enough of our doctrines by now to be able to look at such a situation objectively, not blaming it on any individual, but seeing it from the standpoint of organization. Upon Mr. Whyte's advice Mr. Wiley called the crisis to Mr. Smith's attention in the following manner.

First, Mr. Wiley sketched the situation as he saw it. Then he tried to point out why it arose. Mr. Kraus was reacting to our program in a negative way. Through Mr. Smith's efforts his policemanlike activity was being checked, but that wasn't enough. Since he was being hemmed in on one side, doors would have to be opened to him on the other. He was resident manager in name only. Actually he didn't have control of the hotel at all. He needed to develop his leadership skills before people would accept his leadership, but Mr. Smith had already shown that he could guide Mr. Kraus. Could he also help him to develop a more effective leadership pattern?

At this time the front office was undergoing a major change and Mr. Wiley suggested that it be formally brought under Mr. Kraus's jurisdiction with Mr. Smith following the situation very closely and giving Mr. Kraus painstaking guidance at all critical times.

Mr. Smith listened carefully to what Mr. Wiley had to say. He asked him pointed questions and seemed to be making mental notes but it wasn't until a month later that there was any evidence of a response. Then, in great excitement, Mr. Smith called Mr. Wiley to his office and informed him that the prophesied event had actually taken place. The chef and Kraus had come to him saying, "This is the end!" Warned by Mr. Wiley, Mr. Smith was ready to make his decision and to act forcefully and effectively in this crisis situation. The chef told Mr. Wiley about it later.

> Finally I had to go to Mr. Smith. He's smart, he agreed with me! He saw right through it and told Kraus that the chef should know how to run a kitchen. Well, it was funny, after that Kraus stayed entirely away from the kitchen for about two months. He never came near us.

For Mr. Smith this represented a turning point in our work. Mr. Wiley, as one who could foretell events, rose in his estimation. Now, the whole Kraus problem came up for review with Mr. Wiley as well as Mr. Whyte sitting in on the discussions in Smith's office.

One force that was driving Mr. Smith and Mr. Kraus apart was their different attitudes toward money. Both men had worked in the hotel industry during the depression of the thirties. As representative of an auditing firm, all of Kraus's training had been in cost cutting. Now times had changed and profits were pouring in. Mr. Smith, who was about 15 years younger than Kraus, apparently threw off the inhibitions of the depression years. He looked upon money as something to be spent. He wanted a hotel which would bring him admiration from all over the nation and was prepared to pay the cost. He began to insist that Kraus find ways to invest $5,000 more a month in the business (since otherwise the government would drain off this much money in taxes). It was too big a change for Mr. Kraus to make easily. He couldn't bring himself to spend somebody else's money. Add to that the fact that after a lifetime of autocratic action he was being asked to encourage his employees to speak up, and it becomes immediately apparent what a strain the man was under.

It would have been the easy way out to encourage Mr. Smith to replace the Resident Manager. Perhaps that is what should have been done, but we were reluctant to admit defeat so long as there was a chance of finding a better solution. We knew Kraus to be intelligent, loyal, and hardworking. If Mr. Smith was willing to work with him, we welcomed the opportunity of trying to win over a person whose views were so opposed to our own. Mr. Wiley pointed out to Mr. Smith that Mr. Kraus had no real training for his present duties. This was the first time he had ever found himself in the position of executive. He needed not only guidance but reassurance; he needed praise. Mr. Wiley suggested that Smith give him a job to do which was pretty clearly defined, then express appreciation when it was done acceptably. It was decided that Kraus and Wiley should work together on the problems of the checker-cashier situation. Mr. Smith was to consider putting him in charge of the now reorganized front office. Both Mr. Wiley and Mr. Smith were to talk continuously in terms of organization and thus try to get Mr. Kraus accustomed to the idea of delegated authority, to see himself as chief coordinator rather than one who had to run the whole show. It was repeatedly stressed that the job of reconstructing Mr. Kraus was up to Mr. Smith. We could only advise him. If nothing came of this plan after a suitable time, a replacement had better be considered for the resident manager position.

It is difficult to say how much of this plan was actually put to test. Mr. Wiley did finally succeed in getting Mr. Kraus to work with him on the cashier-checker study, but whether Mr. Smith attempted to do his part we just don't know. Mr. Kraus was not placed over the front office. There was no sign of his gradual growth in responsibility.

Instead, shortly after Christmas, Mr. Smith announced suddenly that he was planning to tour South America where he hoped to study the hotel industry. He was placing Mr. Kraus in full control of the hotel during his absence which would probably be a period of two months.

Showdown with Kraus

The news caused a flurry of excitement throughout the hotel. Mr. Kraus took his new responsibility very seriously and worked longer hours than ever. One might have expected that he would be so busy with plans and preparations that he would storm less at Mr. Wiley, but that wasn't how it worked out. His anxieties and tension being greater, he became more belligerent than ever. Grapevine stories began to circulate about the hotel that Mr. Kraus was just waiting for Mr. Smith to leave before he would force a showdown in the hope that Mr. Wiley would throw up his hands and quit. Instead it was Mr. Wiley who called the showdown and Mr. Kraus who backed down!

What happened was this: Miss Dickson, now assistant personnel manager, had been having her troubles. As the tensions grew between Mr. Kraus and Mr. Wiley, she found herself acting as liaison between the two offices. Whenever Mr. Kraus wanted something from the personnel office he would call her up to his office, and this pressure began to make her nervous and irritable. Always somewhat erratic in her behavior, she began taking time off without notice and complained to Mr. Wiley that her position had become untenable.

> I have been in the middle between you and Mr. Kraus. I know you don't like it when he calls me up to his office. I go there and try to speak up for this office but that is hard to do. I have to think of my own job, you know. After all, he is the resident manager and he's over me. I have too many bosses. You are both over me. One wants me to do things one way and the other wants it another. I can't stand that, I don't know how to handle it.

Mr. Wiley was aware of the problems involved but was temporarily at a loss as to how to correct the situation.

> I have tried to take the pressure off you by getting between you and Mr. Kraus, but I can't make him realize that I am between you when you go up there on frequent occasions. I know he likes to talk to you when there is pressure on him and I think perhaps you both enjoy it. When there is pressure on him he lets it off to you

and that saves the rest of the organization. Perhaps you didn't realize it, but you have done the whole hotel a great service.

While he was pondering over this problem, word came to him that Mr. Kraus had just advised a new department head:

> Don't go to Wiley, he's a dope! Go to Dickson if you want something in Personnel.

That was the last straw. Mr. Wiley now went to the Resident Manager's office to have it out. (See the detailed report of the encounter in Appendix C.)

Mr. Wiley took the offensive from the start and this in itself represented something new in their relationship. Until then he had been trying to woo Mr. Kraus with kindness. The first subject, concerning turnover figures, wasn't too controversial, but the difficulties growing out of the transfers of waiters and waitresses among dining rooms constituted a "hot" topic. (See Chapter 3.) Mr. Kraus was so obviously responsible for the mess that Mr. Smith must have been putting heat on him. Mr. Wiley pointed out bluntly that this sort of thing was just what he had been hired for. It was the task of the personnel man to carry the hotel through such situations, and, if he had been taken into Mr. Kraus's confidence beforehand, the trouble might have been avoided.

This subject was followed by a bit of chitchat and then Mr. Wiley launched into the cashier-checker situation. For the first time Mr. Kraus expressed his willingness to cooperate on this problem.

Then came the big blast, the issue of his relations with the personnel office. The matter of Miss Dickson's "spying" on him was, of course, a figment of his imagination. Once the whole subject came out into the open, it was possible to do something about it and Mr. Wiley did. With a nice combination of firmness and appreciation of Mr. Kraus's good qualities, he swung the Resident Manager over into an entirely new relationship with the project.

From this time on Mr. Wiley was master of the situation. He

contacted Mr. Kraus at least once a day, preferably early in the morning before the current tensions could get tempers ruffled. He consulted with him on Mr. Kraus's problems. It was a rough and bumpy road, for at one time Mr. Kraus would be sympathetic and warm and a half hour later he would be roaring at Wiley in front of employees because he had found roaches in the men's washroom. We would inch forward and begin to congratulate ourselves, when Mr. Kraus would slip back again. On the whole, however, things were greatly improved. Mr. Kraus reported this to Mr. Whyte on a subsequent occasion.

> That little misunderstanding we had is all cleared up. He came in to thrash things out with me before Mr. Smith left for his vacation, and we got things all straightened out. Now when anyone comes to me on a personnel problem, I call in Wiley right away. We sit down and handle it together or else I'll turn it over to him. I don't want to handle anything alone. We're getting along better with the union, too.

The following departmental reports will show just how much difference this made in our work. The King Cole situation would have been much more difficult to handle if it hadn't been for the sympathetic support of the Resident Manager every step of the way.

Chapter VII

CASHIERS AND CHECKERS[1]

In talking with various waitresses, we had heard a good bit about their difficulties with the food checkers. One of the girls commented:

> Kate is very hard on the girls. She is much too strict, I think. I mean she yells at us. I remember once when I was still new, she yelled at me because I forgot something and it upset me for days. Every time I went near her I'd be afraid for fear I was short of something.

This situation wasn't new to us. In our study of restaurants in Chicago we had found very similar stories about difficult food checkers every place we went, so we were sure it wasn't simply a case of any one person's being hard to get along with. There must be something much deeper than this.

THE JOBS

Checkers and cashiers are linked by the fact that they usually report to the auditor as their superior. At the Tremont they were considered as belonging to one department, although actually their work had little in common. A food checker works in the kitchen. As the waiters and waitresses are about to leave with their laden trays, they stop at the checker's stand where their

---

[1] E. L. H.

food portions, arrangement of food, choice of chinaware, etc. are checked for correctness and the prices rung up on the customer's check. The beverage checker may be in the kitchen (as in the case of a service bar) or dining room, and she scans the drinks and checks to make sure the waiter is charging the proper amount. Usually she also rings up the prices on the saelscheck. Cashiers, on the other hand, always work in or very near the dining rooms. They handle only checks and money, never food. Like the checkers, they exert a degree of authority over the waiters and waitresses in that they scan the saleschecks for mistakes in addition, make sure the right cover charge is added, and occasionally criticize the handwriting. At the Tremont the cashiers did their own bookkeeping, keeping track of long columns of figures based on food sales, beverage sales, and various kinds of taxes and cover charges.

THE PEOPLE

It was our custom to stop and talk to the checkers and cashiers just as we stopped to say hello to all the other employees, and by the time we got around to making a formal study of that department we found a friendly welcome. In fact, we were struck by the fact that the turnover in that department, always quite high, began to drop almost immediately with the advent of the interviewing procedure. We found, too, that the checkers seemed only too glad to talk. They would draw the interview out to unusual length and at the end they would make comments, "Thank you, thank you very much," when all we had done was listen to them. Over and over we heard remarks like this:

> Nobody tells us anything. Nobody comes around; they don't know what we're up against.

We found that the checkers and cashiers were lonely people, in spite of work which involved them with several large groups of employees. The auditor gave us some insight into this when he said:

> Who would be a cashier when she could earn twice as much

and only have half the headaches if she were a waitress? Only a a girl who felt too good to wait tables! As it is, those girls are kidding themselves. Those waitresses and waiters downstairs think they can kick the cashiers around all they want to. It's a funny thing, it is just chance that the cashier's job has stayed low in pay and status while the waitress job went up, but that's what happened. If you could raise the cashiers' job and get them to feel surer that they were above the people in the kitchen and dining room, you'd have all the cashiers and checkers you'd want. As it is, the only way I can get people is through my friends. Yes, I'm not above calling them on the phone and begging for help.

With that tip in mind, the personnel records of these girls appeared in a new light. For the four who had waitress experience, sixteen came from white-collar positions. They were former stenographers, bank clerks, insurance office clerks, salesgirls, and the like. In telling of her present position one of them remarked:

> You have to deal with so many people, you can't help but learn psychology. I like to learn how the laboring class lives. You can understand why there is war, after watching these people around here. They need to be educated (softly) in the cultural things of life.

The former waitresses were women who, finding themselves unable to do the heavier waitress work, took checking or cashiering because there is less physical strain involved. One of them commented:

> I used to be a waitress myself. Eight years I waited on tables, so I know how they feel about checkers! Ha, ha, I never thought I'd be one myself. I never meant to be a checker, I can tell you that right from the start. The only thing is, after the last job, my right arm was bothering me so I couldn't waitress any more and I took this. Now that I'm here this long [two years] you know I like it. I really do, I like my work here.

This particular woman, Kate, was the terror of the kitchen. She demanded perfection of the waitresses. Having been pushed

around for eight years by other checkers, she was quite prepared
to do some pushing herself. The Tremont waitresses came to
respect her quite highly, however, because she knew what she
was doing, and she was generally accepted as the best checker
in the hotel.

The other girls, it seemed to us, were having a harder time
adjusting to their present situation. They just didn't fit into any
status group. One spoke feelingly of the last place where she had
worked.

> We had our own biffy and everything, it was wonderful. We
> even had a bed to stretch out on. That's a fine place to work. Here
> you have to share the same room with everybody, you know,
> maids and all. Not that I think I'm better than they are, I don't
> mean that at all.

Actually these women stood alone within the hotel organization. These jobs took them "back-of-the-house" so that they
had no association with the other white-collar workers. The
work demanded that they play the role of policeman and who
loves a cop? It was revealing that the checker, alone of all the
employees interviewed, said she liked having a manager stand at
her elbow as she worked.

> Mr. Kraus and John [the sous chef] stand up for us. During the
> time the chef wasn't here, they would come over every once in a
> while and stand by the desk and watch. They didn't have to say
> much, they'd just stand there and listen to what was going on. Or,
> sometimes Kraus would say to one of the girls, "Where's your
> parsley?" They always complain when I send them back for
> parsley but with him there, they'd trot back without a murmur.
> I think it's a wonderful idea for the manager to stand by, once in
> a while, just to see how things are running.

WORK FLOW

It was at the checkers' suggestion that Miss Lentz spent an
evening at the stand with them, a very revealing experience. We
were able to map the traffic which passed the desk in the course
of an evening. It was plain to see how the tempers rose as rush

hour got under way. Early in the evening the checker would correct a waitress firmly but not unkindly.

> Never put parsley on a creamed dish. Besides, it goes on fish only, not on other foods.

The waitress would flush and reply, "OK; you win."

After eight or ten such corrections, the tempo of business meanwhile picking up, the orders became harsher and the reactions became more acute. By now the checker was seizing the offending parsley and flinging it down on the tray.

> This doesn't go on creamed food! You don't use it on steak either! Now go back and get the proper stuff!

In this last instance the waitress was a new employee. Nobody had instructed her in the use of parsley. She bit her lip and blinked back the tears.

> "What do you mean, the proper stuff?"

The checker ignored the question and the waitress walked uncertainly away. She returned with the proper garnishment (water cress). Evidently she had asked another waitress about it. By the end of the evening the waitresses and checkers could hardly bring themselves to speak courteously to one another.

Cashiers had similar trouble. The management expected them to read the checks and recount them. If the cashier overlooked a mistake, however, the waitress had to pay the shortage. There were rules to be enforced concerning minimum rates. An old and respected cashier could handle problems but a new girl lacked this authority. The supervisor pointed out to us:

> I break in a new girl and try to build up her morale, you know how it is, and no sooner get her started and thinking the job is fine, then a waiter will start barking at her. After all, I have to tell the girl the rules of the house just as they have been told to me. I can't make them over, it's not my job. Then the waiters want her to do it differently.

When the manager had a change in rules to impose, rather

than go to the trouble of telling groups of waiters and waitresses, he would tell the checker or cashier and expect that individual to enforce the change. Since her superior status was not clearly defined, the other employees would resist her fiercely.

These checkers were key figures in the kitchen. Every waiter and waitress had to stop at their desk. A cranky, overworked checker upset all the dining room personnel. When one considers that inevitably some of this tension must have been passed on to the customers, what did this amount to in terms of customer relations?

The conditions so far discussed were basically no different at the Tremont than those we had seen in large restaurants, but there were others which were unique. The Tremont was growing at an unprecedented rate. The distribution of work in the checker-cashier department perhaps made sense at some earlier period, but by the time we arrived on the scene it was completely out of kilter.

There was one food checking stand in the kitchen. All three dining rooms and the room service staff were accommodated here. This necessitated having three workers at this desk during rush hours. The room service phone rang, the impatient waitresses were lined up waiting for service, and the place was a madhouse.

There was one beverage checking stand in the kitchen. At night two girls worked here, one acting as cashier and the other as checker, but during the afternoon one girl did both. The cashier at night told us that the volume of business during the afternoon equaled or surpassed that of the night shift. Everybody said the same thing, that the girl on the day post had an untenable position and was crazy to stay there. The other girls said they wouldn't take her job for a million dollars. Yet both Miss Dickson in the personnel office and the auditor, the checker's superior, expressed annoyance with this girl, saying she was just a chronic griper.

Another bad spot was the cashier's desk in the Coffee Shop. The girls who worked here also handled the Zebra Room business, which meant that from noon until 9 P.M. they were responsible for two busy dining rooms. The rush of work was especially heavy over dinner hour, when two girls could easily have been kept busy but only one was provided. The other rush hour occurred the last thing at night, after the final show closed in the Zebra Room. All the guests would decide to go home at the same time and each waiter would come with his checks to have them added up and rung. When the rush was on, the cashiers were unable to keep abreast of their bookwork, so that when the last waiter left they found themselves with a full hour's work still to be done, and this at 1 or 2 A.M. They did not get paid overtime but were required to stay on their own time to complete their evening's work, the supposition being that if they weren't ready to quit at quitting time it was their own fault.

Along with poor work organization, there were physical problems which served to discourage these women. Everybody testified that something should be done about the poor working conditions which existed in the kitchen, but opinions differed widely about what could be done. The noise was intense and the smells and heat added to the discomfort of all the kitchen workers. The main checking stand was directly across from the dishwashing machines. The beverage stand was next to the service bar with its clatter of glasses, down from the glass washing department, and near the pantry, so that the girls were exposed to a variety of noises. What bothered these workers most was the heat which poured down on them from overhead steam pipes. After incessant complaining, they were given an electric fan which they kept at their feet. The spoke gratefully of this "gift" but it seemed that the benefit was mostly psychological. Actually the fan chilled their feet while their heads baked.

The food checking stand was cluttered with all sorts of supplies. All the saleschecks for the dining rooms were stored here and doled out, package at a time. A month's supply of officer's checks was here, as was tape for the cash registers, and so forth. There was only one cash register, and sometimes three workers behind the desk had to share it.

JOB ATTITUDES

It may appear strange that under the circumstances anyone would take these jobs, but the jobs had their good side too. The girl who worked at the Coffee Shop–Zebra Room cashier's desk got a lot of fun out of her work.

> My friends will say to me, "What, are you still there?" But I enjoy it here. Like Saturday night for instance I got out of here 2:30 in the morning. We worked like the blue blazes, but it was fun, too. It is like an evening out, in a way. It has all the atmosphere of an evening out. We hear the show and sometimes see it too, if we're not too busy. And all the people coming and going—oh, I like it. Of course to a new girl it looks different, I realize that. It is really a very tough job and I don't wonder that we have had a hard time getting people. I've been her two years and know all the people. I know how to handle them.

Being on the job long enough to have mastered the human relations aspect of it is a big help to adjusting to work pressures. It was the new girls who had the most difficulty. Without any orientation, training, standardized procedures, or clear lines of authority, they felt completely lost.

At the main food checking stand the oldest employee was considered "in charge." She was a small, intense woman who prided herself on her efficiency. One of her girls said of her:

> Everything is done for you when Kate is on. She never tells you anything, she goes so fast—why she can do things while we are still thinking about them.

Actually the work was piled too high for even the speedy Kate to handle during her regular work hours, and rather than admit it or call for help, she had been coming in on her own time to get it done.

> I just thought I'd try coming in early, not saying anything to anybody, just to see how I could arrange my work to fit it all in, but I just can't do it no matter how much I try. The desk gets busy right at seven now, seems to me, and I'm always stuck with

the work. I could do it if I just rang up the money and didn't really check the trays. I could do it that way, but I don't really want to. That isn't the way to work, do you think so? I hate to do a sloppy job, but I just don't see how I can fit it all in.

Her eyes were misty and she looked away and swallowed.

I'll have to say something to them, I guess, I'll just have to. I thought coming in early I'd catch up but it didn't work.

The desk was manned by two younger women during the evening, neither of whom had worked at the Tremont very long. Their way of relieving pressure was the one the older women scorned, that is, sloughing off the less important details. For instance, there was a record they should have kept of the silverware and other table appointments which go on room service trays. The waitress pushed such a tray before the checker and she was supposed to check off on a printed list of items just which utensils were leaving the kitchen. They told me:

That's a dumb thing too. We don't keep it too carefully, what's the use? If something is missing when they come back, the waitresses will say to us, "So I guess I'm supposed to go tell the guest he stole it." We just skip the whole thing.

But they went through the ritual of checking off a few items, putting the paper on a spindle, and pretending to scan it when the tray was returned.

The two girls who worked the kitchen beverage stand during the evenings had been together for about half a year and seemed to be working in close harmony. Like the girl who worked there afternoons, they were known as chronic gripers, but that was just the side they showed the world. They reacted to the work pressure by helping each other over the worst spots. One said:

We like to work together, we're lucky that way.

I don't know what I'd do without her. She helps me with my records, otherwise I'd never get out of here nights. I can't help but get behind. Oh, I do pretty well, but when we get rushed, she helps me get caught up. She helps Agnes, too [afternoon checker].

Now there's a girl who is in a bad way. She'd never get out of here if it weren't for Katherine coming in early to help her.

Katherine was arriving ten to fifteen minutes early each day in order to assist the other girl with her paper work. This overtime, like that of the food checker, was not reported to the management so the girl received no pay for it.

Where an employee of long standing will try to adjust to increasing pressure of work, new ones will not. They take one look at the work to be done and quit. One girl who had been on the job a week said heatedly:

One thing I can't understand is that we have to do our bookwork virtually on our own time. The first week I worked with Jean, do you know her? We were never out of here before 2 A.M. Of course, I'm new and not very good yet but even so, we should have had the work finished earlier or at least be paid overtime for an extra hour. Both of us working as hard as we could and it took a whole hour to finish up the work! They think we can keep up with it throughout the day, but it doesn't work out. We have such rush periods that we couldn't possibly keep the accounts and do a good job of cashiering at the same time. I never have worked any place else where the cashier was supposed to do her own bookkeeping!

The supervisor of the cashiers and checkers, a thin, jittery woman, was out sick most of the time this study was going on. Just before she left she commented:

Oh, I've been a mess lately. I'm just tired out, that's all it is, there isn't anything wrong with me otherwise. This place has just run me ragged. . . . The thing that wears me out is all the gripes. Honestly, the things the girls bring up, you'd wonder how anybody would want to even discuss them they are so trivial. But I get all of it, they just pour it on.

WORKERS, MANAGEMENT, AND THE UNION

It was interesting to learn that these white-collar workers with their pride of status had nevertheless joined the Hotel and Restaurant Workers Union just a year before our study began. As the interviewing progressed we listened carefully for remarks which would explain this phenomenon. One little old lady who tended the soda fountain cashiers' desk said:

> We were pushed into it, more or less. Maybe I shouldn't say this, we weren't pushed exactly I guess, but that's what it amounted to. Well, I'll say this for the union, things became improved after we joined. I'll say that for them. They got us a 50¢ a day raise and one meal, but I certainly was against them at first. I was probably the last one around here to join.
>
> LENTZ: For goodness sake!
>
> CASHIER: As I say, we felt pushed even though we didn't have to join it if we didn't want to. They said everybody would be joining and if you didn't, well as changes took place you'd just gradually be, well, pushed aside. That's the way they explained it to me. I'm telling you this straight, just like I would to Mr. Smith. It's just the facts, nothing more. The hotel had a chance to improve conditions and it didn't. We were only getting $4.00 a day then and no meals and working all hours. There was no limit to the day. When they called a meeting just before the union vote came up, Mr. Smith talked to us for a long time. He said that the hotel would see that we were taken care of, we didn't have to go to outsiders. He said the management was on our side. Well, they had lots of time to show it, but they hadn't. Anyway the vote came a few days later and all but one voted for the union. Then as I say, things got better right away. I had to admit I was wrong.
>
> LENTZ: It was really a struggle for you, wasn't it?
>
> CASHIER: I felt degraded. I really did. I never thought I'd be in one of those organizations. Well, maybe there are rackets in everything. There are, aren't there? Business has its rackets too. Anyway, we're unionized now. We got our raise and our meal.

Another cashier was commenting on the Christmas bonus that Mr. Smith had granted them the year before.

> It was right at the time when they were trying to soft soap us out of joining the union. It was all so plain. What did they do but give us a $25 bonus! Can you imagine? MINUS TAX! Yes, they squeezed out the $25 but couldn't bear to pay the tax on it. Gee, did that burn me up plenty! They must have taken us for fools. As if anybody couldn't see through this.

LENTZ: Is that right?

Sure, it was just as plain as the nose on your face. Why, they didn't even say Merry Christmas to us, just that check for $25. The girls were wild. You know me, I'm dead against unions, but I must admit they got us that raise. We never in this world would have got it out of that bunch if the union hadn't gone to bat for us.

What it came down to was that these workers wanted so badly to take a slap at management, they were willing to join a despised union in order to do it! By joining it they had succeeded in getting what they saw to be economic justice, but so far as the work load was concerned, no adjustment was made, and the human relations problems remained as before.

Wages also continued to be a source of dissatisfaction, not so much with relation to the amount per day ($4.50) as on account of the lack of advancement possibilities. The older workers felt that there should be some visible return for long experience but their only hope of getting more money lay in working through the union for a group raise. A group raise doesn't express the superiority of the skilled worker over the unskilled. Of the twenty workers, only seven had worked at the Tremont more than a year. Gradually the experienced ones were moving out to find better jobs elsewhere.

SUPERVISORY RELATIONS

We were used to the gripe "too many bosses" so weren't surprised to hear it in this department. The girls told us:

> We have so many bosses down here. There is the chef, and the sous chef, and the managers—they all tell us different and how are we to know who is top guy?

The reason the chef and the sous chef were giving orders arose from the fact that many food items did not appear on the dining room menus and sometimes each of the several authorities within the kitchen would have his own idea about what price to charge for them. The new chef probably intended to straighten this out once his kitchen organization work was done. Meanwhile the old checkers charged what prices seemed logical to them but the new girls, being more timid, would ask for and receive conflicting orders. Sometimes the day shift would charge one price for an item and the night shift would charge another. The prices were confusing enough without this added complication, since there was a scale of price differences among the Coffee Shop, the King Cole, and the Zebra Room, the latter charging about a third more for everything than the Coffee Shop, the King Cole prices falling between the two.

Within the work group itself there were supervisory troubles. Nobody knew for certain who the supervisor of the checkers was. Most of the girls considered the head cashier to be their superior but she refused to acknowledge this responsibility:

> I had a big fight with Kraus one night. Gee it was a scream. He had a mistake on his check for about 80¢, and he talked to me about it. Well, Mr. Kraus was wild at me because I laughed at him. I couldn't help it, the expression on his face was so funny. He glared and roared, "You're the head checker, aren't you? It's your business, why do you laugh?" I told him, "No, Mr. Kraus, I'm not head checker, Kate is." That only made him madder.
>
> Now Kate is officially head checker and should take responsibility for all her girls, but she doesn't, Miss Lentz, and that gripes me plenty! Especially since she gets more money than I do. Yes, we are paid the same salary but she gets overtime and I don't. Well, I'll be busy as anything and I'll get a call to go to see Kate. I'll go in to her desk and she'll say, "Jean, what shall we do about covering this desk? The girl is sick and can't come in tonight." Now what is that to me? Why doesn't she take responsibility for her own girls? But she doesn't. I wouldn't mind if we got the same money, but her getting overtime and me not, just drives me wild. I like Kate, don't misunderstand. We get along swell. If Kate quit here today I'd walk right out with her.

When Kate was interviewed Miss Lentz inquired of her, "Are you head checker, Kate?"

> Well, that's hard to answer. I thought I was and then Jean was promoted and now I don't just know exactly. I don't know what her relation is to this department. She's head, I guess. Most of the girls come to me when they want to know something about days

off and it makes it hard too. I just turn them over to Jean whenever I can.

Another kink in the relationships was the arrangement for meals. The union contract provided for one meal a day at the hotel's expense but in the course of events various situations had arisen to govern how the meal was consumed. The Coffee Shop cashiers ate within that dining room and ordered from the regular customers' menu. Kate and her main checking desk crew ate at their desks but it was Coffee Shop food they received and they were allowed all of it they wanted. The Soda Fountain cashiers and the beverage stand checkers, however, had to eat at the Fountain, where all they could get at night was sandwiches and soda pop.

SOLUTIONS

Once the situation was reviewed, certain reforms went into effect at once. The most important was the reorganization of the checkers' work flow. There was no room in the kitchen for an additional desk so it was decided to use one end of the beverage checking stand for checking food. The King Cole and Room Service waiters and waitresses were shifted to this desk, thus cutting in half the waiting line and the excitement at the other desk. One of the main desk checkers was moved over to take care of this work at the beverage stand and one new employee was hired to take care of the night shift work here. She also helped the night shift beverage checker-cashier who had had an unusually heavy burden of work before. The supplies of officers' checks and saleschecks were removed to the dining room cashiers' desks where they were more accessible to the waitresses, thus making more room available at the main checking stand. The room service phone, which had been given to the checkers to answer years before on a "temporary basis," was now turned over to its proper department where there were now sufficient employees on duty to care for it. These changes alone made enough difference to change Kate's mind about quitting. She all but cried on Mr. Wiley's shoulder a day or so later.

Honestly, you have no idea how different it is. It's just a new job altogether, that's all. It isn't only that the work is cut almost in half, either, but the confusion is so much less. You see when all the dining rooms were busy at once, before this new stand opened, half the waitresses would go in one direction when they left the stand and the others would want to go the other. They were forever getting into each others' way and we were always afraid of trays upsetting or food splashing over the dishes. Not only that, but we didn't have time to be polite to people. The room service phone would ring all the time and we were just too busy to be courteous. I admit it, I know myself I just *had* to be short with people. We tried to cut out every unnecessary word to save time. Now—oh, I feel swell today. It is like heaven, really it is.

We had hoped that the overtime the cashiers were putting in on bookwork could be eliminated by having the work done the following morning during slack hours, but this couldn't be agreed upon. The night auditors were too proud of their up-to-the-minute accounts. But when it was pointed out that these girls were entitled to be paid for their overtime, this was immediately corrected and they got the regular union time and a half from then on.

Not too much could be done to improve the physical conditions. A new kitchen was in the plans and it was hoped that this would be a comfortable place for everyone. Meanwhile Mr. Smith ordered the heat pipes to be insulated. It helped somewhat to overcome the physical unpleasantness and, even more, it helped to ease the psychological tensions.

The system of the food checkers training the waitresses in proper service came up for discussion and Mr. Kraus pointed out that, properly, new rules and new waitresses should be taken care of by the dining room managers and not the kitchen help. It was agreed by everyone that this course should be pursued in the future.

The supervision tangle was straightened out by the auditor. Since one of the disputing parties was a cashier and the other a checker, it was decided to split this department in two with one head for each, their pay to be equalized. The organizational structure was thus defined so that everybody was relieved and content on this score.

Then there was the problem of food. Mr. Wiley urged that all the women get meals in the Coffee Shop, saying it was pretty difficult to level off downward, but he pointed out that the main thing was to get a uniform pattern. The Fountain was over-crowded all the time, whereas the Coffee Shop had slack periods so that the checkers and cashiers would eat without getting in the way of paying guests. But Mr. Kraus, always careful of funds, thought they should try eating at the Fountain and see how that worked, and it was so arranged.

To provide a continuing method for solving problems, and to give these isolated women a sense of group belongingness, we proposed group meetings but we failed completely to put the idea across. Nobody refused us a meeting. In fact, every time the question came up, the auditor assured Mr. Wiley earnestly that he intended having one at his first opportunity. The time just never arrived.

Once the reforms got under way and the new checker stand was opened, a glow of satisfaction seemed to go through every-one concerned. There was no doubt of its general acceptance. The waiters and waitresses sang its praises:

> Say, that new checker's stand is swell, isn't it? That certainly made a big difference in our service. Gee, we used to have to stand around and all the food would get cold while we waited. Then the customers would gripe. It wasn't our fault, it was just that we had to wait out at that checker's desk. I'm sure glad this new desk is in operation.

The dining room managers, the checkers, everyone remarked on the improvement in service. It served as an example which we used to encourage other employees to give suggestions. We would say, "That was the checkers' idea and it helped everyone, didn't it?" And they would say it certainly had and go on to state in their own words what a difference it had made in their work. Visible changes like this were extremely helpful and made each step in our project somewhat easier than the ones before it.

Chapter VIII

THE FRONT OFFICE [1]

To many of the Tremont employees, the guests were people for whom they worked in an indirect sort of way but seldom saw. Not so the front office employees. The room clerk, mail clerk, the cashier and assistant manager had to talk to the guests face to face and deal with them as people. Consequently, the pressures of wartime traveling conditions were grim realities for these employees. All day long a constant stream of disconsolate persons came through the hotel lobby, begging for rooms, pleading for rooms. There just wasn't enough hotel space in the city to accommodate all the travelers. To be able to say "no" a hundred times a day and do it gracefully is quite a feat. To say "no" only to the poor credit risks and always "yes" to the others is more than a feat, it is a fine art and not many people attain it.

The work at the Tremont was not only difficult, it was underpaid. At the time, stenographers throughout the city were earning from $110 to $175 a month. A Tremont mail clerk earned from $95.68 to $124.80 a month. (The maids were earning $98.88.) Cashiers did a little better, getting $116.48 to $145.00, but even the room clerks, whose positions were most exacting, received a mere $124.80 to $210, not much compared to what defense workers were getting right in the same area.

People were hired for these positions on the basis of appear-

------

[1] E. L. H.

97

ance and education as well as experience. They had to have pleasant personalities, dress well, be able to meet guests with poise. Why did they work here? The work was glamorous and exciting to many employees. They were willing to put up with poor pay in exchange for this impressive public front.

RECENT HISTORY

It would be difficult to appraise the state of affairs existing in the Tremont's front office without getting a glimpse of the situation six months previous to our study, when Mr. Flanagan had been in charge of the office. He was an old friend and business associate of Mr. Smith, one of the "Sheridan clique" who had worked with the boss in a previous venture. Mr. Flanagan was a genial man but not an organizer. With the hotel jammed to the doors with guests, he was kept busy handling individual cases, and when his employees needed him he never could be found.

And they needed him often! The way room reservations were being handled at that time, about ten people were accepting applications and there wasn't sufficient check made of them, so that frequently the house was oversold. The distraught, angry guests who found themselves without shelter when night came would demand to see the person in charge and if he wasn't available they took out their wrath on the defenseless clerks. Other nights there would be as many as 50 to 60 rooms vacant, and this in a city crowded with travelers.

The "queen bee" of the office was Mr. Flanagan's secretary, Susan. Like her boss she was given to sociability and was almost as hard to find as he was. It was one of her tasks to contact "special guests" and make sure they were well taken care of. She handled convention reservations and helped to schedule banquets. Perhaps her main task was to be pretty and entertaining, and this she did quite well. Work was secondary.

As the entire complexion of business changed during the war emergency, little was done to make adjustments in the work load. The cashiers, for instance, had a cubbyhole of their own at one far end of the front office. When business had been moderate, there had been only one cashier on duty at a time. She knew most of the guests on sight and when they came to cash a check, she didn't have to see whether they had identification but could cheerfully and promptly give them their cash. In the less frequent cases of guests who were unknown to her, she had to go to the manager to have him OK the check first but he was seldom too busy to stop and give her courteous attention. Now, with people standing three deep outside her window, the cashier had an assistant who handled the bookwork while she spoke to the guests. This meant that two people were working inside a space meant for one, and there was some irritation arising from overcrowding. There were so many new faces among the guests that even an experienced cashier couldn't keep track of them. Literally a hundred times a day she would have to trudge over to the manager's desk which lay, incidentally, clear across the lobby. And when she had pushed her way through the throngs and reached the desk, often as not he wasn't there and she had to hunt for him. The manager suggested that they keep more strictly to the use of "credit cards," but the guests had been trained in the easy ways of happier times, and they fretted when the girls asked their cooperation in setting up the formal credit-card system of identification.

The files used constantly by the room clerks were so arranged that only one person could comfortably use them at any given time, yet three and sometimes four people were trying to work with the guests at the room clerk's desk at which they were located. There were many other inefficiencies arising out of changed business conditions, but these examples should give the general picture.

The human relations problems were many. Some members of the staff (Flanagan and Susan) were busy being "greeters," while others, partly because of this, were so grossly overburdened with paper work that their jobs seemed untenable. It isn't strange that turnover was high even among these white-collar workers. When pressures increased, clerks quit, and it seemed to the despairing ones who remained that each replacement was inferior to the last.

The fact that eventually Mr. Flanagan was replaced by his assistant was regarded as a revolution in itself. (Mr. Wiley had nothing to do with this; it occurred well before our study of the department.) The notion of the "Sheridan clique" was firmly embedded in the minds of many of the staff, but here was a member in good standing being replaced by a man who was an old Tremont employee and of independent spirit at that. True, nobody called it a demotion to Mr. Flanagan's face. He was officially considered the night manager from this time on, but everybody knew it was a step down for him.

No sooner had his successor, Mr. Hume, taken over the office than things began to change. One of the first and most far-reaching innovations was the change in room reservation procedures. No matter who took a reservation for a room, even though he be the General Manager, he had to clear it through Mr. Hume's desk. This meant that a close check could be kept on the number of rooms available and the phenomenon of an oversold or undersold house became a thing of the past. This wasn't as simple as it sounds. The demand for rooms was so great that patrons were willing to pay almost any bribe to get them. Channeling the flow of business through one desk also meant channeling the flow of tip money and gifts, and that wasn't accomplished without grief. Nevertheless, the rule was passed, the General Manager upheld it, and it worked sufficiently well to establish order.

The second set of innovations changed the physical arrangement of the office. Files were made more accessible, the office was enlarged, and the manager's desk was brought within the main enclosure, thus making him available to employees when vexatious problems needed his attention.

With these obvious changes went more subtle ones. The new office manager wasn't the sociable man that his successor had been. The employees remarked enthusiastically, "He's always there when we want him," because he could be found at his desk, surrounded with paper work, most of the time. As the opportunity presented itself, he clarified positions of his staff members and outlined more precisely what their duties were. One of the most popular changes had to do with salaries. These had been absurdly out of line with one another, and instead of raises the people had been getting promises which were seldom fulfilled. Mr. Hume got together with Mr. Wiley and worked out a system for a sliding scale which gave most of his staff a small initial raise at once and provided a promise of progressive raises in the future. Mr. Hume explained:

> The problem is, first, to get good people on the job; then encourage them to stay a long time and get rid of those who don't pan out.

This is approximately what he did. The less adequate ones he managed to drop from his staff. The new "queen bee" of the office was his secretary, a woman who put business before pleasure, while the former secretary to Mr. Flanagan wilted under the new regime and finally quit.

In general, one might say that with the change of office managers went a formalizing of office procedures, more convenient physical arrangements, and a stabilizing and improvement of employment policies. When we arrived in the department, three months after Mr. Hume took over the office, there was little we could do to suggest improvements in these conditions. What we could and did do was to observe as carefully as possible to see what effect his work was having.

RESULTS OF THE CHANGE

It was plain that the evidence of intelligent planning had sent the general morale on an upward swing. Every employee interviewed responded in similar vein. A mail clerk said:

> It is much better lately. Since all the improvements went in, I mean. We used to have to stand up and type, did you know that? Two and three hours at a time! All my friends just about died when I told them that, they never heard of anybody having to stand up and type but we did. Now we can sit down, thank goodness. They are talking of getting us a new machine, too, and we have the files conveniently placed. It is much better, there is no comparison. Then for another thing, I'm making more money

now. It didn't go over so big when I was here for a year and making less than anybody else. Now they raised it and so I feel much better about the job. It's worth working for now.

While the feeling of gratification was genuine and universal, there appeared to be little feeling of participation in these changes on the part of the staff, and this sometimes tempered their enthusiasm for the new regime.

After remarking that things were much improved, the chief room clerk added:

> Smith said he wanted suggestions before we went about making all those changes. I don't know whether he meant it or not. I sent up a long list of suggestions, I know that. Whether the others did or not is something else again. Anyway, far as I can see they just ignored the whole thing. I never heard another word about it and I can't see that any of the suggestions were considered. He asked for them and I gave them, that's all I know. Maybe they weren't any good, they never said. So now if I have any ideas I go to Hume and tell him. If he thinks they are any good he can pass them along.

At least this man, an employee of 25 years, went to Hume with suggestions. Many of the others looked baffled when asked to whom they should take a suggestion.

> CASHIER: "Well, I'm not sure who to go to with a complaint, tell you the truth. I haven't been here long enough [four months]. If anything goes wrong, I just yap good and loud and somebody comes along and fixes it for me.

When Mr. Hume talked to us before the formal study of his department began he commented:

> I don't know why the spirit should be as low as it is, tell you the truth, but it's low right now. What happened is this: say you have four mail clerks, two on a shift. One girl will take a day off and the other one has to do all the work. It's too much for one person, see? She works like a dog all day and it makes her sore. She thinks, "Why should I sweat and slave to make up for her? I'll take tomorrow off to rest up and let her try working for both of us, see how she likes it." They are always trying to get even with the

other one. It never occurs to them to set an example, to put things to rights. If they would cooperate, try to get the job done right, why everybody would benefit, wouldn't they?

After Mr. Hume had been on the job long enough to have given the employees a sense of a new order being established, it seemed to us that this attitude changed. Weeding out the undesirables on the staff had a lot to do with it. A mail clerk told us:

> We had a succession of clerks, one worse than the next. It was very discouraging. That's another reason why I feel happy about my job now. Virginia is a sweet kid and we get along fine. She's energetic and more than willing to do her share of the work.

A room clerk had a similar account to offer:

> We have a pretty nice team down here all around. For some reason they have weeded out the gripers and the ones who are left take an interest in their jobs.

A reservation clerk said:

> Of course it makes you mad to have somebody laying down on the work so that you have to do yours and theirs too. I didn't particularly like doing the work and seeing somebody else get the credit. You just can't pull together when people get along as badly as that.

While the consensus seemed to be that within each work group people were cooperating with increasing harmony, there still was room for improvement between work groups. A cashier gave us some insight into this:

> We cashiers stick together, naturally, doing the same work all the time, but I always think of myself as being part of the front office. We have to work together to get the work done. I don't think there is enough understanding, though, I think it could be better. I've wondered about that, how to improve it I mean. If we could only get over to them how badly we need those folios! [She went on to explain the dependence of the cashier on other parts of the front office.] I don't know, maybe if they studied our work for a half hour some slack day, wouldn't that help? Then we could

go over to the other desks and see what goes on there. We probably need to learn that work too, so we could see what they are
up against.

It was essential that all parts of the department pull together. The
cashier was by no means the only one who needed the sympathetic support of other groups.

The front office was one of the departments which had not
yet begun having regular monthly meetings and it interested us
to hear the employees requesting one.

> If Mr. Hume would get all of us together so that the mail clerks
> and room clerks and cashiers could talk things over—gee, that
> would be a swell idea. We used to have meetings like that years
> ago, but it has been so busy lately, maybe they figure they can't
> take the time. People should be able to speak up face to face and
> get things off their chest, don't you think so? Instead of us griping
> about a mail clerk, if we all got together we could straighten things
> out so easily. I'd like to see us all get together.

Mr. Hume occasionally held meetings for the small work
groups. He held one for mail clerks while our study was going on
and it was illuminating to hear the comments afterward.

> Then another good policy here, they have meetings for the
> employees. I like that. We had one for the mail clerks and it
> helped a lot to clear things up.

> Those meetings help. We had one just lately and it's a good idea,
> I think. When you have a lot of new people doing a job, each one
> does it a little differently. What Mr. Hume did was to bring in a
> little notebook and suggest that we each jot down the things we
> wanted discussed. We put in our suggestions and then we discussed
> all of them. Then Mr. Hume said what way he wanted it and that
> was that. It was what we needed. Once he said that was the way
> he wanted it, everyone was satisfied.

The attitude the staff took toward Mr. Hume was a rather
mixed one. They gave him and Mr. Smith full credit for improving their working conditions and raising their salaries, yet
there was little warmth expressed for either of these two men.

They would speak of Mr. Hume, then hesitate and quietly add, "He's all right" without much enthusiasm. Occasionally one would be harsher.

> I thought when Hume took over it might be different, but he thinks he's so darned much that no one likes him. He never asks you to do something, he orders you to do it.

We were inclined to think that this went back to the lack of participation the people felt in the new changes. Mr. Hume had been "benevolent" in a somewhat autocratic way, and, while they appreciated his efforts on their behalf, they resented them too. The reservation clerks, working with him in the same office day after day, spoke with more fellow feeling, saying how hard he worked, but the others had little to add once they mentioned the fact that the physical changes were good. Mr. Hume himself told us:

> It might just be what is needed down there, to have somebody talk to those people, do you know that? I'd love to do it myself. I'd like nothing more than to have time to sit and get to know them somewhat. Do you know I haven't had time to sit down with even one of them and get to know him individually? There just isn't opportunity. The phone rings and the guests come in with demands, a man just can't do it.

It was true that the office hummed with activity. As things quieted down with the passing of the wartime frenzy, this condition might have been remedied. It was our feeling, however, that Mr. Hume was normally a man of great reserve who would find it difficult to be "folksy" with his employees. Where Mr. Flanagan had been the "personality boy" type, so necessary in a hotel, Mr. Hume was the organizer, also necessary and particularly scarce in the Tremont.

PUBLIC RELATIONS

The biggest problem of any front office employee is how to get along with the guests. All day the phone rings and guests crowd around. A clerk philosophized:

This job either makes saints or madmen, I should imagine. If you can master it, you acquire the ability to keep calm while everyone else goes crazy.

The first problem to be met was, whose reservations were to be given priority. When so many more people were applying for rooms than could be accommodated, it was possible to be highly selective, but there seemed to be no uniform way to do the selecting. The older employees knew many of the steady patrons and their tastes but a new clerk was left to flounder. Most of the staff agreed that businessmen from well-established firms should have preference, but which firms were to be considered well established was left to the individual to decide. Mr. Hume ultimately reviewed all reservations but his final check didn't help much when people came in person for rooms and wanted to know at once about their chances. Some of the clerks took pity on women and soldiers. Others would never take in a soldier if they could avoid doing so. Some favored big city residents, other small town folk, and so on.

The chief room clerk commented on some employees he had known.

> We have had some lemons in here, I'm telling you. Some of them were really hopeless. They would get so nervous and the guests would complain to me—it was a headache.

The trouble was, a new clerk had to learn the hard way. When a man constantly ran into trouble with the guests, everyone suffered. The way most people learned the ropes was by watching the older employees, especially the assistant managers. When a man mastered the art of getting along, he acquired prestige accordingly and much was forgiven him.

> He's a wonderful man, though. He knows how to handle people. You should see him at work! People come in here just demanding rooms. They act as though they are thinking, "Either I get a room or I never walk into the Tremont again!" And after they talk to him they think "Well, after all if they haven't any rooms left, they just haven't! They would help me if they could." He's wonderful that way. . . .

Mr. Stevens, an assistant manager was suddenly demoted amid a flurry of excitement. We expected a lot of fireworks over that, and some occurred, as we shall discuss later. But some of his fellow workers weren't as upset by the shift as we expected them to be. When they got around to discussing it, this is what they said:

> He wasn't the man for that job, he's so nervous. You'd be surprised, you might not know that but he is. He wasn't right for that job at all. Now take the matter of okaying checks, especially for old ladies, he was downright rude to people. He would say, "Do you have any identification?" Well, an old lady doesn't know what identification means and she might say, "I have a charge account at the department store." Then he'd say, "MADAM, I said do you have any identification?" The poor woman wouldn't know what to say. She might say, "Well, the other Assistant Manager—" and he'd say, "MADAM!! I SAID. . . ." Well, by that time we were all feeling so sorry for that poor woman, it was all we could do to sit there and not say something. . . .

The same thing was true of a clerk who got excited; he made everyone else suffer.

> Those others get so het up, they take it too seriously. I had a lady come up to me the other morning. She's the wife of a banker in a small town near here and she's a very nice person. She said to me, "I guess in times like these we can't complain about how we are treated, but believe me when good times come back, we won't take the sort of abuse we took last night." That was all she said. She meant the other shift, see? They had been pushing people around again. What happens, they get so excited when things get tight and then they take it out on the guests.

THE KENT CASE

Following Mr. Flanagan's fall from grace, the notion of the "Sheridan clique" had lost vitality. It had been quite some time since we had heard any really biting remarks along this line, when suddenly the old prejudice flared high.

There was a young man, Mr. Kent, who had worked at the

Sheridan Hotel when Mr. Smith was manager there. He was to all appearances an exceptionally able and attractive young man. When the war started he was called into the armed services while the older men stayed on to run Mr. Smith's hotel for him. While Mr. Kent conducted himself honorably in the army and became an officer, he also married Mr. Smith's secretary. With the end of hostilities he returned to civilian life and what could be more natural than that he should come to Mr. Smith for a job.

It was just before Mr. Smith left for South America and perhaps he was laden with too many details at the last minute to handle the situation well. In any case, Mr. Kent was hired at top salary and Mr. Kraus was given the job of demoting Mr. Stevens, one of the assistant managers (and a "Tremont" not a "Sheridan clique" man) and putting Mr. Kent in his place. Mr. Kent's new supervisor, Mr. Hume, was curtly informed of the new addition to his staff. Nobody was consulted prior to Mr. Kent's hiring, and the first Mr. Wiley knew about it was when the grapevine began carrying hot rumors. Mr. Smith went off to South America in blissful ignorance of the tempest, and Mr. Kent and the rest of the staff were left to adjust to one another as best they were able. A few days later the demoted man whose place Mr. Kent had taken was up in Miss Lentz's office pouring out his grief.

> Miss O'Brien's husband is getting my job. I'm being moved down to make a place for him. I'll be a room clerk. They weren't big enough to let me keep the title even [Assistant Manager]. That would have helped. Mr. Hume is going to make it as easy for me as he can. . . . I don't know how they expect to keep up morale. Everybody down there wonders who will be next. What else can they expect of us? Hume knows damn well he will be next.
>
> LENTZ: No fooling?
>
> STEVENS: Sure, they'll never let Miss O'Brien's husband work under Hume, you know that. It's only a matter of time before he gets Hume's job. Hume said to me just now he's expecting the knife. . . . That's how it is around here, always has been and still is. If you belong to the Sheridan clique you get ahead; otherwise you don't.

(*speaking of Kraus*) He's one of the most reasonable men in this hotel, that's a fact. Now take this business with me. He was decent about that. God knows it wasn't an easy job for him either, to hand out that stuff. He told me right out that he didn't like it. He was against it, he said. . . . Well, that's neither here nor there, but it was decent of him to say that. He broke the news to me as well as anybody could do. After all, it isn't his fault. . . .

Well, it's nothing new, none of us have the right to be surprised, I guess. That Sheridan clique always did run this place. This is just more of the same. Nobody downstairs will feel like working, who can blame them? If they can bring somebody in over your head like this, and it doesn't matter how hard you work.

We wondered how much truth there was in the statement that Hume was "expecting the knife." He had done such an excellent job in straightening out the front office that we would have been sorry indeed to see him discouraged to the point of leaving. We soon found out that this was the case. Mr. Kent's arrival had increased his woes in more ways than one:

One thing about morale in that office, when a person feels secure in his job and that he is in line for promotions, he will work hard and get pleasure out of it. But when a new person can come in over his head, well, what can you expect? Now I don't have anything against Mr. Kent's coming in here. Personally I think it was right that he should be brought in. After all, he was a veteran and he had worked for Mr. Smith before, he was entitled to his job. But when he came in, I had four men come to me all upset, wondering what it meant to them. Sure, that made us an extra room clerk. The jobs were overloaded and they knew it so each one wondered whether he was to be bumped. I had to sit down with each one separately and discuss it with him and try to explain how it happened. Then another thing, Mr. Kent's coming from the Sheridan didn't help matters much. We have an old feeling around here that anybody coming from the Sheridan has a natural "in" with the boss. The rest of them figure they can't compete with that, they feel out in the cold. So everybody knows that Kent is a Sheridan man and has the jump on them. . . . As I said, I think it was right to bring in Kent, I'm not trying to take a crack at him. But my point is, if they do this over a period of time, you have to expect people to feel insecure and consequently to fall down on their jobs.

Now you take Mr. Stevens, maybe they didn't think he was good at the job, I don't know how they feel. But if that's the conclusion they came to, why didn't they let him go? That man put in two, three years at honest endeavor, trying to do the right thing. Then they demote him to room clerk. They didn't take his salary away, just his title. What's the sense of that, can you see? It wouldn't have cost them anything to let him keep his title, would it? It doesn't cost anything and think what it means to him in prestige, not only here on the job but at home and with his friends too. I can't see that at all (*pause*).

Well, I talked to each of them separately and tried to explain how it was. That's life, isn't it? One darn thing after another. You can see why I wonder whether any progress is being made.

Mr. Kent, fortunately for us all, had a pleasing personality and could handle the public well. Women on the staff said he "seemed awfully nice and interested in the work, too." The women were not made insecure by his coming as some of the men were.

Two months later the reverberations were still running high. Mr. Hume was talking to Mr. Wiley about the possibility of a raise in salary for his secretary. He was in favor of it, but Kent, Flanagan, and others felt the woman was too officious and shouldn't be encouraged. Mr. Hume commented to Mr. Wiley:

Many times I have done things that I knew were wrong, but I couldn't do differently because if I did, I conceded a point to the Sheridan crowd and I weakened my own position. That's the way it is with this raise. I don't like to break the cooperation down there even if it is just on the surface; but on the other hand I can't let them get the better of me either.

It had become a tug of war. Mr. Hume felt he had to maintain a balance between the new and old cliques but found himself naturally on the side of the Tremont clique and opposed to the Sheridan one even to the point of doing things he felt were wrong.

If the bad feeling had confined itself to the front office, things would have been bad enough, but since Mr. Stevens, being an old employee, had friends throughout the hotel, the unhappiness spread. We got repercussions from all over the house:

> There is one clique around here that's the whole show. Flanagan, Kane, O'Mara, and now Kent. They all came from the Sheridan and they all know Mr. Smith from way back. They are the hotel. The rest don't count. . . . Everybody hates them, they won't work with them because they are from the Sheridan, and that's not right either. . . .

Here was an instance where Mr. Smith's new personnel manager could have been a help to him, had he been consulted in time. Mr. Wiley was by now well enough versed in hotel patterns of thought to be able to predict what happened in such a case. It wouldn't have been too difficult to introduce Mr. Kent in a way that would have won him early approval and acceptance.

The Kent case disrupted our own plans as well as those of Mr. Hume. It had seemed to us that Mr. Hume had handled very well the problems of work flow, layout and equipment, work procedures, and salary administration. We had had no desire to introduce changes in these areas. We felt at the time that a regular pattern of group meetings might help to bring Mr. Hume closer to his staff, to improve relations among employees performing interdependent functions, and to provide guidance in handling the public. Under other circumstances, Mr. Wiley might have been able to work with Mr. Hume toward the development of such a program. As it was, Mr. Hume was too troubled by the Kent case to undertake anything new.

Mr. Wiley at least did whatever he could to support Mr. Hume. He gave Mr. Smith a glowing report on Hume's achievements in the front office, and Mr. Smith complimented Mr. Hume shortly thereafter. Mr. Wiley also sought to reassure Mr. Hume directly. We hoped that, with time, Mr. Hume would feel more secure and would again be able to take a constructive approach to his job.

Chapter IX

THE KING COLE ROOM[1]

The King Cole was one of those dark, wood-paneled places where people go for drinking and fellowship. It seated 150 persons but at smaller tables than the other dining rooms, and, where the swankier Zebra Room used white linen tablecloths, the King Cole used red and white striped place mats. It was known everywhere. Mention the fact that you worked at the Tremont, and out-of-towners were sure to say brightly, "Oh, that's where the King Cole is, isn't it? Do you know Larry?"

Larry was as much a local tradition as his room. He had been headwaiter for something like 25 years and looked just right for his role, being short, stout, and bald headed. His jovial personal approach had a great appeal for the customers. His dining room was jammed to the doors all the time and the cash rolled in most satisfactorily.

Larry was one of the supervisors who greeted us most cordially. He gave us the same hearty welcome he gave every guest, but we had hardly got upstairs before the rumblings of trouble began to reach our ears. His employees complained that he played favorites. He had "lieutenants" who exerted authority over other employees of the same status level, and this was resented. He was said to be shaking down his waiters for tip money; he was too affectionate with his waitresses; he was no gentleman. Most of these charges came from disgruntled em-

---
[1] E. L. H.

112

ployees as they shook the dust of the Tremont from their heels, and we withheld judgment. It was evident that Larry was a financial asset to the hotel, and since we lacked time to look into his department more than superficially, we felt our job was to get along with him for the present and try to lay the ground-work for closer relations in the immediate future.

Two occasions earned us Larry's good will. On V-J Day he was placed in charge of the Coffee Shop, which not only was the sole Tremont dining room to be open but one of the three dining rooms in town which attempted to give service that day. It was a wild time. Edith Lentz spent the day helping to set tables and clear off dirty dishes, and, from that day on, Larry was her friend. Then, at an early supervisors' meeting, Larry came in for a public chastising by Mr. Kraus, and, when the meeting was over, he poured out his chagrin to the willing ear of Meredith Wiley. As is usual in such cases, the role of the good listener won for Mr. Wiley Larry's confidence and he developed the habit of dropping into our office from time to time to chat about his work.

Mr. Kraus had jumped Larry about his failure to hold group meetings for his employees after he had been specifically ordered to do so, and Larry's reaction to this revealed his attitudes to-ward supervision in general. He said to Mr. Wiley:

> You know, Mr. Kraus thinks I should hold meetings, but I have meetings with one of the employees at least every meal time. You have seen me sitting there. I usually have some waiter or waitress with me, talking to them. That way I get to know them. I don't see how you can get these problems solved in a big meeting. Every person is different. I understand every one of my little chickens. I try to help them out, even their problems at home because the home problems affect their work and everything that affects their work affects me.

He told us on other occasions that his idea of a good supervisor was one who acted sympathetic, like Christ. Larry's interpreta-tion of this ideal was that he should be sympathetic to the weak, but he couldn't tolerate strength or independence.

Mr. Wiley encouraged Larry to try holding group meetings, pointing out that there were common problems which affected the entire department and could be handled most speedily in this fashion. Since top management was driving him in that direction, Larry acquiesced and began to hold meetings regularly. He was proud of his "democracy" and would speak of it at every opportunity. He told us of how he had his employees elect their own supervisor on the night shift.

> I did it by group vote. What I did, I said to them that we needed somebody to take over John's job and I said I thought a woman should be in that job. I told them right out that I personally preferred Betty. So I told them to speak up and give me their opinion. I said I wanted them to be perfectly frank. I wouldn't mind if they thought somebody could do it better, and I knew Betty wouldn't either. I went around the group and asked each one just what she thought about it. I said, "Do you think Betty would be a good person," and they each said, "Yes." It was yes, yes, yes. One girl was slow in speaking up and I said to her, "Now none of that slow stuff. Speak up, do you or don't you think she's the best person?" So she said "Yes." I believe in democracy. If they didn't want Betty, nobody would have been able to force me to put her in charge. I made sure they all wanted her before she was put in that job.

We hoped that Larry's meetings would improve with the course of time, but they didn't. Larry stated frequently that he wanted people to speak their minds, but the few who took him at his word soon found out otherwise. Three employee comments express the prevailing view:

> We have those meetings and he says we are to express our viewpoints. Then if we do, we get it in the neck! Nobody dares speak up. I'm getting so I just hate to go to those meetings. There are so many things I want to say and don't dare.

> It isn't that Larry isn't nice, but we don't have confidence. Like with the meetings, we are supposed to speak up and say what we want. But when we had a meeting about the busboys, one of the girls said that the trouble was, as soon as we got a good busboy

Larry took him for the day shift. Well, two girls were going to be laid off for that. He threatened to lay them off for two weeks because he said they didn't show the right attitude. Well, you can see how we feel about talking up. I know every time I have opened my mouth I've been sorry for it afterwards.

Now what kind of meetings are they if you can't talk up, would you tell me? Isn't that the damndest thing? They ask you to speak up and when you do, you get clipped. If you keep quiet, they say you're not interested in your work! Well, don't worry, from now on I'm keeping my mouth shut, interested in the work or not. I learned my lesson!

One of Larry's techniques for getting participation in his meetings when executives were present was to call upon people to express an opinion. He would start at one side of the room and work his way around, calling on everyone in turn, but his topic would be a carefully selected one. For instance he started a round once by saying:

Now, Geraldine, you have been here three years, you must have seen some improvements. What do you think has improved since you have been here? Do you think we have done a better job down here?

Each employee in turn then had to say how much better the dining room was becoming.

Since there was so limited a freedom to speak within the department, the employees turned to their union when the going got too tough. Larry hated the union above all else, and he had reason. It was the only agency which was effectively limiting his freedom. In the case of sharing tip monies with the busboys, for instance, he did everything he could to dissuade his workers from taking the issue up with union headquarters. He said in a special meeting called to discuss this issue,

There are two places where you can go for advice. The first is to your superiors. You can find out what you can do, the right way to do things, by watching those above you and asking them questions. . . . The other place you can get advice is from the outside. The people outside do not have the interest of the House at heart. They aren't interested in you. You can get advice from them but you will suffer if you do. The right place to go if you want prestige and advancement and to better your livelihood is to the people above you on the job. Don't go to outsiders!

Now I don't want to criticize you, I like you . . . [but] we must admit to ourselves that management is shopping. Management is always shopping for employees. Right now we have plenty of work but that might not continue. You and I know that we have good times and bad times in this business and if bad times come, management will have to shop among you and pick out the workers who do the best job. I'm not trying to worry anybody, I'm just putting you wise that it is to your best interest to do a good job.

In spite of his advice, they went "outside" and the result was that Larry had to backtrack on his ultimatum that the busboys should be raised 25¢ a night in tips (the waiters and waitresses to foot the bill). The union would have none of it.

The union came into the picture, too, when the waitresses were transferred from the Zebra Room to the King Cole Room although in this instance the heat was not put on Larry but on Mr. Kraus and the Zebra Room manager. In the cases so far mentioned, Mr. Wiley stood on the sidelines. He was naturally involved insofar as he was Personnel Manager, but he didn't have to take direct action. In the case of Shirley he did. Shirley had a quarrel with one of the King Cole captains and he promptly suspended her, whereupon she went to the union and the union ordered that she be reinstated. About a week later, Larry decided to fire her for good. He came to Mr. Wiley and said that the girl was still fighting with the captain and it was an impossible situation.

She thinks she can run the place. I tell you, Mr. Wiley, if I can't run the King Cole I might just as well leave. I can't do a thing. We do everything for the employee.

WILEY: You feel you aren't being permitted to run the King Cole?

LARRY: Yes, whenever we do anything the girls run over to the union. Now Mr. Wiley why don't you try to decide these things for the hotel? It's just as easy to decide them for the hotel as for the employees. You have a lot of influence with the union.

WILEY: Well, I'll tell you just exactly how I have tried to decide such things. I try to get all sides of the story. After I have all the facts I try to see whatever is fair and right is done. I can't do it any other way. . . . There are other ways of punishing an employee than firing her. I'll tell you, Larry, I'm afraid you are going to have trouble with the union if you let this girl go, in view of the fact that we had all this trouble with her just last week. You see it looks like you might be holding a grudge.

Mr. Wiley finally persuaded Larry to scold the girl and then give her another chance. He did this and subsequently reported a marked improvement in her conduct.

In the case of Grace, Mr. Wiley had to play an even more dominant role. Grace was a perky little waitress who was in the habit of speaking her mind. She and Larry had never got along for this reason. When her husband returned home after his overseas service in the army, she asked if she might have a month's leave of absence for a second honeymoon. In view of the fact that she had worked for the Tremont through the war, Mr. Wiley felt she was entitled to it. Larry, however, wouldn't give her an answer on the matter although she had asked him several times. Would Mr. Wiley please settle the thing for her? Mr. Wiley did. He didn't make any attempt to influence Larry's decision either way but simply inquired whether he wished to grant the leave or not, without any comment. Larry agreed the girl could have her leave.

Several weeks later, while the girl was still on her leave of absence, Larry sent a "final card" through on her (signifying termination of service). Miss Dickson just happened to catch it and recalled that Grace was the girl who had expressed mistrust of Larry, fearing that he would pull a dirty trick on her during her absence. Miss Dickson took the case up with Mr. Wiley before sending the final card through and Mr. Wiley went at once to Larry to see what it was all about.

WILEY: Wasn't this the girl we gave a leave of absence to?

LARRY: Yes, but I changed my mind. She isn't very good and I thought I'd let her go.

WILEY: You remember I talked to you about her. Of course after that talk I told her that she would be put on "leave of absence" status. It would be pretty difficult for us to go back on our word and call it a discharge. I really don't think it's right, do you? She probably won't stay with us long after she returns, her husband is back from service, you know.

LARRY (*tearing the card up*): All right, Mr. Wiley.

He didn't look happy, but there were no more comments made at this time. When Grace returned after her month's leave was up, she reported for work and Larry's lieutenant told her that her station was filled by another girl, and there was no job available for her. Grace came up to our office, shaking with emotion, and again Mr. Wiley had to go to bat for her. Larry said angrily:

We haven't got any station for her. Am I supposed to fire somebody to put her back on?

Mr. Wiley explained as patiently as he could that the girl was entitled to her job back. After considerable conversation it was revealed that another waitress was planning to quit in two days, thus leaving a station open, so Grace was advised to take off two more days and that she would definitely get her post back at that time, so a compromise was effected. The next day Grace telephoned us from her home. She said nervously:

Larry didn't like me talking to you last night. He said he didn't like the way I had gone over his head and that if I ever did it again, I was *out*. So I guess I can't come up to Personnel anymore. I thought you would want to know that.

A few days later Larry was up in the office telling Miss Lentz about a small matter he had fixed to his satisfaction. One of his employees had done a bad thing. (She had cursed in the dining room.) Instead of firing the girl, he had talked to her and got the matter straightened out. It seemed to us that he was trying to get back into Mr. Wiley's good graces via Miss Lentz, trying to show us that he really wasn't such a poor supervisor after all. Miss Lentz responded warmly to his account and he left looking happier. Our relations with Larry moved onto a more stable plane for a time, although we continued to be troubled with reports that King Cole people felt it was "unsafe" to be seen in close proximity to us.

Just about this time we began to hear new rumors that the union was out gunning for Larry, and there was talk of their pulling a strike if any more trouble occurred in the King Cole. At the same time Mr. Smith began to inquire crossly why the King Cole turnover figures weren't going down in the same proportion as the other dining rooms. He announced to Mr. Wiley that he planned to get Larry up to his office and tear into him. "He's getting so he thinks he owns the place." It seems that the union had been telling Mr. Smith of their difficulties with Larry, which was probably the cause of his sudden concern for the management of the King Cole.

The subsequent meeting was remarkable. Mr. Smith tried in vain to get Larry to face the fact that his turnover was running too high. Larry insisted on citing individual cases.

> SMITH: I don't think we care so much what each one of these people said was the reason they left. What we want to know is the underlying cause. People will give any kind of a reason for leaving, not necessarily the right one. Maybe we can get at the base of the trouble.

Larry was completely unable to answer Smith's probing questions and finally, over his protests, Mr. Smith suggested that Miss Lentz make a formal study of his department. At the time Miss Lentz had her hands full, but, since the King Cole situation had become so critical, other things were dropped and a study of Larry's department got under way at once.

We knew well enough that it was on the night shift that most of the King Cole trouble lay. Larry himself worked days, and he had built up an excellent staff, partly by transferring the preferred waitresses and busboys from the night shift. However he accomplished it, it seemed a closely knit team that was doing a good job. We were interested in discovering why the day shift worked so much more cooperatively than the night one. It seemed to us that a careful comparison of the two groups would give us more insight into the situation than would comparing the King Cole with the Zebra Room, for instance.

Miss Lentz consulted Larry on how to proceed, as was our custom in beginning a departmental study, and he promptly suggested that she interview his day crew. We agreed to that procedure only to find to our dismay that nothing seemed to come out of it. Everybody was happy. They all loved their work. They loved each other. They loved Larry. The Tremont was a wonderful place to work. We were willing to grant that the King Cole day shift was a good outfit—but a perfect one? Something was fishy.

We didn't believe in pressing people when they were reluctant to talk to us. Miss Lentz's procedure was to put the person being interviewed at ease by offering him a bit of chit-chat, a cigarette, and then letting him talk as uninterruptedly as possible. Occasionally it was necessary to put a few questions to him to get him talking on the subject of his work, but we tried not to regiment the interviews any more than we had to. Sometimes it was tantalizing. There was one waitress, for instance, whom we knew had had grave trouble with Larry only a month or so before. She was a shy person and unquestionably a "good" girl whom Larry had deeply offended by making improper advances to her in front of witnesses, with the result that she spent one afternoon crying in the girls' room. She had never reported it to us but the witnesses had. Now she sat in our office, her body tense with anxiety.

> I haven't anything to suggest. Everything is just fine as far as I can see. And Larry is a wonderful boss, he is so considerate. [Her eyes pleaded with me.] I couldn't say a thing against him, he's just fine to work for.

What could we do? We decided not to try to push our way in. When the time ripened, they would come to us willingly.

The night shift was something else again. When consulted about the best time and place to talk to these employees, Larry first tried to persuade Miss Lentz to interview the group all at one time, rather than individually. Finding that unsuccessful, he began to alibi about the night shift situation.[2]

By now Larry was feeling perfectly wretched about the whole thing. To do him justice, he didn't know what was expected of him. Up to this point Mr. Smith had given him almost perfect freedom to run the dining room as he chose. Now out of a clear sky (so far as he was concerned) Mr. Smith, the union, and the personnel office were ganging up to make his life miserable. For the life of him he couldn't understand it.

Shortly after this interview we were presented with proof of what we had been suspecting, that he had been trying to terrorize his employees into keeping quiet in our office. There were two girls who reported this to Mr. Kraus and he called Mr. Wiley in to witness their complaints.

GRACE: And there's another thing, we were told what to say to Miss Lentz.

KRAUS: You mean that somebody told you what you were supposed to say up there?

GRACE: That's right, Mr. Kraus, they did.

KRAUS: Who's they?

GRACE (*names* LARRY, *the night captains, and some of* LARRY'S *henchmen*): They have been coming up to us all the time, telling us that we had better say the right thing. We better say that we like it the way it is, that we don't have any trouble down there at all.

The other girl was more reluctant to talk. Mr. Kraus had called her up to verify some of the things Grace had said, and, when the personnel office was mentioned, she became excited and began to talk swiftly and indignantly.

MAY: Well, I don't think it is right. We are supposed to talk to

---

[2] Appendix F gives the transcription of this revealing conversation.

Miss Lentz and tell her how we feel. I thought that was a very fair way to do things but then when we were ready to come up, they all came around and told us that we should tell her we liked it here and that we don't want any changes. I don't know what to do. It isn't fair the way it is down there, and I can't say that it is all right and be honest. I can't understand Ruth, either. When we first talked about this, Ruth very strongly thought that we should have rotating stations, but I guess they must have talked her out of it because she was telling me that I should change my mind. She said whatever we say won't make any difference anyway, we better be careful if we know what's best for us. . . .

It was difficult to see a clear way out of the situation into which Larry had put us. Of course, there was always the possibility of making an open accusation of his trickery, but we wanted to hold that off as the final choice. It may have been vanity on our part, but we could never quite bring ourselves to take overt action against people like Larry or Mr. Kraus. We were bound and determined to win them over by pacific means.

The interviewing of the night shift got under way and again the first contacts were valueless. Then, suddenly, the tide turned. There were several "cliques" on that shift. We knew enough about human relations to realize what was happening. Each clique was seized with the fear that the others were squealing on them and that their only defense lay in offense. Once they began to open up, they told us everything. We learned a lot of things about human nature which weren't particularly pertinent to the King Cole but also received considerable insight into that turbulent place. We found out what lack of leadership did to a place of work. That was really the crux of the matter. As Larry himself had once remarked, the night shift were "orphans." He always worked days and left the night shift to the care of a long succession of night managers, none of whom stayed more than a few months. Whether deliberately or not, he had kept these men weak in authority and perhaps this was why the turnover among them was so high. In the absence of any established law and order, the stronger spirits on the staff began to prey on the weaker ones. The clique of aggressors divided the good stations among themselves. They grabbed off the good tips. They were also indulging in some drinking on company time and were effectively barring all attempts to correct this situation. This, we found, led to guilt feelings on the part of the aggressors and considerable frustration on the part of the milder members of the staff.

Larry's "pet" waitress, according to all reports, was in a particularly tough spot. A relatively new employee, she nevertheless was getting so many plums that even the clique of aggressors was griping about her luck. She had the largest station of them all. It was near the door, so she had the most rapid turnover of customers, resulting in the most tips. It was also nearest the kitchen and supply boards so she spent the least amount of time on nonpaying trips back and forth. And she was the girl whom Larry had managed to get "elected" by his democratic process to position of night "lieutenant." This gave her control over regulating days off, late duty, vacation assignments. Nevertheless, the others spoke well of her. They said it wasn't fair that she get all the breaks, but in the next breath they would testify that she was an excellent waitress and very fair about the way she assigned days off. One revealing fact was their praise of her for putting system into the late duty schedule. Until she got this job, it had always been handled in an exceedingly arbitrary way, they told us.

> You know we never used to know when we would have to work late. Every night there was a fuss down there. Now Betty has it all laid out in advance so everybody knows just when she has to work late. You have no idea what a difference a little thing like that made. It was the best thing ever happened down there (*laughs incredulously*). It's amazing, isn't it, that such a little thing should make so much difference, but it's a fact.

One main source of complaint, we found, centered around the business of stations. (A station is a group of tables assigned to one waitress.) We made Larry nervous by sitting in his dining room drawing pictures of it, but the results were most revealing. There was scant resemblance between work stations on the two shifts.

We inquired and found that at one time they had been alike. What had happened was that through the constant turnover of night managers, tables were swapped back and forth and never restored to their original stations. Perhaps an experienced waitress left and a novice replaced her. The novice might be unable to handle the station on busy nights and therefore one of her tables might be given to the waitress next to her, on a temporary basis. Should the manager who thus assigned them decide to leave, the experienced waitress might refuse to give up that extra table. In such a fashion the distribution of tables grew ever more awry.

It wasn't only that some stations were larger than others, but the arrangement of tables within them was poor. The girls would show us on our diagrams how one table of theirs was behind a post in respect to their other tables, and hence apt to be neglected. Another table, conveniently placed, would belong to the girl who had the next station. If the two girls were friendly, they might work together on such matters, switching tables in an informal fashion. We came upon "systems" among a clique of girls where each one was looking after a table or two of another, with a third girl helping the first one out, and so forth, the favors not being returned to the same person but within the group working out fairly enough. This sort of arrangement was tenuous, depending upon informal relationships built up through contacts at work and outside. The turnover among waitresses and the high state of tension within the department served to discourage such cooperative systems.

Many of the girls proposed that the stations be "rotated" as a means of ending the alleged favoritism. That meant that each night the stations would be assigned anew in such a way that every waitress would move about the dining room handling the stations in turn, thus getting a chance at all of them in the course of a fortnight. There were strong feelings about this proposal. Mr. Smith had suggested such an arrangement to Larry without much effect. It would have reduced drastically Larry's ability to mete out rewards and punishments if stations were assigned so methodically.

How the waiters and waitresses felt depended, naturally, on

which station they held. Some of the employees with the most seniority had the worst stations, and they were all for the change. The ones with the prize stations preferred to keep the *status quo* and threatened to quit if it were tampered with. They advanced excellent reasons for leaving things as they were. The best, it seemed to us, was that a waitress or waiter builds her own business over a period of time. Her satisfied customers return to her station regularly, and it is helpful to them to know where to find her. It is also good for the House since, knowing they could get good service, the guests would return to the King Cole. These waitresses looked on their jobs as an entrepreneur looks on his business. They felt they were entitled to the rewards for hard work and didn't want to share them.

We found that some of the best workers were on each side of the issues. Through interviews we intended to relieve the excess emotional tension, to encourage discussion within the group, and finally to settle the issue by taking a vote and letting the majority rule.

Then Larry popped up with another trick. Quite abruptly and without notice to us, he announced to both his day and night crews that starting immediately, *all* stations were to be rotated, orders of the personnel department! Whether he just wanted to take the initiative away from us, or whether it was a full-fledged plan to sabotage our project entirely by creating a wave of reaction to us through crediting us with such arbitrary action, we will never know. What he didn't consider was that by now the fear of us had abated considerably. We deliberately hadn't pressed anybody to talk to us and the group had decided that we were "fair." No sooner had Larry made his fateful announcement than waitresses from both shifts came running up to our office with the news. Was this our idea or wasn't it?

It was one of those places where, looking back, we can see how sharply we deviated from our original plans of action. We certainly had never contemplated going into a man's department and ordering him to hold a meeting of all his employees. Where was the velvet glove there? But that's what Mr. Wiley did. He asked Larry in front of some of the workers if meetings might be

called, and of course Larry had to acquiesce. In his address to
them Mr. Wiley made it quite clear that we had no wish to force
anything down anyone's throat. It was a "misunderstanding." To
the day crew he said that, as far as we could determine, people
were satisfied with things as they were. We had no intention of
changing anything for the present. To the night crew he pointed
out the dissatisfaction which was being expressed and listed all
the proposals that members of the group had made to Miss Lentz.
As he read off the list, people around the room nodded in recognition of their suggestions.

1. Keep the stations as they were.
2. Reassign the tables arbitrarily so that each station had the
   same number as all the others.
3. Reassign the stations in order of the seniority of waitresses
   and waiters.
4. Keep the stations as they were but put them up for bids as
   people quit, seniority ruling whose bid would win.
5. Rotate the stations every day or once a week.

He went on to say:

> I think the thing to do is to show you the possibilities you have
> and let you think them over very carefully. I cannot ask you not
> to consider your own personal benefits. I can't and I won't. I
> would like you, however, to look at this fairly and clearly as you
> can. I would like to have you consider not only yourself but con-
> sider the other fellow too and try to arrive at the best solution for
> everyone. My interest is to see that you get what you want and
> to see that the fairest and best method is chosen. Keep in mind
> that it's for everyone's benefit to have the fairest system. You
> can't expect cooperation otherwise.

He made it clear that no changes were to be made until everyone
had had the opportunity to speak to Miss Lentz privately, and
that then probably a vote would be taken to decide the issue.

Right at this time, when our minds were full of station distribution, a young fellow came in for a job as waiter. He had worked
in a room which corresponded closely to the King Cole, and
which was situated in the Tremont's biggest rival, the Hotel

Clinton. He had quit this well-paying position, not because he had the worst station there, but because he had the best one! Here's the way he looked at the situation:

> The thing was, they only had three good waiters down there so they gave us the three heavy stations. That made the others sore, especially the older men. They felt they had worked there a longer time than we had so they deserved the best stations. Well, they just couldn't handle them, see? They just couldn't. Sam put me on this big station and as I say, he had good reason, but it wasn't worth all the grief. Everybody was bickering all the time. I couldn't see it. It wasn't worth it to me. If you don't have co-operation, you can't do a good job. At least, I can't.

We watched the King Cole staff face this same problem, and saw how the issue grew and changed under the impetus of events. When the matter first came up in the interviews, it was shot through with bitterness and recriminations. Only the chronic gripers were complaining, the satisfied few insisted. It was only these Zebra girls who had resented being put into the King Cole; they were never happy here; they were troublemakers.

The "Zebra girls" were a study in themselves. While two of them were indeed highly dissatisfied, the other two spoke enthusiastically of the King Cole and of Larry. Our interviews help to interpret these differences.

Katherine was one of the two who got along well. (Like the other satisfied "Zebra girl," she worked on the day shift.)

> KATHERINE: I liked the King Cole from the first day. That's funny, too, because I didn't expect to like it. I always dreaded going in there and the girls still kid me about it. I told them I'd quit before I went in there, but the first day changed my mind.
> LENTZ: How come, Katherine?
> KATHERINE: Well, there seemed to be so much confusion. When I got in there I found there really wasn't any at all. Everything goes like clockwork. I never worked in such a well run place, Larry has it running perfectly. It is very busy but everyone knows just what is to be done. I can honestly say I never had a job I enjoyed more than this one. I like the room and I like working for Larry, he's a very fine man.

(*Later*) The way I happened to move into the King Cole, I have been on the night shift and then the men returned from service so I went on days. [This was the excuse finally given the girls for the forced transfer, that the hotel was forced to rehire these service men who had returned from the war. Actually the men were not former employees of the hotel and therefore we were entirely free to hire or not hire them.]

I couldn't make any money on daywork, it was so slow. Then George [headwaiter in the Zebra Room] asked me if I wanted to go over to the King Cole. He was very nice about it, he said I didn't have to go if I didn't want to but that a vacancy was there and I was the first one in line if I wanted it. I thought I might just as well try it so I did and I like it very much.

Katherine, then, transferred feeling that it was of her own volition. Her supervisor did her the courtesy of consulting with her before putting the transfer through. Her companion spoke similarly.

In the case of the first two girls to be moved, this wasn't so. They were informed one day that the next they were being shifted to the King Cole and arguments were of no avail. This was at Mr. Kraus's orders. He commented to Mr. Whyte that some of the employees didn't like it but that the hotel wasn't being run for their convenience. Nevertheless, when the girls went to him with protests, he tried to console them with promises.

ENA: You know Mr. Kraus and George were so sweet to us. They still are, they both tell Sophie and me to come to them immediately if Larry pulls any shady tricks. When we went into the King Cole we knew they were in back of us, so that helped.

LENTZ: Is that so?

ENA: Yes, and Larry knew it too. He said to Sophie and me, "One of you will have to work days." Well I just told him, "I'm sorry, Larry, but I always worked nights and I'm going to continue to work nights." Sophie told him, "I have children going to school and I can't possibly work days." Larry got sore right at the start because of that. He said, "Who do you think you are that you can come into the King Cole and start running things your way?" I told him, "Larry, I'm not trying to run the King Cole, I'm just telling you that I'm going to work nights. Mr. Kraus said we weren't to be pushed around." That made him furious, just furious. He turned and walked away; he wouldn't even talk to us any more . . . . You know Larry is afraid of losing his job . . . . He's afraid because he knows Mr. Kraus isn't too fond of him . . . . He's afraid of us, too. I know he's afraid of me, I can tell the way he stays away from me. We hardly say a word to each other except on business. He doesn't like us because he knows Kraus is fond of me and Sophie. Well Kraus is, he thinks we are nice girls, and he knows we understand good service.

The two who transferred feeling that they went of their own free will made satisfactory adjustments. Nobody mentioned "protecting" them from Larry's "shady tricks." They were put on the day shift where things presumably were well organized and where the group was well knit. In a very short while they had adjusted so well that the other girls never mentioned their being Zebra girls at all.

The other two were transferred arbitrarily—and with a warning against their supervisor. Also they went onto the King Cole night shift, which lacked a clear organization and was split up into cliques. These two waitresses complained frequently of Larry's favoritism. They continued to feel discriminated against and presented fair evidence to prove their point. Both girls wanted the stations to rotate, saying that in the Zebra Room they had always had rotating stations and it had worked well. These girls had the longest of any interviews with Miss Lentz. She let them talk out all their discontent and made herself readily available for repeat interviews as they felt the need of them.

The other waitresses were quite correct in saying that Sophie and Ena had never been happy in the King Cole, but they were wrong in thinking that all the other King Cole girls were content. We found that many of them certainly were not content but that they were hesitant to express their viewpoints for fear of Larry's reprisals. Now the issue which had been festering under the surface came out. It was discussed everywhere, in the kitchen, in the dressing room. Girls with mediocre stations began saying that for the sake of justice and peace they were willing to see changes made.

There was June, for instance. Her station was fairly good but definitely not the best. She stood to gain nothing by rotating stations. In fact, the chances were that she would lose by it since her regular customers might find her difficult to locate on a busy night.

> JUNE: Well, I'll make it short and snappy. I like my station as it is.
>
> LENTZ: Uh huh.
>
> JUNE: But on the other hand, if the griping and complaining will stop, I say let them rotate. I'll go along with it if the rest want it. The way I see it, I was here for nine months before I got this station. Meanwhile I saw new girls come in and pick off the best stations in the house. Yes, I really did, and I didn't have nerve enough to speak up about it. Then I thought to myself, "Well, if I don't speak up I'll never get anything!" So I spoke to Larry and sure enough, he gave me this station I have now. It isn't the best in the house but it suits me, I like it. And yet if it will stop the griping—well Mr. Wiley said the other day that we shouldn't think only of ourselves. I was all for keeping my station until he said that. Now I think if it will stop this griping, it would be worth it to rotate. So you can put me down as being willing.

Talking to "outsiders" helped clarify the issues and helped take the heat of passion out of them, making rational consideration more possible. By the time we had finished the interviewing, the real business of discovering basic problems and figuring out a better order was done for us. All we had to do was to present our findings.

Appendix G gives the report of the meeting in Mr. Kraus's office when Mr. Wiley presented his summary to Larry and the latest night manager. Mr. Wiley didn't have to force a solution on the department. Once the basic problems were clear, the supervisor was willing and able to handle them himself.

As we saw it, these were the points at issue:

1. The main difficulty centered around the lack of adequate lead-

ership. In the absence of law and order, it was inevitable that cliques should form and the strong should prey on the weak. We felt that the staff would welcome the establishment of a consistent discipline.

2. In order to achieve this, one person would have to have the authority to deal with problems as they arose. Since Larry was on the day shift, his night manager should be this person. Since he was a very new employee, he would require Larry's public support. To win the respect of the workers he would have to show respect for them and their ideas by encouraging their participation in settling present issues.

3. The unequal size of the stations on the night shift was creating considerable tension. Since the day crew stations were being accepted as fair, would it help to make the night stations resemble the day ones?

4. There were disciplinary problems but we felt the night captain could deal with them once his leadership was established. (We had in mind the drinking problem, which was worrying Mr. Kraus particularly. We felt it was the sort of thing which the night man could handle better without interference.)

5. We would do our part in improving the staff's morale by passing along their suggestions and criticisms of the kitchen, etc. Some of their ideas were quite helpful and could easily be implemented (such as a slight modification of the checker system).

We carefully avoided pointing any fingers. Our study of the situation had caused us to feel that this wasn't so much a matter of personalities as it was a lack of system. What was needed was a sense of a just order and the security which could grow out of it.

It worked out beautifully, from our point of view. Larry amazed us by coming up with the suggestion that the night stations be changed to resemble the day stations before Mr. Wiley made the point. He had tried to pass the responsibility for the night shift to his new night manager when things were hottest, so Mr. Wiley could give him credit for the idea that the night man have full authority. Larry was so relieved, evidently, that nothing was done to take his job away from him, that he cooperated to the fullest extent in putting the new system into effect.

When it was announced in group meeting that the stations were to be redivided according to the present day-schedule system, the night girls accepted it as their own idea. A vote was taken on the rotating once a week. This may or may not have been the best long-run decision. We had our doubts, but at least it did solve the immediate need for visible justice and they were free to change their minds at a later date and vote permanent stations back in again. Nobody quit, not even Larry's "pet" who was most inconvenienced by the change of events. On the contrary, a general relief was expressed that something was done to settle the troublesome issues.

At the end of the study, therefore, all was peaceful in the King Cole. At least on the surface. We had succeeded in making changes that most of the staff felt were desirable. We had won the confidence of the night crew. We had established the fact that the Personnel Office did not put the heat on individuals but could open the way for effective action on common problems. By that token we hoped that in time the day crew would also come to have confidence in us. And, as far as we could see, Larry was feeling a new respect for our office. He cooperated fully in putting the new measures into effect, and he and the night captain appeared to be working together closely to map out the new organization and procedures.

An unfinished matter was the waitresses' request for more training. The younger girls especially envied the older waiters their craftsmanship. They wanted to learn the niceties of supreme service. As in the case of the front office, talking to the employees had also shown us their deep respect for the people among them who had good public relations. They wanted to know more about human psychology, and we began to plan how to fill that need. The King Cole still had a long way to go.

Chapter X

MR. KRAUS: TOO LITTLE AND TOO LATE[1]

By now Mr. Kraus had long since given up fighting us. He had agreeably sat in on the cashier-checker discussion with Mr. Wiley and the auditor but contributed nothing to the solution of the problems involved. Similarly he sat in on all King Cole discussions, having little to say but not rejecting anything we said. That was the role he now undertook, following Mr. Wiley's lead and co-operating to the best of his ability in all personnel matters.

From what we could gather, he had been worrying about union relations during the time of Mr. Smith's South American trip. Immediately before this there had been a series of nasty incidents: the Zebra Room transfer, the busboy wage matter, King Cole grievances. There had been whispers of a strike if any more trouble came from Larry. Instead, relations with the workers and their organizations continued to improve steadily so long as grievances were channeled through Mr. Wiley and that, evidently, was not lost on Mr. Kraus.

He was very anxious to keep life running smoothly at the hotel during the two month absence of Mr. Smith. Everything pointed to the fact that he realized he was "on trial." He carefully side-stepped every possible pitfall in order not to disturb the equilibrium. Actually, the hotel did run smoothly during his administration. There were only two unpleasant events of any importance.

[1] E. L. H.

The first, the hiring of Mr. Kent and demotion of Mr. Stevens to make room for him, was Mr. Smith's doing rather than Mr. Kraus's. The second involved Mr. Kraus more directly.

Mr. Daly, a young man fresh from a hotel management school, had been brought into the hotel by Mr. Smith to act as assistant to Mr. Kraus. Mr. Kraus didn't want an assistant, felt embarrassed to have one, but, no matter, Mr. Smith's mind was made up, so another bright young man was added to the staff. Mr. Smith's idea was that Mr. Daly would take over some of Kraus's catering responsibilities, thus permitting Mr. Kraus to spend more time on overall coordination of the hotel. It was evidently part of his scheme for the retraining of Mr. Kraus. He made no suggestions as to how Daly was to be broken in or what duties he was to be assigned. Perhaps he wanted to see how well Mr. Kraus could handle the situation.

If so, the results were tragic. Mr. Daly received all the impossible odds and ends of jobs, nothing he could sink his teeth into. He was never properly introduced to the organization and when, at Mr. Kraus's bidding, he would venture into a department with a complaint, the department head would wonder what business it was of his to criticize. Mr. Daly was a very ambitious young man and wanted desperately to succeed, but after a two-month period Mr. Kraus informed him that he wouldn't do. There were too many complaints being registered against him, he said.

It didn't help morale among the other supervisors to see a man dismissed so curtly. The chef, in particular, was upset by it. He said to Mr. Whyte:

I felt very bad about that. I'm sure that Mr. Kraus just didn't want the man to succeed. From the beginning nobody knew what he was supposed to be doing. Daly was just given the dirty jobs to do. He wasn't given any real responsibility. I think Mr. Kraus wanted him to fail, he's afraid of having any strong people under him. I'll tell you what happened in the kitchen. He sent Daly in there to check the food as it went by the checker's stand. Remember, I told you how I had had it out with Mr. Kraus about him checking the food and I had told him that I wouldn't stand for it. Why did he send Mr. Daly in there? Because he wanted me to complain and that would be held against Daly, but

I knew what he was trying to do and so I just smiled at John [the sous chef] and said, "Look what Mr. Kraus has done."

When Mr. Smith came back from South America after a two-month absence, this was one of the things upon which he pounced.

> I had a little talk with the chef the other day and he told me he had been very much upset by this Daly incident. He had been on the point of buying a house, but when this happened he said to his wife, he certainly didn't want to invest his money here if people were treated that way. If Daly could be fired, he could be fired too. You know, we can't do things like that anymore, it's very damaging to the organization.

The fact was, Mr. Smith had returned from his trip with his mind already made up to let Mr. Kraus go. It perhaps wouldn't have made too much difference how well things had gone during his absence. Four days after Smith's return he commented to Mr. Wiley:

> Things have to change here. I have been thinking it over. You have a lot of time to think while you are riding on an airplane for 18,000 miles. I have told Mr. Kraus that he was holding up what we have been trying to do with employee relations. He couldn't see it. He said he didn't do anything. I told him that that was just it, he hasn't accepted what we have been trying to do and that's held us back.
>
> WILEY: I think he has come a long way. There has been a big change in him from the way I remember him when we first came in here. There is no question but what he still needs a lot of training . . . but I feel confident we can bring him around. How long it will take, I don't know.
>
> SMITH: Still we have been held up a long time. If we are ever going to get anyplace in this organization, we have got to take a hold on it. I'm through with just sitting back and hoping things will happen. I did an awful lot of thinking. We're going to straighten things out even if it means someone has to leave.

Once Mr. Smith began to look around for reasons to let Mr. Kraus go, he found plenty. The chef wasn't far wrong when he complained that Mr. Kraus was driving out the strong men under him. Several of the most able department heads had quit because of their inability to tolerate his autocratic manner. Now the chef and the head of the Zebra Room, two important figures in the hotel, were on the verge of quitting. The manager of the Zebra Room told Mr. Wiley:

I'm going to have an operation in a couple of weeks and I know before I come back that some of these things are going to have to be straightened out. I have an ulcer and that's what I'm going to have the operation for. This place has got my ulcer on edge all the time.

Take these busboys, that's a good example. If I had a head busboy I wouldn't have to worry about watching them so close. I have ten busboys now, that ought to be enough to have a head busboy to take charge. We could pay him just a nickel an hour more. Kraus told me I could have one, once, but when we got around to fixing the wage he backed down. You remember that? Well the other night he came in here about 1:30 A.M. Imagine, 1:30 after we had been busier than the devil all night, and he says the back room is a mess. Well all it was was a few tracks on the floor. Now if it wasn't a little dirty I'd think something was wrong, wouldn't you? Seems to me we would rather be busy and have it dirty than not busy. Well anyway, what did he do? He jumped on me! So I said, "Look, Mr. Kraus, if you would let me have that head busboy like you were going to, I could see that that place was kept clean." Now that would just be a nickel more an hour, but he won't go for that.

I don't mean to be critical, this is just between you and me, but a resident manager is supposed to see to it that there is coordination between all departments. I'll tell you one thing, Wiley, I just don't have the guts to go in and tell those bartenders they are doing a lousy job, or to fire a busboy. Yet that's what Kraus told me to do. He told me to jump on Frank the bartender and to get rid of one of those barboys. What's he got a head bartender for? I told him that wasn't my job and he said, "Yes, you're in charge in there." Now what am I going to do? By God, I don't know. If I come back here after my operation, I'm crazy.

The pity of it was that Mr. Kraus had really tried to do a good job. His reform insofar as we could tell was genuine and enduring. It was just that the change took time and people were impatient, Mr. Smith in particular. Mr. Kraus said to Mr. Wiley in private:

> You know, it's hard for me to say that I'm wrong, I don't like to do that, but I was wrong about you. I think what you and Mr. Smith are doing is the right thing. I didn't think so before, I admit that. I thought it was a lot of nonsense, but I can see now that those meetings are a good thing. You can't have just a head of a department or one person doing all the talking. You have got to let the employee say something. I can see the psychology behind that now. They feel they are working for the hotel and that makes them like their job better. Now you take the King Cole meetings, they are no good. Larry talks and talks and talks and he says the same things over and over. They get sick of listening and they don't hear a word he says. If he would let them talk they would do things a lot better. I can see an awful lot of improvement here since you have come in and I'm the first one to admit it. I think you are doing a fine job.

So, just as Larry had realized his mistakes through observing the error of Mr. Kraus's ways, now Mr. Kraus saw the light by looking at Larry's mistakes!

We had no reason to doubt the sincerity of Mr. Kraus's change of philosophy. He went about the hotel preaching the gospel of good human relations. He told people over and over:

> It takes a big man to admit he was wrong.

and

> You can't be a leader without having followers.

> Times have changed. It isn't any more that one man can tell a lot of people what to do. It isn't that way in the hotel industry or any other industry. It's all changed now, I know that now.

Two things were happening to Mr. Kraus which seemed to be responsible for this change in his attitude. First, he had been exposed to a new philosophy of management through the combined efforts of Mr. Smith, Mr. Wiley, and Mr. Whyte. It is reasonable to suppose that something of this was seeping through his mental processes into his behavior patterns. Secondly, Mr. Smith had been expressing impatience with him to the point where Mr. Kraus had become afraid of losing his job. Mr. Wiley sounded Mr. Smith out concerning this and received an entirely frank reply:

> I have told him that he hasn't accepted what we were doing and he's held us up. I even told him he was our main problem. We were trying to do something good for this organization and he was stopping it, whether he knew it or whether he didn't. And I told him that it's got to the point where he or the chef have to give in and get along or one of them was going to have to go. . . .

How much of his reaction was due to fear and how much to faith cannot be measured. Perhaps he himself couldn't have said.

Unfortunately for him, while his behavior was being modified for the better, his ability to grasp the essentials of organization was not. A typical example of his blind spot in this respect is the following story told by the chef:

> When I came in here the place was all in confusion and everybody was working overtime. Today we're doing 50 percent more business with the same number of people and we hardly have any overtime. That was accomplished through organization. I drew up a large chart of the organization to place on the wall and I also put up a schedule of working hours and days off. There's no secret about such things. People should know the organization and they should know just what their hours are. That way if a man wants to change his day off he knows what people to go to to trade. Well Mr. Kraus came into the kitchen one day and saw that on the wall. He said to John, the sous chef, "What's that chart doing?" John told him what it was and Mr. Kraus said, "Take it down. I just want good food."

A series of such incidents served to close Mr. Smith's mind against him. During Smith's absence Mr. Kraus had failed to handle several important matters. He neglected to prepare for a predicted meat shortage, for instance. He had allowed the hotel to drift into trouble with the U.S. Office of Price Administration. Mr. Smith had asked him to work on a plan for new uniforms for the entire hotel staff. He wanted something novel and ultra-modern which would be in keeping with the spirit of the hotel, but upon his return from South America all Mr. Kraus had to show him was a catalog of stereotyped uniforms he had sent for from a mail-order house. These things plus repeated complaints from such persons as the chef and the Zebra Room manager con-firmed Mr. Smith's opinion that Mr. Kraus was making progress too slowly. He consulted Mr. Whyte about the advisability of re-placing the Resident Manager and Mr. Whyte, realizing the hope-lessness of the situation, agreed that it was probably necessary. Just before the first year of our project was up, Mr. Smith con-fided to Mr. Wiley:

> I've been talking to Mr. Kraus a lot the last few days, I've been giving him an awful lot of heat. As a matter of fact, I have been trying to make it so tough that he would want to get out. And he just sits there! He isn't himself, he just takes it like a father to son talk. I don't know what to make of it. I know I have got to act, I have got to quit stalling this off. I have got to do something!

The planned program for retraining Mr. Kraus never did materialize, to our knowledge. There was just this turning over the hotel completely to Mr. Kraus for a two month period, Mr. Kraus's attempt to swing the job, and Mr. Smith's dissatisfaction with the job done. We had sincerely tried to help Mr. Kraus and had succeeded in winning his confidence. He turned to Mr. Wiley constantly during the last month or two of his stay at the Tremont, yet we did not do him much good. His old authoritarian patterns were broken but the new ones hadn't developed in time to save his job. He was confused and weary. About a month after the last conversation quoted above, he resigned his position at the Hotel Tremont.

Chapter XI

EPILOGUE [1]

In June, 1946, the contract between the Tremont and the University of Chicago expired. Smith was pleased with the results of the program, and expressed the desire to have Miss Lentz stay on with Wiley at the hotel. However, when Miss Lentz had originally accepted the assignment her plans were to take just one year from her academic training and then return to the University. Her decision at this time was to abide by that plan. Whyte knew a young man at the University who had been following the program closely and was interested in becoming a part of it. With this man in mind to replace Miss Lentz, Whyte submitted a new contract proposal to Smith following the lines established during the previous year. Smith replied that he had some additional things he wished to discuss with Whyte, and, since Whyte was to be away from the University for the remainder of the summer, he suggested they get together in the fall to arrange the new contract. Whyte informed Miss Lentz's replacement of this development. The young man was interested in taking the assignment on the basis of gaining experience in human relations research, and decided that without definite assurance that the University would be connected with the project, he could not risk starting on the job. This turn of events was a real blow to Wiley, for though he believed Smith planned to sign the

---

[1] M. W.

contract in the fall, being without a research assistant would cause a delay in the work, together with a serious loss of momentum. Wiley was keenly disappointed, and for a moment he, too, considered resigning. However, he decided to stay on and try to keep the project on the track until fall. By fall it had become evident that there would be no new contract.

THE UNION AND COSTS

It was not long after this that the new union contract came up for negotiation. The postwar pattern of wage increases had been substantial. Thus, the Hotel Workers' Union was able to negotiate a very favorable contract with the Trade Association.

Wiley had impressed upon Smith the need for a research assistant to keep the project moving. Because there was no one immediately available from the University of Chicago, he secured Smith's approval to employ a local young man whom Wiley felt could be trained in the human relations research approach. The man had barely started on the job when Smith insisted he be let go. Smith stated that it was imperative to keep costs at a minimum, that the hotel had reached a loss position and was forced to embark on a cost reduction program. And, Smith indicated, he would like Wiley to coordinate this program.

This was another bitter pill for Wiley. First, he was told he would no longer have an assistant, and now he was asked to do cost reduction, a job for which he had no taste. Cost reduction is not characteristically a personnel department activity, and though the approach at the Tremont had not been sterotyped, it seemed to Wiley that cost reduction was definitely too far afield. He had further feelings of uneasiness, for while both management and employee needs had been met in the past, these needs had originated principally from the employees. Cost reduction would be an activity arising from management's goal of a profitable organization, and he questioned his ability to integrate it with employee objectives. And Wiley was distressed by the punitive aspect of the cost reduction role. Some people would get hurt as a result of the program. Up to this time, a cardinal principle had been that Wiley would give neither rewards nor punishments.

Whyte and Wiley had a number of discussions regarding Wiley's taking the cost reduction assignment. Whyte encouraged him to stay and give it a try. There was still hope, of course, that the University would sign another contract with the Tremont, and it was Whyte's feeling that, as cost reduction coordinator, Wiley would be in a better position to protect the gains made in human relations during the past year than someone else in that position. Whyte also felt that insofar as the cost reduction program would affect people, in its broadest sense it was a personnel problem. From a research point of view, Whyte felt that a study of the cost reduction program would provide some new and valuable information on a type of change problem that occurred frequently, and about which little was known. Wiley considered the situation and finally agreed that the personnel department would help see that the best possible job was done in meshing management's objectives with employee objectives. Though Wiley was still concerned about the punitive aspect of the role, he felt he might be able to cope with it by concerning himself primarily with the policies, procedures, and coordination of the program. He took consolation from the fact that his relations with the employees were good, and from the knowledge that people will accept things, even unpleasant things, when they know they are necessary.

Wiley decided to stay on as personnel manager at the Tremont. Working with him was Miss Dickson, his secretary/assistant. In addition to furthering the human relations program that had been established, they now had a new objective, to cut costs—but Smith held off on the cost campaign during the summer.

WILEY ON HIS OWN

Miss Dickson was needed to carry on the employment and record functions of the personnel department. Wiley was to carry out the human relations program as well as he could alone. Seemingly, this could best be done by keeping as well informed as possible and by emphasizing one of the key tenets of the program —to helping build an organization able to solve its own problems.

Since Wiley's role was well established in the hotel, employees continued to come to him when they had problems. The executives had by now established a pattern of seeking him out when they were making plans or when something unusual came up. Wiley also helped keep himself informed by periodically circulating throughout the hotel and stopping to talk with the employees. To try to anticipate trouble spots, Wiley requested and received copies of all financial and statistical reports compiled by the hotel. While line management characteristically used these reports as controls and checks on subordinates, Wiley used them solely to keep informed on what was transpiring, and never referred specifically to an item in such reports in his conversations with executives and supervisors. If he noticed something unusual on a report, he would make himself available to persons in the department concerned. Wiley also kept himself informed by attending departmental meetings, or, if he was unable to attend, from receiving reports of the meetings. With this information, and with the knowledge gained from the research the previous year, Wiley was able to anticipate certain problems, though this approach was certainly no adequate substitute for a research assistant.

Wiley concentrated on building the organization. He continued to work directly with the executives on their plans and problems. He got Smith's approval to conduct Monday morning breakfast meetings. These meetings opened with a free exchange of operating information to help the department managers with their planning, but the major portion of the meetings was devoted to improving the understanding of the human relations approach and developing management skills. The topics came directly from the department managers and usually involved problems confronting them at the time. Sometimes an executive would wish to remain anonymous, and in these instances Wiley would present his problem for him. At other times Wiley might present case material related to happenings at the Tremont. In addition to group discussion, some problems were acted out in role playing. The department managers responded enthusiastically to these meetings, and there was always good participation in the discussion portion. Wiley felt that he could see favorable changes in the behavior patterns of some of them.

The new human relations approach seemed to be flowing from the top down. The executives were learning new approaches to problems and new skills in discussion through their weekly management meetings. They practiced what they were learning and developed further skill and understanding as they conducted group meetings with their subordinates. On an individual basis, Wiley consulted with them, not to provide solutions, but to help them to analyze their own problems. The rank and file employees became involved in the process of change as they participated in discussions with their supervisors and found individual supervisors more receptive to complaints and suggestions than they had been before.

Of course, progress was not even throughout the house. Some departments seemed hardly touched by the program, while in others the supervisory process had been completely transformed. The first department we studied, the Coffee Shop, carried the new approach farther than any other unit.

THE COFFEE SHOP TRAINS ITSELF

During the course of a meeting conducted by Miss Paris, Department Manager of the Coffee Shop, one of the waitresses said:

> I think it's a shame the way we treat new girls here. Of course we're nice to them—we treat them just like we treat everyone else, but I think we should go out of our way to help them. They might not leave so quick if we did.

Wiley stayed after the meeting was over to discuss the statement with Miss Paris. She was much concerned over the rate of turnover among new waitresses and was eager to do something about it. Wiley suggested that it might be good to make a film on introducing new employees into the department, and that if she wished he would be happy to work with her on it. She was somewhat awed by the idea at first but became more and more enthusiastic as they discussed it, and together they worked out the procedure.

The following week, at the regular Coffee Shop meeting, Miss Paris said that she had been especially interested in improving the introduction of new employees into the department. She then presented the film suggestion, explaining that the plot would be simple—perhaps taking one particular problem a new girl might have in the department and then showing how this problem was solved. The girls responded, and there was a good deal of discussion on what the problem might be. Before the meeting was over they had agreed on one and had worked out a rough story outline. Wiley offered to have copies of the story outline typed up for all of them so they could bring ideas for changes into the next meeting. In addition, they should be thinking about characters for the plot and dialogue. At the next meeting, they revised the outline, filled in details, and decided on the parts. During the third meeting, they completed the dialogue. At the fourth and final meeting, they selected people from the department to play the parts, and decided on the pictures they would need to convey the story. All that remained was for the parts to be read into a tape recorder, and for Wiley to arrange with one of the busboys in the department to take pictures of the scenes with a 35 mm. camera.

Miss Paris conducted all of the meetings. There was a free exchange of opinions and suggestions, and the girls were able to reach consensus on each point. Wiley's secretary recorded the proceedings, typed them, and distributed them after the meeting so that each girl would have a chance to study the record before the next meeting. Wiley attended all of the meetings, and after each one he and Miss Paris would discuss the progress and make plans for the next meeting.

The Coffee Shop film project took about one month to complete. It had a great effect on Miss Paris, helping to build her confidence in human relations skills. The waitresses not only had fun in the preparation of the film but also learned much about the principles used in meeting one particular problem. The project gave everyone in the department the opportunity to use creative energy, and increased insight into the problem of orientation of new employees. New waitresses commented on the unusual warmth and helpfulness of the girls, and employee turnover of new employees in the department dropped from 16.2 percent a month to 3.12 percent.

UNION RELATIONS

In the handling of union grievances, as in other areas, Wiley sought to develop an organization that could solve its own problems. At the beginning of the Tremont Study, the University of Chicago group had assumed that Wiley would not get involved in union grievances. As we have noted, since grievances simply were not being handled within the hotel, Wiley found he had to fill in the void. As the union business agents were increasingly satisfied with his grievance handling, he found himself becoming in effect a grievance arbitrator. The unions did not appeal adverse decisions over his head.

With the expiration of the University contract, Wiley felt that he should be working toward more indirect action on union grievances. He tried to get the parties in a grievance to come to their own agreement. Rather than encouraging compromise, he tried to help them come to a new arrangement that would be mutually satisfying.

To achieve this type of grievance settlement, Wiley would first interview the parties separately, encouraging them to talk freely. He wanted them to "talk out" the problem, which not only would dissipate much of the emotionalism involved, but would sometimes result in the perception of a solution. This approach also gave Wiley a better understanding of the problem. Wiley then would ask the parties to the grievance to meet together with him. At this time, he would define his role as not judging either of them. He would state that he was not going to hand down a decision, that he was there to help them come to a creative understanding. He stated further that if either party had reservations, then the meeting would continue until the "right" answer was found, that the responsibility for an answer to the problem was theirs, that they would need to be open-minded, objective, and imaginative, that differences of opinion might appear unpleasant on the surface, but that underneath they could be the means of leading to something new and better. Wiley would also say that he did not believe this approach would be easy, but that it would be a challenge—one that he thought they could meet, with results being more satisfying than any other approach they could use. He would ask them not to put blame on other people, to avoid name-calling, bringing personalities into the picture, or judging the other fellow. As much as possible, Wiley said, he hoped they would try to understand their own behavior rather than the other person's, for the more they could understand their own behavior, the more they could see both sides, and the better would be their conclusions. Wiley would then hear both sides of the story without interruption, asking that the participants define the problem in as broad terms as possible. Concentrating on the positive aspects of the problem, Wiley would encourage both participants to think of possible solutions, emphasizing the areas of common agreement. He sought to get the participants into a feeling of "this is *our* problem and we want to work out a good solution." As soon as they had this "we" feeling and had become immersed in the creative aspects of problem-solving, it was only a matter of time before they came to a mutual understanding. There were a few instances in which more than one meeting was required before a solution was reached but, on the whole, one sitting was enough.

PLANNING FOR COST REDUCTION

During the summer months of 1946, Smith had decided to postpone the organized cost reduction program. About four months after the signing of the union contract Smith wanted action in reducing costs and called Wiley in to discuss the matter. Wiley had agreed to coordinate the cost reduction program earlier, and at this time presented Smith with his plans. The largest single cost item was payroll, and both Wiley and Smith agreed that efforts should be concentrated in this area. Because a person who does a job knows that job better than anyone else, and because the department managers best knew their own particular departments, Wiley recommended that these people study the jobs themselves and suggest improvements necessary for more efficiency. Wiley further recommended that he establish the procedure and then work with the department managers and employees on how to go about studying their jobs and deciding how to do their work more efficiently. It was Wiley's feeling that the gains made from this approach would be more solid, and the method was in line with the idea of organizational development. Smith accepted the recommendations, but wanted the hotel to show a profit as quickly as possible. He stated that the hotel would need a 5 percent reduction in payroll costs immediately, which would be cutting out approximately 25 people. Wiley reminded Smith that the union contract provided for layoffs on the basis of seniority by job classification, and he recommended that there be, not a flat 5 percent reduction in each department, but that the percentage be an overall hotel figure. Some departments, Wiley pointed out, would be better able to take the cut than others. For example, some positions in the laundry and house-keeping departments had already established work standards, while the kitchen, which had received new equipment reducing the work load, had still maintained the same number of employees. On the other hand, in the dining room, a reduction in the number of employees could bring higher tips to the remaining waiters. Wiley recommended that the department managers be consulted on the extent of the layoffs in their departments. He further advised that there be a discussion with the union about the layoffs before any action was taken. And, finally, he recommended to Smith that the policy of giving people a two week notice of termination be strictly adhered to, that it could be handled as two weeks severance pay. Wiley not only wanted the unions to have definite assurance that there would be no further layoffs but he wanted them to know that further cost reduction would come about through normal employee turnover, and this only after job methods had been improved. Smith did not feel it was necessary to discuss the layoffs with the union but went along with Wiley's recommendation. He was much opposed to giving the union assurance there would be no further layoffs, but Wiley was able to show him that normal employee turnover would take care of further cost reduction. Previously, in matters of timing, the approach had been to move slowly and have thorough discussion among the people concerned before introducing change. For the layoffs, however, Wiley felt that it was better to have the blow fall all at once and then work on rebuilding morale, instead of reducing the work force gradually and thus prolonging the anxiety.

Tying the Fire Underwriters' Knot

While Wiley was working on plans for the cost reduction program, Smith upset him by a new program idea. He proposed bringing in a Professor Rogers to conduct a War Manpower Job Instruction Training Program at the hotel. Wiley argued against this, stating that the organization would have enough to absorb with the cost reduction program, but Smith informed Wiley that the man had already been retained.

Wiley talked with the Professor when he arrived, informed him of the cost reduction program to be launched, and suggested he conduct a Job Methods Training Program instead of the Job Instruction Training Program. However, the man was not familiar with this other aspect of the War Manpower Commission job training programs, so he proceeded with his original plans. Further, the Professor busied himself around the edges of the cost reduction program, which was a thorn in Wiley's side. Wiley was disturbed, too, because he did not feel he could discuss the matter with Smith without being accused of professional jealousy. Wiley finally concluded that his best response was to carry out the cost reduction as originally planned, meeting any problems the Professor introduced as they came along.

The Cost Reduction Program

The first step in the cost reduction program was to hold a meeting of the department managers. At this meeting, Smith pointed out that the hotel was operating at a loss and that it was imperative for everyone to work together to get back to a profit picture. Smith made his presentation along the lines of the conversation he had previously had with Wiley concerning the layoffs, the union contract, and the severance pay. He then requested that the department managers go over their departments with an eye toward laying off recently hired employees. He asked each department manager to determine, right at this meeting, how many people he could lay off without seriously jeopardizing his department. Some managers persuaded Smith that they could not lay off as many as 5 percent. In other cases, Smith prodded them to lay off more. For the hotel as a whole, Smith was able to attain his 5 percent objective. When this phase of the meeting was over, Smith said that he had asked Wiley to coordinate the program, and asked him to present his ideas.

Wiley opened by stating that his role of coordinator was one of helping the department managers with a procedure—a way of approaching the job. He said he would help them in every way possible, but that he was not going to interfere with the operation of their departments. After the layoffs, the next phase of the cost reduction program would be an effort to simplify the jobs wherever possible, so that fewer people would be required to do the work. The essence of this plan was to have every employee prepare a list of the tasks he performed. It would not be difficult, nor would it require a high degree of intelligence: the employee would simply write down his tasks on a sheet of paper as they were performed. For example, when a maid changed a bed she might write, "Removed linen from bed. Put dirty linen in cart." After each task the employee was to note the time started and the time completed, and if it was the kind of thing he did every day. At the bottom of the page employees were asked to list any tasks that were not done on a daily basis, and their frequency. Wiley would be available to answer any questions they might have. After the lists were prepared, they were to be turned in to the department managers so that copies could be made and one returned to the employee. Because some of the department managers did not have secretaries, Wiley offered the services of his department in making copies. In this way, the department manager and the employee could study the lists simultaneously. When studying the task lists, the department managers and the employees were to ask the following questions:

1. What is the purpose of this task?
2. Is it necessary?
3. Can it be eliminated?
4. Can it be combined with another task?

5. Can the order of the tasks be improved?
6. Who is the best person to do this task?
7. When is the best time to do this task?

After the employees had studied their lists, answering the seven questions, they were to turn in their lists to their department manager, who would compare the employee answers with his own answers and then write a new description of the job where it seemed warranted. Department meetings would be held approximately four days after the task lists were turned in, at which time the department managers would present the proposed new jobs and ask for suggestions from the employees. New jobs were to be on a one-month trial basis. In Wiley's closing comments he pointed out that the program could stand or fall on the effectiveness of the department managers in getting the employees behind it. He stated that problems could often be eliminated or eased if they were anticipated. After the 5 percent layoff, the remaining employees would more than likely feel insecure, despite the fact that they had been told they would be kept on the job. And, as far as the task lists were concerned, they would be bound to wonder how this study would affect their future. Wiley pointed out that change in and of itself could cause restlessness, and there would be some changes as a result of the program: changes in the social environment, changes in the size and composition of work groups, and, because of the redefined jobs, changes in status of the workers which would affect their relations with fellow employees and supervisors. Changes in the nature of their jobs could cause feelings of either greater or lesser importance. Wiley concluded by saying that the department managers could do much to offset this restlessness through just thoughtful consideration—by recognizing the importance of employee contribution, by complimenting good work, and by keeping their employees informed of the progress on the job study program.

After Wiley's remarks, there was a group discussion. A number of questions were asked on the preparation of the task lists and the study of them. One department manager asked if his department would have fewer employees after the job study program. He was told this would happen only if it seemed the right thing to do, and this would occur only through normal turnover. Another asked Wiley to conduct the meeting when the plan was presented to the employees in his department. Wiley agreed to be there and to help in all phases of the program, but it was his feeling that the department manager would lose status with his employees if Wiley conducted the meeting.

The afternoon of the same day, Wiley had an appointment with the union business agents. Wiley explained that because the Tremont was losing money, the hotel was going to have to reduce costs, which would mean a layoff of some of the employees. The business agents' first reaction was that this was a typical Smith story—that Smith was trying to keep the union off balance. Wiley quoted the percentage of decrease in revenue at the hotel in the past six months, and the percentage of increase in costs. And he particularly called attention to the percentage of increase in payroll costs since the new union contract. The business agents replied that the Hotel Workers' Union had received no greater increase than workers in other industries, and added that Smith had signed the contract and therefore had no one but himself to blame. Wiley pointed out that Smith was not trying to welch on the contract or to put the blame on anyone, but was forced to reduce his costs. The hotel's plan was to lay off 5 percent of the employees, and this action was in line with the present contract. They were discussing it with the union before the action was taken because it seemed the fair thing to do. The business agents asked to see the list of those persons who would be laid off and Wiley presented it to them. Although the business agents did some complaining about the size of the list, they did not make a strong argument. Wiley assured the union there would be no further layoffs, that future reduction in force would come about through normal turnover. He explained the job simplification study to them.

Although the business agents were not easy on him, Wiley had expected far more trouble. When he parted company with them they expressed appreciation for having been approached before action was taken and stated that this had been a new experience for them. A parting shot to Wiley, however, was that if things got out of line later on, it would be necessary for them to step in.

As the cost reduction program got under way Wiley would periodically call the business agents of the union to keep them informed and to ask if they had heard any unfavorable comments. He made it a point to hold the initiative with the union.

Through the cost reduction program, payroll was reduced by more than 5 percent. Its success was difficult to measure in other ways. Wiley was personally at the center of it, and one in that position is usually the last to know when things are not going smoothly. Further, he was very busy working with both the department managers and the employees on the preparation and study of task lists, although he did make it a point to interview during these contacts on reaction to the program. There was the expected unrest at the outset, but there was considerable enthusiasm once the purpose had been explained, and employees generally got into the spirit of it. Employee turnover continued to drop and the Tremont got back into a profit position. Wiley was relieved at the results of the program but did not feel as close to the employees as he would have liked. A research assistant working along with him would have provided a smoother introduction of change and certainly would have given a better assessment of results.

THE FIGHT FOR THE HOTEL

Up to this point, President Jones had been Mr. Smith's silent partner. Now the two had a falling out and got into a struggle for control of the hotel.

Jones forced Smith out, and the fight over Smith's half interest was waged in the courts. Since Smith had bought his share largely on the basis of loans from Jones, the President was reluctant to buy out his former partner. Without any reference to the law case, Jones wrote Whyte to say that, since he was now operating the hotel, it would be very helpful to have a copy of the final report of our research. Apparently Smith at the time had remarked that the report was very critical of him, and Jones wanted to see if he could use it in court. Kept informed by Wiley but feigning innocence, Whyte replied that he had submitted the report to Smith and suggested Jones ask Smith for it.

Smith got several millions for his share and went on to bigger things.

The President asked Green, now purchasing agent, to take over temporarily as general manager. For some time Green had been talking out his problems with Wiley. Now that he was general manager, he called on Wiley more than ever, and it soon became apparent that he was asking Wiley what to do and what decision to come to in nearly every matter. Since Wiley's role was to help build a healthy organization, he set about putting Green on his own by gradually playing less and less of a direct role in his decision making, and by working to build his self-confidence.

Green was starting to develop some independence in his position, when the President of the Tremont asked Kraus to return to the hotel as general manager. Wiley had some misgivings about this, but from the start Kraus showed that he had learned something of the human relations approach. He was too busy as general manager to walk about the hotel checking up on people, but he could have used other means of checking up if he had been so inclined, and he did not do so. He occasionally lost his temper, but no longer stormed at people, nor did he reprimand his subordinates when others were present. Although it never came easy for Kraus to delegate, at least he tried, and Wiley would call it to his attention when he missed. Kraus worked closely with Wiley and accepted his recommendations much of the time. Wiley encouraged him to have the departments submit long-run plans to help him get away from much of the day-to-day decision making and at the same time encourage delegation. Kraus was not the imaginative, dynamic builder Smith was, but in the main he did a good job.

TAKING LEAVE

In the summer of 1948 Wiley attempted to review the total progress at the Tremont, a difficult job because much that had been accomplished was not readily measured. The most significant results were in the area of feeling tone, and here the gains

were positive. People like Kraus and Larry, who had once opposed Wiley, were now his staunch advocates. And morale was
stable and at a relatively high level throughout the hotel. The
hotel was operating at a satisfactory profit, business had increased,
and, though general costs had risen, the number on the payroll
had decreased from 500 employees to 467. In January of 1945
employee turnover was 22.5 percent a month. In January, 1948,
it was 3.55 percent. Employee absenteeism had dropped similarly; in the Coffee Shop, for example, it dropped from 11.0 percent a month in June, 1945, to 0.5 percent in June, 1948.

Wiley felt that the biggest part of the job was done. He had
never visualized a career in the hotel industry, so in August, 1948,
he left the Tremont with an armload of gifts, one of which was
very reassuring: an engraved watch given him through the insti-
gation of Kraus.

Chapter XII

THE STRATEGY OF ACTION RESEARCH AT THE TREMONT[1]

One of the achievements of the Tremont project was the establishment of a new role for the personnel man. The new role was initially established as part of a research contract, but Wiley's experience at the hotel following termination of the contract indicates that at least some of the aspects of this new role could be maintained without the direct support of research. Let us review how this new role was established and maintained.

This report has made it clear that we did not foresee in any detail the nature of this new role that we were establishing. We did envision some of the essential aspects—that Wiley would become an interpreter of human relations research findings to management people and that he would also serve as a consultant and trainer in human relations. This conception gave us some general objectives but we were far from any specific blueprint.

DEVELOPING THE PERSONNEL MAN'S ROLE

At the outset we shied away from even calling Wiley a personnel manager because we feared that he would get involved in the routine administration of personnel activities and thus be blocked from carrying out the new functions we had in mind. It might have been possible to maintain this position if the necessary func-

---

[1] W. F. W.

tions of personnel administration had been being adequately carried out at the time we entered. As it was, personnel activities
were being carried out in a haphazard manner. Personnel policies
were either unformulated or else subject to differing interpretations in different departments. The union was threatening to take
drastic action, and the union leaders were frustrated at not being
able to handle grievances within the hotel. There were thus things
that urgently needed doing, and Wiley was the only person qualified to do them.

There were also things that were expected of Wiley, which he
had to decline to do. For example, he found that in the past it
had been customary for the personnel manager to handle the
firing of all employees. The departmental managers had made the
decisions about discharges but had turned over the dirty work to
be done by the personnel manager. As Wiley began to take up
some of the necessary personnel functions, he told supervisors
and executives politely but firmly that they were going to have
to do their own firing.

The establishment of the new role for the personnel manager
depended most importantly upon winning the confidence of
Smith, the vice-president and general manager. His signing the
contract with the University was an indication of overall confidence in the project, but it did not mean that at the outset he had
confidence in Meredith Wiley. Wiley had to win that confidence
in action. He found himself in a most difficult situation because
we had counted on his handling of research findings as the most
important aid in winning Smith's confidence, and yet, in the
nature of research, there would necessarily be a period of some
weeks before he had anything from research upon which he could
take action.

The first three months were the most difficult for Wiley. It
was in this period that Whyte had to carry the burden of a relationship with Smith and seek to keep the pressure of the dynamic
executive off of Wiley. While Smith had been told that it would
take some time for the results of our program to show and had
accepted this statement rationally, he was nevertheless a man of
action who was accustomed to thinking in terms of quick results.

Witness his detailing to Whyte and Wiley a ten-point personnel program that he wanted carried out in the hotel. If Wiley had assumed responsibility for carrying out any of these ten points, he would have become so involved in Smith's programs that it would have been impossible to build a new role.

Whyte's most important contribution in this period was to block the ten-point program and to persuade Smith to await the results of research with a bit more patience.

While Wiley recognized the crucial role of Whyte in this period, his dependence upon Whyte and the University did not make for a happy situation among the three of us. Wiley's anxieties were further increased by the disadvantage he experienced in relation to Edith Lentz in the contacts with Whyte and the University. According to the original plan, Whyte would spend a day a month at the hotel. This meant that he came up in the late afternoon of one day and spent all his time until late in the evening with Wiley and Miss Lentz and then met with them one or more times the following day. In their relationships with Whyte at the hotel, Wiley and Miss Lentz were therefore on an equal footing. However, plans called for Miss Lentz to come to Chicago once a month for two days to go over with Whyte the development of the research and to consider its implications for action. While Miss Lentz conscientiously sought to report Wiley's point of view, this arrangement naturally tended to put the man who was to be primarily responsible for action into a position in which important decisions regarding his actions could be tentatively arrived at without his participation. This situation, adding to the natural tensions of the personnel manager's job in the early stages, created a certain strain within the project group. Fortunately, we were all aware of the sources of this strain and were able to take action to eliminate them. Miss Lentz suggested that Wiley substitute for her on the third monthly trip to Chicago. This enabled Wiley and Whyte to have a thorough discussion on both the research and action aspects. It also led to the decision that from this time on Wiley would be responsible for making the action decisions. We hoped that the three of us could be in close enough communication so that we could arrive at agreement regarding actions important enough to affect the basic strategy of the project, but we recognized that Wiley would be in an untenable position if he were not free to respond to the needs of the situation as he saw them. This decision further served not only to relieve Wiley's anxieties but also to give him more confidence in facing the future.

Even before we were in a position to take action on research findings, Wiley began to make progress in his relations with Smith. The first gain came through Wiley's taking over the handling of union relations. While Smith may not have understood very well what was happening at this time, at least he could recognize that the business agents were no longer bothering him and were no longer threatening strikes.

A second gain came through the prediction Wiley gave Smith regarding the impending clash between Kraus and the new chef. Smith appeared to pay no particular attention at the time, but when, several weeks later, the clash did occur, Smith recalled the prediction and gave Wiley credit for it. This appeared to be a major turning point in the relations between the two men. Wiley gained prestige as a man able to foretell the future. (Actually, this was not a very difficult feat, for anyone who was close enough to observe the two men in action would have realized that a major clash was unavoidable. However, the fact that Wiley did not have a special crystal ball does not affect our analysis. The prediction had its effect.)

By the time Christmas came, we had already reached the point of acting on certain research findings, but the Christmas party provided another important boost to the standing of Wiley with Smith, quite independent of the research. Smith was delighted with the success of the Christmas party and recognized that Wiley and Miss Lentz were the ones primarily responsible for the success. On the other hand, the Christmas party placed a further strain on the relations between Wiley and Kraus, for Kraus had remained aloof from the party activities and had even obstructed them in certain respects.

THE STRATEGY OF ACTION RESEARCH

While we sought to keep from getting involved in activities that would divert us from our major purposes, we did aim to bring about three major types of changes, which we expected to be interrelated and mutually reinforcing. These were:

1. Changing the work environment.
2. Changing the symbols of success and failure.
3. Changing interpersonal relations.

If we had not been able to effect changes in the work environment and in significant symbols, we could have made very little progress in changing human relations directly. Let us note some of the significant changes that fall under each heading.

Changing the Work Environment

Technological change almost inevitably brings about changes in human relations. Sometimes technology can be modified to take the requirements of the social system into account. While the technology was on a relatively simple level in the hotel, it nevertheless provided us with illustrations of this proposition. For example, the introduction of the water spigot into the Coffee Shop dining room was a change of this nature. Not only did it markedly reduce the physical strain in the job, with attendant effects upon human relations; it also symbolized top management's concern for the employees just as the lack of the water spigot earlier had symbolized management's disregard for employee welfare.

Work flow tends to channel relations among workers and to influence worker-management relations also. If frictions arise directly out of the flow of work, it may be that changing the flow of the work provides the best means—in some cases, the only means—of eliminating the friction. Changes in layout, equipment, and flow of work led to a marked reduction in friction between waitresses and checkers—not to mention an improvement in the speed and quality of service.

The formal organization structure—the official allocation of positions and assignment of activities to positions—also presents an influential aspect of the environment of the particular work group. In some cases, it may be necessary to change the formal structure before much constructive work can be done directly on human relations. In collaboration with Kane, Wiley worked out a structural change in the Housekeeping Department that had the effect of eliminating a large part of the friction between the department head and his assistant.

Changing the Symbols of Success and Failure

Organization members need to know how they are doing. Even if the boss were much more communicative on such matters than the average boss tends to be, reliance solely on the expression of personal opinions would not make for a healthy relationship. It encourages dependence of the subordinate on the superior. In his preoccupation with pleasing the boss, the subordinate tends to lose sight of the objective problems in the work environment with which he must deal.

To relate himself to the work environment, the individual needs some symbols that will represent the performance of himself and of those for whom he is responsible. What symbols are available?

Before our project began, the predominant symbols were those associated with costs. The records on costs were elaborate and systematic. Other records were sparse and disorganized. The supervisor knew that if his costs went up, he would suffer for it.

One of Wiley's first efforts was to develop systematic records of labor turnover. This proved to be a powerful set of symbols. Smith and others must have been vaguely aware that labor turnover was high, but when they did not have the symbols representing turnover set before them, there seemed no need to do anything about it.

When Smith first had the chart representing labor turnover set before him, he was delighted. He seemed to study it with just as much relish as he devoted to his cost records. We were able to establish in his mind a connection between costs and labor turnover. The cost of advertising for new employees was the most obvious connecting link, but he also agreed that there were costs associated with training new employees and with the inefficiencies that must arise when so many employees have little experience on the job.

We also persuaded Smith that high labor turnover was in part a response to the pressures of autocratic management.

Subordinates now discovered that Smith's questions about their operations were not limited to matters of money. If labor turnover went up, he wanted to know why, and he was not satisfied when a supervisor told him, as Larry did, "I can explain why every one of these people left." Smith became just as concerned as we were with establishing the point that high labor turnover indicated that a poor human relations job was being done.

We did not have to establish a connection between turnover rates and supervisory leadership in the scientific sense. Smith let it be known that high labor turnover signified poor management, and that was more influential than the most solid statistics we might have been able to present.

My discussions with the management group were aimed at getting them to think in terms of a social system and to recognize heavy downward pressures as presenting problems for employee morale and productivity. I presented the notion of group meetings as a device for allowing workers to initiate activities for their superiors and in that way to relieve some of the downward pressures. Even if the idea were grasped intellectually, the value of the idea had to be reinforced. Our success in the Coffee Shop provided the necessary means of reinforcement. My report regarding the success Miss Paris had achieved with her group meetings—supported by Smith's strong endorsement—was designed to symbolize for members of management that a new pattern of managerial leadership would be rewarded.

Changing Interpersonal Relations

In working directly on human relations, our aim at first was to relax the downward pressures and to stimulate initiative upward. Group meetings provided the primary vehicle in this program—but they were not automatically effective. Therefore we needed to examine the problems of developing effective group meetings.

It seemed to us that the group meetings were most effective in those departments where they were launched after a period of research interviewing and consultation between Wiley and the department head. This sequence of action enabled Wiley to present a preliminary picture of employee reactions to the department head and to help the department head prepare himself intellectually and emotionally for handling the kind of criticisms and suggestions that would come up. Interviewing was also important as a follow-up on meetings. As Miss Lentz reported back certain adverse reactions to the meetings in the Housekeeping Department, Kane and Mrs. Grellis were able to change the conduct of the meetings so as to retain the advantages and eliminate the defects. This is our explanation of the success of group meetings in the Coffee Shop and the Housekeeping Department.

By contrast, let us consider two other examples. In the King Cole Room, Larry was simply ordered by Smith to institute group meetings before he was at all prepared for them, in fact when he was feeling greatly threatened. Larry either would not or could not give up his tight control of the departmental meetings. He seemed most secure when he called on people to speak and they spoke only in response to questions he had phrased. Workers learned that they might be penalized if they ventured to break this pattern.

The same points seem to apply to interdepartmental meetings. At one time, the waiters and waitresses in the Zebra Room were complaining about the problems they were having in the kitchen. The Zebra Room department head persuaded the chef to come in and meet with them. While none of us observed the meeting, we received reports that the waiters and waitresses had spoken up to the chef in a most aggressive fashion. The employees later expressed satisfaction with the meeting. They had certainly got a great deal off their chests. They also reported that things seemed to have changed for the better in the kitchen, but this seems much more doubtful to us, judging from the reaction of the chef. He expressed great indignation to Wiley about the way he had been attacked by the Zebra Room people. He was so upset by the experience that he would have found it difficult to respond to criticisms in any constructive fashion.

Note that in arranging the Coffee Shop interdepartmental

meeting with the chef, Wiley spoke to the chef on two or three occasions before the chef could see any point to having such a meeting. Wiley was also able to orient the chef as to the sorts of problems that were going to come up and to suggest that if the chef were able to absorb some of the heat from the girls, this might contribute to a more harmonious relationship between the two departments. Thus prepared, the chef was able to go in and handle the meeting in a masterly fashion, which brought marked improvements in relations between the two departments. Without any such preparation, he was unable to withstand the criticisms the Zebra Room employees poured upon him, even though this came after his successful Coffee Shop experience.

Two further notes of explanation are perhaps in order. The Zebra Room waiters and waitresses had had more years of experience in the trade, and our previous research had indicated that such people tend to be more aggressive than the newcomers. Furthermore, the Zebra Room employees had not been meeting regularly with their department head to discuss their problems so that their meetings with the chef took place in sort of a crisis atmosphere. By the time the chef came into the Coffee Shop meeting, the girls had met with their department head often enough and successfully enough so that they did not carry with them so much pent-up emotional heat.

We also found that departmental meetings present a problem in developmental sequence over time.. If the department head is emotionally prepared to deal with a group meeting and really to encourage free expression, he has little difficulty in conducting the first few meetings in such a way that they yield general satisfaction. Many complaints and suggestions are just waiting to be aired. After two or three meetings, these pre-existing complaints and suggestions will be drained out, and the department head may have to ask himself: what do we talk about now?

In both the Coffee Shop and the Housekeeping Department, the department heads found that, in order to maintain employee interest, they had to take steps to provide at least initial structuring to the meeting as time went on. No longer could they just sit back and be confident that people would have things to bring up.

They found that the discussion leader needs to present some problem for discussion, some information the people will need to know. In time, the meetings may become explicitly involved with training at least to a certain extent, with the department head describing and demonstrating how he wants things done. As long as the department head continues to encourage people to speak up with criticisms and suggestions of the material he introduces and also provides some time for bringing up problems directly from the floor, he can retain the constructive human relations aspects of meetings without allowing them to degenerate into a routine where members no longer have much interest in what is going on.

We gave great emphasis to these group meetings in our work in the hotel, and in a sense they are the key to much that we accomplished. We were not only communicating to department heads and supervisors the problems we found in their department; we were helping them to develop skills to get at these problems directly through discussion with their employees. We aimed to use the research interviewing and the consulting process as means to aid the supervisor in the development of these essential skills.

THE ROLE OF THE PERSONNEL MAN

In carrying out the action-research program, Meredith Wiley played a role quite different from that ordinarily occupied by the personnel man. The following features of that role seem of greatest importance:

1. *Keeping confidences.* The notes of the field researcher and of the personnel man were not available to anyone within the organization, no matter what his position of authority. (Kraus made several attempts to see the notes and was rebuffed.) Similarly, neither Miss Lentz nor Wiley ever identified a particular individual as the source of a complaint. At first, Smith would want to know, "Who said that?" Wiley would then have to point out that he had promised not to reveal this information and that, if he did so, this would destroy his usefulness to Mr. Smith.

Reports to higher management always involved the presentation of general ideas, distilled out of the statements of particular individuals. If such confidential relations cannot be maintained, then employees, supervisors, and managers themselves will not be willing to talk their problems over freely with the personnel man or with the research worker.

2. *Blame or interpretation?* The personnel man seeks to avoid laying the blame on particular individuals. Instead, he seeks to understand the bases of human problems and to interpret this understanding to supervisors and managers. His first responsibility is to understand *why* people behave as they do and to communicate this understanding to those having responsibility for parts of the organization.

3. *Working with the man most immediately responsible.* Wiley sought at all times to work primarily with that supervisor immediately responsible for the problem area. As much as possible, he avoided placing himself in the position of reporting errors and inefficiencies to the top. Through working closely with the departmental supervisor, he was able to help that supervisor to improve the performance of his department. Then Wiley, in reporting to the top, was able to describe progress being made as well as problems encountered. This made it possible for supervisors to look upon Wiley as someone who could help them to do a better job—and to get them credit for improved performance.

4. *Consultation with the top man.* Smith naturally wanted to be kept informed regarding the progress of his program. Wiley sought to meet this need by letting the boss know what department was being worked in at a given time, and, in a most general way, what he hoped to accomplish. He sought to avoid pressure from the boss to give him information regarding the details of any given study or action program. He led Smith to expect that fuller reports would be presented when the action program was further advanced.

Wiley also sought to alert Smith regarding any anticipated developments of major importance to the hotel. In the case of the predicted clash between Kraus and the chef, we can see how important this function was.

Wiley also sought to help the top executive to understand his own impact upon the organization. In this he was not as completely successful as in some other respects, as we have already seen.

5. *Utilization of research data.* Wiley used research data in consultation with executives in different ways in different stages of the program. His utilization of these data went through three general stages that may be characterized as recommendation, statement of alternatives, and aid in interpretation.

In the early stages, Wiley used the data to make specific recommendations. For example, he told the supervisor and then Smith himself that the Coffee Shop waitresses were upset about the lack of a water spigot in their dining room. He explained that this was not just a physical problem; it also had an important symbolic meaning, suggesting that management had no interest in the employees. He recommended that a water spigot be installed.

In the next stage, Wiley withheld recommendations but pointed out possible alternative lines of action to meet problems brought to light by research. He encouraged executives to explore these alternatives in discussion with him but to make up their own minds.

At a later stage, he refrained even from pointing out alternatives. He presented the data to the responsible executive and aided him in interpreting the data. He then put it to the executive himself to move from interpretation of data to statement of alternatives and to a decision.

These changes were in line with our general objective: to build a problem-solving organization. Wiley was not concentrating on solving particular problems revealed by the research. He aimed to strengthen people in the solving of their problems, and this he did in part by giving them increasing latitude in utilizing our research findings.

While these stages followed a general sequence of time throughout the hotel, the techniques used had to be adapted to individual cases. Kane in the Housekeeping Department quickly caught on so that Wiley could simply present data to him and give him a start at interpretation. After Wiley had broken down his resistance, Kraus remained much more dependent on Wiley for advice than we would have liked. And, finally, Larry in the

King Cole Room was so concerned with protecting his position as father to his people that he never made any voluntary use of the research data at all.

6. *Responsibility for rewards and punishments.* Wiley avoided getting directly involved in the administration of rewards and punishments for supervisory and management personnel. We believed that it should be the responsibility of the operating executives to administer the rewards and punishments. Of course, our program had an important impact on the administration of rewards and punishments. As we got our program established, it became apparent that those who were able to lead their units according to the pattern we were seeking to establish would be rewarded whereas those who did not follow the pattern would run into negative sanctions. Wiley sought to help people fit into this pattern so that they themselves could earn the rewards from the operating executives.

Did we deviate from this principle when Wiley got involved in the cost reduction program? It seemed to me that we did not. Wiley was not the one who decided that 5 percent of the employees would be discharged. Neither did he set quotas for each department, much less select the particular individuals who would be discharged. It was Smith who established a new set of symbols whereby performance would be judged: each department had the responsibility of reducing its work force by 5 percent (more or less)—this without losing efficiency and with a minimum of disturbance from the employees and the union leaders. These objectives having been established, it was Wiley's responsibility to work with the executives and supervisors so that they could win the rewards of recognition by Smith and escape the penalties of his displeasure. (It was Wiley's responsibility to handle the union leaders directly.)

7. *Counseling and control.* Insofar as possible, Wiley sought to avoid the direct exercise of control. His aim was to consult with people so that they would understand the possibilities of the new pattern that was developing and so that they themselves would be able to solve their problems in line with the new pattern.

Throughout most of this period, Wiley was able to hold to

this approach, but in dealing with Kraus and with Larry in the King Cole Room, Wiley found himself taking direct and forceful action. Does this mean that our approach was faulty. Were these impulsive acts that should have been avoided? Or can we find some characteristics in the particular situations that require a different sort of handling than that generally applied?

I think we must conclude that Wiley had to act as he did with Kraus and Larry. Let us examine those cases.

Wiley knew for a long time that Kraus wanted to get rid of him. The normal human reaction to such knowledge would be to fight back and try to get rid of Kraus. However, we reasoned that this resistance to Wiley was to be expected and simply presented us with a problem with which we had to deal. As long as Kraus did not stand directly in the way of Wiley's carrying out his functions with department heads, supervisors, and workers, no direct action against Kraus seemed necessary. It is, of course, not easy to draw the line between the personal resistance of a key executive and the interference he provides through influencing other people, and Wiley might well have confronted Kraus much earlier than he did. However, by the time we learned that Kraus was telling other hotel people to pay no attention to Wiley, the interference had become too obvious to ignore. If Wiley had not intervened at that point, the whole program would have been jeopardized.

With Larry the point of direct intervention came when Larry announced to the waiters and waitresses that stations would now be rotated—by orders of the personnel department. The statement was not only false; it was in complete violation of the understandings we had with the employees and with the philosophy of the program. If Larry's statement had been allowed to go unchallenged, it would have been impossible for Miss Lentz and Wiley to carry the program any further in the King Cole Room, and, no doubt, word of what had happened in the King Cole Room would have jeopardized our work everywhere.

We can sum it up in this way. The personnel man should regard personal resistances as entirely normal and simply as presenting problems that he has to contend with. At the same time, he must have a clear idea of his own role and functions. He must be prepared to explain them fully when asked. He must also be prepared to take a firm initiative in cases where others take such actions as may jeopardize his role.

PERSONNEL PROGRAMS

From the beginning we sought to lead Smith away from considering personnel's function as consisting of a series of programs. It was not that we considered programs unimportant; it was rather that we felt that personnel programs should grow out of the needs of the organization. Our research was designed to establish what the needs were. By that logic, personnel programs should have developed as we went along, even if we did not call them such.

Indeed they did develop. Wiley developed a scheme of wage and salary administration. He clarified and rationalized personnel policy. He established new procedures for handling union grievances. Finally, a large part of our program might be regarded as training or management development. It was on-the-job training, built upon problems people were actually encountering. In the group meetings, executives, supervisors, and workers discussed human relations and technical problems, but the cases they dealt with were not provided by Harvard or Cornell or any outside agency. They discussed the cases that they were actually experiencing, and this might be expected to provide for a maximum carry-over of the learning.

In addition to handling a number of the common types of personnel programs, Wiley worked directly on certain aspects of organizational problems which are usually outside the scope of the personnel man. He dealt with technology, work flow, and organization structure. We have sought to show that, if he had not been free to tackle these aspects of the organization, the progress we made would have been much more limited.

Chapter XIII

THE BALANCE OF SUCCESS AND FAILURE [1]

This chapter will attempt to sum up the successes and failures we experienced during the period of the action-research program. Let us consider our successes first.

WHAT DID WE ACHIEVE?

The gains can be summed up under six main headings:

1. We were able to establish *a new role for the personnel man,* as discussed in the preceding chapter. Without success here, none of the other gains could have been achieved.

2. *Improvement in the quality of interpersonal relations.* Here we have no precise measures. Ideally, we should have had a questionnaire administered to all employees before we began and then a similar questionnaire at the end of the year. We did not do this for several reasons. We were frankly afraid to introduce a questionnaire at the outset. We recognized that people were quite anxious about our presence, and we felt that a questionnaire would contribute to this sense of alarm. An equally compelling, but less scientifically justifiable, reason was that none of us at the time had any great faith in the questionnaire nor any special competence in this method.

Although we do not have any precise measures of changes in quality of interpersonal relations, we do have voluminous interview data in which employees in various departments comment

---
[1] W. F. W.

freely and fully upon their relations with supervisors, fellow workers, and workers in other departments. In case after case employees spoke about the reduction of interpersonal tensions. Supervisors and executives also reported that interpersonal relations were going much more smoothly than they had at earlier periods.

3. *Labor turnover and safety.* Our first efforts in the Coffee Shop demonstrated—perhaps in part spuriously—that our efforts led to marked reductions in labor turnover. The Coffee Shop figures over succeeding months indicated that we had unwittingly had the advantage of season fluctuations. We began in the late summer, and by fall turnover in that department had dropped sharply. The following summer turnover went up again in the Coffee Shop without any apparent change in the internal human relations situation. A number of the girls just took off for summer resort waitress jobs.

Since some of the hotel departments were small enough so that large percentage changes in turnover figures could take place in the short run more or less at random, we probably have a better indicator of achievement in the turnover rate for the hotel as a whole. Here there was no marked drop from the initial figure of around 22 percent a month during the 12 months of the project, but beyond that point turnover did drop sharply, so that it leveled off around 6 percent at the 18-month mark, and then had dropped to below 4 percent in another 12 months. This raises two questions: why no significant drop within the first 12 months? Why then a drastic drop in 6 more months?

Assuming that a smoothing out of interpersonal relations should result in a drop in labor turnover, we can only speculate regarding a possible lag. We might perhaps assume that our stabilizing efforts would not show immediate results but would only show up after some latency period.

Could the sharp decline from 12 to 18 months be explained in terms of labor market factors? If jobs became somewhat more difficult to get, we might expect people to remain longer in their jobs even when dissatisfied, and this would show up in lowered turnover. The best way to check this possibility would have been to compare the Hotel Tremont figures with those of other hotels in the city for the same period. Unfortunately, the other hotels at the time were not keeping turnover records that would have made such a comparison possible. We can only say that other hotel personnel managers did not have the impression that they were experiencing any marked change in their labor turnover situation at a time when the Tremont turnover was dropping by 60 to 70 percent.

In the field of safety, the hotel received a National Safety Council award in recognition of a reduction of average man-days lost from 25.5 in July, 1945 (when the project began), to 1.0 in July, 1948 (toward the end of Wiley's tenure as personnel manager). Interestingly enough, this drop was not associated with any formal safety program. We assume that the reduction in emotional tension in the organization may have contributed to the lowering of the accident rate.

4. *Management development.* A large part of our work might have been considered a management development program. As we relieved the pressures down from the top on the department heads and lower level supervisors, they were able to assume more responsibility for the planning and organizing of their own activities. We sought to avoid imposing direct solutions of problems. Our effort was directed rather toward helping individual managers and supervisors to analyze their problems more effectively and to work out their own solutions. Our study shows that we made some progress in this in certain parts of the organization. It was perhaps in the area of leadership of group meetings that the most specific management development progress could be shown. In the Coffee Shop and in the Housekeeping Department, the key managment people learned how to conduct group meetings which contributed to solutions of technical problems and also to improvement of the morale of the work group. (We certainly do not wish to claim credit for the quality of group meetings in the King Cole Room.)

5. *Efficiency and productivity.* Our successes here might be evaluated in two ways: in terms of objective standards of performance and in terms of the opinions of key management people.

We have nothing in the way of objective standards that enables us to claim that our project contributed to the productivity and efficiency of the organization. Such measures may be difficult to devise in a service industry. Certainly it would have required a major research effort for us to establish any reasonably adequate standards.

With reference to the second criterion, there is no question of our success. As far as public opinion was concerned—at least the opinions of the key decision makers in the hotel—there were strong sentiments indicating that our project had helped the hotel to do its job more efficiently.

6. *The transfer of initiative.* When the project began, I was the only one in a position to initiate activities for Smith and the other main power figures in the hotel. Since we were aiming to establish the personnel man as an agent of change in the field of human relations, our program would not have been successful if the initiative had remained with me backed by the prestige of the University. The record shows that Meredith Wiley became steadily more effective in iniating activities at high levels. Wiley achieved a major victory with Kraus, in that he was able to establish a cordial consulting relationship. With Smith, he achieved substantial progress, although the relationship there left much to be desired. The problems we had with Smith will be more thoroughly explored below.

WHERE DID WE FALL SHORT?

We achieved our most complete successes at the departmental level. At higher levels, we progressed far enough so that at least we opened the way for constructive action at the departmental level. With Smith we never did achieve the sort of relationship we had hoped to establish. With Kraus, we achieved more than we had expected—but less than we had hoped.

Subordinates testified to marked changes in the behavior of Smith. He seemed to become pleasanter to talk to. He began noticing people as he passed them in the corridors. He made an effort to compliment people on work well done. People commented that he handled his management meetings much better than he had before he was exposed to the management discussions I conducted. However, we could not say that we had been successful in establishing a new *pattern* for managerial leadership. Smith seemed to accept our analysis of the Kraus problem, and yet he failed to take any constructive steps to resolve the problem. He simply changed his mind about Kraus and then proceeded to needle him in hopes of getting him to resign.

Smith continued to make impulsive decisions that sometimes had far-reaching adverse consequences. The case of Mr. Kent in the front office provides perhaps the best example of the impact of an ill-considered and ill-prepared management decision.

Finally, we were never able to get Smith to see the pattern that we thought existed in our program. He was accustomed to thinking of individual good ideas. He continued to think of our project as a good idea, but he also had an enthusiasm for Professor Rogers and employed him to teach the supervisors the J.I.T. program, without any real consideration as to how this activity would fit in with the personnel program already established in the hotel. Perhaps our criticism of the Rogers course smacks of professional jealousy. Another professor was moving in on our monopoly. While we cannot deny feelings of personal resentment, we can say with objectivity that the decision to bring in Professor Rogers was made without any consideration of the place his course would occupy in the existing pattern of personnel activities within the hotel, nor was this matter discussed with Personnel Manager Wiley. By the time Wiley was informed the decision had already been made. Even if Professor Rogers' course had been much better than we considered it to be, the question of integration could still be raised. Our philosophy was that specific personnel programs should grow out of the needs of the hotel, and these needs should be established through research and discussions with management people. While Smith gave verbal acquiescence to this approach, he did not always conform to its requirements.

Smith's failure to renew the research contract beyond the first year must also be counted against us. It is interesting to note that if Edith Lentz had been free to continue with the project, Smith would have signed the contract without question. He saw the project in somewhat personal terms. He was convinced that Edith Lentz had contributed importantly to the improvement of hotel management, and therefore he was prepared to continue with her. He was not so sold on the research-action program in general that he would leave it to us to decide who could appropriately succeed her. Perhaps we should not argue too strongly against his judgment in this case. The effectiveness of such a program depends in a very high degree upon the caliber of the individuals involved, and Wiley and I both had serious misgivings about our ability to find a replacement that would come close to the standard of performance Miss Lentz had set. Furthermore, the termination of the project after one year did have at least one significant advantage for us. It enabled us to show that even this short time was sufficient to establish some relatively permanent results. We refer not only to what was achieved during the year but more importantly to the fact that Meredith Wiley was able to carry on the spirit of the program for two additional years, even without a university connection and a research project to support it.

Our limited success with Smith naturally raises the question as to whether we handled him well enough. Here the responsibility was primarily mine, and my relationship with Smith left much to be desired—on my side and probably his side also. I should confess at the outset that I never felt at ease in dealing with Smith. Perhaps my insecurity stemmed in large part from my youth and lack of much previous experience in dealing with management people. Beyond this, Smith was known even to his associates as "a hard fellow to get to know." He did not encourage informality. My meetings with him were generally held in his office, with an atmosphere of strictly business. Even when we had lunch together, the businesslike atmosphere prevailed. Had I been able to see him more than once a month, it might have been possible to reduce these barriers, although I am convinced that much of the problem would still have remained.

I now feel that my approach to Smith was too indirect and cautious. While I found many shortcomings in his pattern of managerial leadership, I never discussed these with him directly.

Our talks centered on what he should do with Kraus, how group meetings might be stimulated, and so on—all matters in which Smith necessarily played a prominent role. No doubt he could infer from things I said some criticisms of his own behavior, but in our discussions I never confronted him with these criticisms.

Apart from my own timidity, I must confess to another inhibiting influence. I wanted to get the research contract renewed. Suppose I did confront Smith with some of the problems he himself created? This might antagonize him, I reasoned, and then he might just cut the project off at the end of the first year.

Here I fell into a trap that claims many consultants, and it is interesting to note that I did so even though I had nothing to gain *financially* (as would a consultant) from the renewal of the contract. My salary at the University of Chicago was in no way affected by the Tremont project, and I received no consultation fees from the hotel. My career at the University depended much more upon my performance of other activities, and, in fact, some of my colleagues probably looked askance at my getting involved in running a hotel and would have considered two years at this task twice as bad as one.

If I had no financial or concrete career interest in the contract renewal, what then did trap me? As the psychologists would say, I had become ego-involved in the project. I was happy with the progress we had made, but I could see much still to be done. Smith's acceptance of the project was one indication of our success. If he rejected us, then somehow we would have failed. So I rationalized that I should put off confronting Smith with criticisms of his leadership style until he had signed the contract for the second year. After that point, I could watch for my opportunities and gradually work toward a more direct approach to the Smith problem.

Subsequent events convinced me that my rationalization had been dead wrong. By the time I was writing my report to Smith on our year of work at the Tremont, it was clear that the contract was not going to be renewed. Having nothing to gain through holding anything back, I decided to build a main part of the report on our analysis of Smith's leadership style. In fact, I presented him with the ten points used in analyzing his behavior in the present book. (See Chapter 2.)

I came to town to deliver the report in person. Smith was so eager to get it that he locked himself in his office immediately and read it straight through. When he called me in, it was to express enthusiasm particularly for my analysis of his own executive behavior. Later, he called his management group together and told them that he had just read my final report. He said further that I had pointed out that he was the main personnel problem of the hotel, and that he intended to profit from the criticisms I had made.

This response left me in a somewhat dazed condition. As I thought it over later, I convinced myself that I should have taken the initiative much earlier, and confronted him in discussions with our view of his leadership behavior and of its impact upon the organzation.

Could I have done this effectively? I am not sure. While effective consultation requires the consultant to adapt his approach to the personality of the client and to the nature of the situation, I am afraid we are all limited by our own personalities, so that we tend to follow a distinct personal style in consultation—to some extent independent of the nature of the situation and the personality of the client.

Some years later, when I was working on a project with Chris Argyris, I saw in action a very effective "confronter." He would bring out into the open thoughts and feelings that I would be unable or unwilling to express. This is not necessarily to say that his particular style is more effective on the average than my own. The experience simply suggested that there are a number of different styles and that one style may be more effective than another with a particular client and situation.

If I had it to do over again, I would have contronted Smith much earlier with my criticisms of his leadership. However, it would oversimplify the problem to assume that the issue was to confront or not to confront. In working with management people at the department head level and below, we were involved in human relations training in a very real sense. We had no training strategy for Smith. Should we have tried to train him? If so, how? I shall leave those questions for a final chapter, for they involve some important general issues in the fields of human relations research and training.

WHAT TO DO WITH MR. KRAUS?

Why did we make such an effort to remodel Kraus? Wouldn't it have been better for the organization if we had got him discharged at an early stage? Whenever I describe this case, these are the most popular questions that come up in the discussion.

We recognized quite early in the project that the chances of turning Kraus into a good manager were small indeed. Why, nevertheless, did we try and keep trying?

In the first place, we tried because we thought we had something to learn from the effort. Discharging a man was no new solution to a human relation problem. We knew that the replacement of Kraus by a different personality would lead to important changes in human relations. We knew very little about the possibilities of changing human relations through attempting to change the behavior of a key executive. On this problem we wanted to find out as much as we could.

In the second place, we did not move to get Kraus discharged because this was contrary to the philosophy of our project. The nature of this philosophy will be discussed in the next chapter. For present purposes, let us consider what might have happened if we had indeed moved to get Kraus discharged.

We must first recognize that this would not have been an easy thing to accomplish—at least in the early stages of the project. When Mr. Smith elected to be out of town on the day our project was to be launched, he put us on notice that our position was far from solid. Even when Smith finally did decide to discharge Kraus, he had a great deal of difficulty in bringing himself to take action. Note the lengths to which he went in trying to prod Kraus into resigning. Presumably a time did come when we could have hastened the departure of Kraus if we had sought to influence Smith in this direction. On the other hand, if we had sought to intervene in this direction as soon as we were fully aware of the inadequacies of Kraus, we would have been risking a good deal for an uncertain outcome.

Suppose, nevertheless, we had intervened—successfully—to get Kraus fired at an early stage. Presumably then our influence in the matter would have become known throughout the hotel. What then would have been the effects upon the relations of other executives, supervisors, and workers to us? Since many people would have been glad to see Kraus go, might we, through this action, have improved our standing with members of the organization? Even if those who would have rejoiced at his departure had been more numerous than those who would have regretted it, which was probably the case, I question whether our contribution to his discharge would have helped our position.

Such action would have involved a major change in our roles. It would have made evident to people throughout the hotel that we held a great deal of power in our hands. If we could get Kraus fired, presumably we could get other people fired—and who would be the next one to go? It would then have appeared that the individual's progress or loss of position in the hotel was dependent upon his relationship with us. What then would have become of the consulting relationship Wiley enjoyed with executives and supervisors?

They did of course come to recognize that he enjoyed a good deal of influence or power, but it was power of a different sort the nature of which will be explored in the next chapter. Knowing that Wiley would not directly intervene to reward or punish them, they continued to express themselves rather freely and frankly as they discussed their problems with him.

Consider the return of Kraus. As it was, Wiley and Kraus were able to work as cooperatively together when Kraus returned to be in complete charge as when Kraus had been resident manager. Had he credited Wiley with an effort to get rid of him, this continuing cooperative relationship would have been impossible.

While the return to a key position of an executive who had been discharged is certainly unusual, events with the same social meaning happen frequently in organizations. Let us say that there is a struggle between faction A and faction B. The personnel man intervenes with actions that help the cause of A. Faction A wins out, and the personnel man enjoys a solid and powerful position, but then the situation changes, and faction B comes out on top. Where now is the personnel man?

If we were justified in trying to remodel Kraus instead of firing him, it does not necessarily follow that our approach to the problem was sound. Although I do not see how we could have been more effective in the long run, it now seems clear that the cooperative relationship between Wiley and Kraus could have been established much earlier. Here we were misled by our own faith in the power of interviewing. Partly from our experience and partly from the influence of Carl Rogers,[2] we had come to look upon a more or less nondirective interview as an exceedingly powerful force in human relations. I am afraid we were inclined to think that it could do all things with all men if only we knew how to use it effectively enough.

For many weeks Meredith Wiley pursued Kraus, in hopes of interviewing him. Kraus simply would not be interviewed.

It now seems clear that we were naïve in expecting this approach to work with a personality like that of Kraus. For our purposes, one dimension of his personality was of special importance. Following William Schutz,[3] we would call this "control." Schutz examines personality in the three dimensions of inclusion, affection, and control. His FIRO questionnaire is designed to measure the importance for the individual of having control expressed toward him and of expressing control toward others. We may assume that if we had had Kraus's FIRO scores on the control dimension, he would have shown up as exceedingly high both in needing to express control to others and in needing to have control expressed toward him. Certainly his behavior gave this indication. His tendency to order subordinates around at all times make obvious enough his need to express control. His behavior in relation to Smith shows equally clearly the other side of

---

[2] Carl R. Rogers, *Counseling and Psychotherapy; Newer Concepts in Practice* (New York: Houghton Mifflin Co., 1942).

[3] William Schutz, *FIRO: A Three Dimensional Theory of InterPersonal Behavior* (New York: Rinehart & Co., Inc., 1958).

this dimension. Note that he was so submissive toward his boss that Smith had great difficulty in driving him into resignation.

Kraus seemed to interpret all human relations in control terms: either he controlled or someone controlled him. He had to get the control question decided before he could establish any stable relationship.

In this context, it is clear why Wiley's interviewing approach could not possibly succeed. Probably Kraus at first was apprehensive toward Wiley, assuming that Wiley was going to try to establish some control over him. When Wiley's behavior did not fit this control picture in any fashion recognizable to Kraus, the Resident Manager jumped to the conclusion that Wiley had no control and therefore could be disregarded. Witness his advice to other executives: "Don't go to Wiley. He's a dope!"

While we were surprised at the dramatic turnabout in the Wiley-Kraus relations that followed in the showdown meeting that Wiley initiated, if our analysis of Kraus's personality is correct, the outcome should not have been surprising at all. Wiley moved right in and structured the situation in detail. He indicated that in certain types of situations there were certain things that Kraus *had to do* with and through Wiley. As they argued over these matters, they worked through to a resolution of the control problem and at last they had a basis for working together.

This is not to suggest discarding the interview as a technique for the personnel man. Mr. Wiley's skill in interviewing enabled him to establish relations of confidence and trust with many of the management people. They felt he was interested in their problems as he encouraged them to talk about those problems. The Kraus case simply indicates that interviewing is not an all-purpose technique for all men.

Chapter XIV

ON THE THEORY AND PRACTICE OF ACTION RESEARCH [1]

Now the story has been told, but if it is received as simply an interesting case, we will have failed in our major purpose. We feel that the case can help to lead us toward some conclusions of general significance for both the theory and practice of action research. In this final chapter, we hope to explore these points of general significance. We shall begin with theory.

In this examination of theory, I shall not attempt to distinguish between what we think we know now and what we knew at the time we carried out the project. The general theoretical orientation that led us at the Hotel Tremont has remained the same, but that experience and many others have led to a further development of our theoretical ideas. Therefore I shall try to re-examine the case in terms of theory as we now see it.

In our theory,[2] *activities*, *interactions*, and *sentiments* are the basic concepts. *Activities* refer to the physical actions carried out by the people we observe. In a work organization, they can range all the way from the carrying out of work itself to the social activities in the coffee break and in the lunchroom and in other informal social contacts.

Interaction refers to certain aspects of interpersonal relations

---

[1] W. F. W.

[2] For further development of theory see William F. Whyte, *Men at Work* (Homewood, Illinois: Irwin-Dorsey Press, 1961), chaps. 2 and 3.

that we can observe and quantify. We can note how often A talks with B and how long each such interaction lasts. We can also note who initiates the interaction, that is, whether A contacts B or B contacts A.

In observing *activities* and *interactions*, we are particularly interested in noting instances where interaction gives rise to change in activities. This sort of observation provides the key to the study of leadership and interpersonal influence. In a sense, every time A contacts B and gets his attention, we can observe B modifying his behavior in response to A at least at that moment. However, for the study of organizations, we are less interested in the moment-to-moment adjustment than we are in the changes in activity that may follow it. As examples of such changes in activity, we see a checker finding something wrong on the tray of a waitress and telling her to return to the kitchen. We observe the waitress responding by so returning. Or we see Resident Manager Kraus telling Miss Paris and the waitresses that he is ready to start the meeting, and we see the meeting getting started.

Sentiments refer to the mental and emotional reactions we have to people and physical objects. They have the following three elements:

1. An idea about something or somebody; that is, a cognitive element.
2. Emotional content or affect.
3. A tendency to recur, upon presentation of the same symbols that have been associated with it in the past.

According to the theory, the social system of the organization is made up of activities, interactions, and sentiments which are in a state of mutual dependence. That means that a change in one will necessarily involve changes in the other.

This theoretical approach would indicate that change in the organization can be introduced through activities, interactions, or sentiments. However, for most theoretical and practical purposes, we can regard sentiments as a dependent variable, responding to changes in activities and interactions. To be sure, we sometimes note changes in sentiments that are independent of the interactions and activities currently going on inside the organization. For example, let us say that the workers are reasonably satisfied with the wages they are receiving. Then they hear that workers in the same industry in another plant in the same city have received a substantial wage increase. The workers in this other plant had previously been below our own workers in earnings but now have surpassed them. Under these circumstances, we can expect the workers in our case to become less satisfied with their wages, quite independently of changes taking place in interactions and activities within the organizational social system.

While changes of this nature may frequently occur in response to events outside of the organizational system, when we are concerned with producing changes within the system we will generally find it futile to make a direct approach to sentiments. Much research has indicated that telling people what they should believe and feel is very unlikely to have the desired effect upon them. If the effort is made to change sentiments through group discussion, then we are at the same time changing the pattern of interactions and activities at least for the period of the discussion program. Our theory suggests that for sentiment changes brought about by training group discussions to persist within the life of the organization requires the production of supporting changes in interactions and activities in that organization.

If we conclude that this direct approach to sentiments can only be effective insofar as it involves interaction and activity changes in the organization, then it seems to make good theoretical and practical sense to look first at activities and interactions in order to bring about sentiment changes—not to mention changes in performance with which we will deal later.

In a work organization, the activities people carry on are strongly influenced by the technology, the flow of work, the formal distribution of tasks, and the location of individuals in the formal structure of the organization. This structuring of activities in turn will strongly influence which people come together in interaction, how frequently, and for how long a period. In many situations, the most effective approach to changing interactions is through changing the technology, work flow, formal organization structure or assignment of task responsibilities, and thus changing activities. On the other hand, influence can move in the other direction. While tasks may be formally assigned to groups of workers, we often find that, in the process of their interaction together, they reorganize the distribution of these tasks and thus the activities within their group.

As so far stated, the theory might seem to imply that activities and interactions provide their own motive power. Of course, this is not the case. While each one of us needs some sort of interaction in order to maintain his emotional equilibrium, interactions alone are not sufficient reward in themselves to bring people into organizations and then keep them interacting together. The same may be said of activities. While certain people find certain activities intrinsically rewarding, these intrinsic rewards are never enough to keep an organization of activities in being. To maintain or to change a given pattern of activities and interactions, the organization must provide both rewards and penalties: rewards for carrying out certain activities in a certain way, penalties for failing to do so, rewards for interacting along certain lines, penalties for failing to do so. We are dealing here with what psychologists call *reinforcement*.

For human beings, rewards or penalties are not always immediately associated with a given action. In fact, in a complex organization the association is often remote indeed: the reward (or penalty) may be forthcoming only after a long series of actions has been evaluated by an organizational superior. On the basis of past experience, man learns to anticipate reward or punishment long before it comes and to adjust his behavior in terms of these anticipations. He develops *symbols* of performance that enable him to evaluate how he is doing as he goes along.

Some of these symbols he picks up from the immediate interpersonal situation. A smile or a frown from the boss may be interpreted by the subordinate as approval or disapproval, even though, in any given case, they may be more directly caused by the headache from which the boss is suffering at the moment or by recollection of a good joke he heard earlier.

An organization also provides more patterned symbols of per-

formance: figures on output, costs, incentive earnings, labor turnover, absenteeism, number of grievances, and so on. While costs
and turnover will exist whether they are measured or not, the
measurement and reporting of these items by management tends
to produce two results. In the first place, it establishes the importance of certain symbols—for management would hardly make
the effort to measure and report if the figures were not considered important. In the second place, it provides a regular pattern of symbols, furnished at regular intervals, to which people
learn to respond in a patterned manner. If people simply had impressions that turnover was high, there would be a variety of
interpretations and responses to this phenomenon. The provision
of turnover figures at regular intervals greatly narrows the variation in response.

The behavioral connection between symbols, performance,
and rewards and penalties does not automatically occur. Let us
illustrate again with turnover: what do high turnover figures
mean? Suppose the key executive believes that turnover is high
because unstable and incompetent people are being hired. In that
case, we are likely to find the personnel department responding
by trying to recruit and select more stable and competent people.
The work of the operating departments will continue to be
hampered by high turnover, but the supervisors will incline toward the view that this problem belongs to the personnel department and is beyond their control. On the other hand, suppose
the key executive makes known his conviction that high turnover
is due to poor supervisory leadership. In that case, recruiting and
selection efforts will assume secondary importance, and the
supervisors will become more concerned about their relations
with their subordinates.

Note that this analysis holds true regardless of what the
causes of the high turnover may be in any given case. We are
not now trying to establish scientifically the relationship between turnover and supervisory leadership. We are simply saying that if the boss begins using turnover figures as one measure
of results and lets it be known that he thinks turnover is related
to the way supervisors handle their subordinates, then supervisors

will become increasingly concerned with their relations with subordinates.

Of course, this increasing concern will not guarantee favorable results. It will simply increase the supervisors' readiness to change their behavior. Whether the changes tried out prove to be more effective is another matter. That will depend upon the insight and skill of the supervisor and upon the intervention of others who may be able to help him to restructure interactions and activities in such a way that the turnover symbols will reflect improved performance.

(Each organization necessarily develops its own sets of symbols to indicate good or poor performance.) We often find situations in which an executive advocates one type of behavior whereas a set of symbols he himself uses tends to point his subordinates to an opposite type of behavior. The skilled executive recognizes such possible conflicts and seeks to learn how subordinates interpret the prevailing symbols and seeks to develop new sets or new ways of using symbols to bring behavior more in line with his objectives. (The change agent may make a significant contribution through analyzing responses to symbols and helping the executive to devise new sets of symbols and new ways of using them.)

While certain symbols become linked in men's sentiments with anticipated rewards or penalties, this is not the only kind of linkage which occurs. (In time men come to consider as *right* or *good* the behavior called forth by these symbols, quite apart from eventual rewards or penalties. Psychologists refer to this process as *internalization.*)

Kraus provides us a good example of internalization. At first he stopped cracking down in the Coffee Shop because he knew it would bring penalties from his superior. Only later did he come to believe that a leadership pattern that avoided crackdowns was a good thing in and of itself. So thoroughly did this sentiment become internalized that he did not revert to crackdowns even when he returned to the hotel as its top operating executive and had no Smith to police his actions.

(When we speak of a social system being made up of mutually

dependent parts, we mean that a change of one part will not be confined to that part but will have an impact on other parts of the system. This does not mean that a change in one part of the system will necessarily be felt in all other parts. A change in activities and interactions in one department may have an observable impact upon adjoining departments and upon one or two levels of supervision above the department but have little noticeable effect upon more remote parts of the system. On the other hand, one who wishes to introduce change into an organization must think in social system terms and recognize that to some extent he is dealing with the whole organization, even as he seeks to have a direct impact only on one part of it. This does not mean that the change agent must work on all parts of the organization at the same time. This is clearly impossible. Even if his goal is to make major changes in the functioning of the total organization, he must start somewhere and concentrate his efforts. If the change agent is constantly aware of the relations of the small part on which he is directly working to the social system as a whole, he may be able to move from part to part, gradually reshaping the whole system.

LEADERSHIP AND GROUP PROCESSES

An examination of the literature of small group research may help us to understand the role that Wiley was playing in the Tremont.

As Bales[3] and others have shown, even in a small group there tends to be differentiation between two leadership roles: the task leader and the social-emotional leader. This is observed by asking the members of the group after each session which members contributed the most to getting the group moving toward its objectives and which members they would most enjoy associating with socially. In the first meeting or two of a group, it is common to find the same individual standing out in response to both questions, but, as the group proceeds from meeting to meeting,

---

[3] Robert F. Bales, "Some Uniformities of Behavior in Small Social Systems," in G. E. Swanson, T. M. Newcomb, and E. L. Hartley, *Readings in Social Psychology* (rev. ed.; New York: Henry Holt & Co., 1952), pp. 146–59.

the general pattern is for one member to assume the task leadership and another to assume the social-emotional leadership role. (The task leader rarely remains the most socially chosen individual.)(On the other hand, neither does he drop to the bottom in this category. Typically, he occupies an intermediate position in the social choice scale.)

This small group analysis should enable us to see in microcosm the problems of leadership that any organization faces. In work organizations, we can expect two leadership roles to be played. Especially in a work organization, the task leader will carry the primary leadership role, but this alone is not enough. The group must maintain itself, motivate its members to put out effort, and keep the members sufficiently satisfied to remain in the organization, or else the work will not get done.

According to this logic, there should be no simple relationship between productivity and social integration. At one extreme, where leadership emphasis is almost exclusively on the task, social integration may be lost, people will leave the organization or else band together in slowdowns and strikes, so that the progress of work is slowed or stopped. At the other extreme, where effort is concentrated upon meeting the social-emotional needs of members, will productivity similarly drop? Based on small group studies, there is some reason to believe that this would be the case. As group discussion approaches a decision point, we observe a rise in the expression of disagreement and tension, and a loss in social integration. In other words, the group will decide to move in a direction that some members welcome but other members resist, so tensions necessarily will arise that would not be present if the existing routines were continued. Even in a small group, this leadership dilemma cannot be avoided. If the members simply put off making decisions as to what they are to do, eventually they themselves will begin asking what they are there for and will lose interest in the group. Thus even a small group will necessarily experience a rise in tension as it approaches decisions, but the tensions of task progress can be dealt with where social-emotional leadership is present. In other words, the group needs leadership to get it moving and keep it moving, but it also needs a type of leadership that will give attention to the social stresses and strains involved in task progress and will act to maintain the integration of the system.

ORGANIZATIONAL INTEGRATION AT THE TREMONT

If we apply this analysis to the Tremont, we can say that at the time of the beginning of the project task leadership was very heavily emphasized and no provision was made for social-emotional leadership. Some supervisors were indeed concerned with problems of social integration, but they had no support from the administration. For example, Miss Paris in the Coffee Shop did the best she could to maintain the equilibrium of her department, but the heavy pressures from above severely limited her effectiveness and even made her wonder whether what she was trying to do was appropriate.

In these terms, it was the role of Meredith Wiley to provide social-emotional leadership at a high level and to make it possible for this role to be played at lower levels. If the term social-emotional leader seems inappropriate in a business setting, we might equally well refer to Wiley as an *organizational integrator*. It was not his responsibility to determine the tasks that should be done, but it was his responsibility to develop means for building and maintaining the integration of the organization, in the face of the demands of task leaders.

How can we measure his success and that of the project? At first I was inclined to think that productivity should provide the really important criteria for success, and we all felt frustrated since we did not see how we could develop useful measures of productivity in this situation. As my colleague, Leopold Gruenfeld, has pointed out to me, according to the line of analysis here used, to judge the effectiveness of Wiley's role and of the project, we should not be looking for indices of productivity but rather for indices of social integration. In this area, we had abundant though not readily quantifiable expressions of sentiments indicating that the level of integration did indeed increase greatly. Turning to more concrete figures, we note the marked reduction in labor turnover. Wiley also cites one example in the Coffee Shop of a sharp reduction in absenteeism. Unfortunately, we do not have systematic absenteeism figures for the whole organization over time.

In some organizations and with some types of personnel, labor turnover seems to remain fairly constant over long periods of time, in spite of changing conditions within the social system, and even absenteeism is not very sensitive to such changes. We could not therefore always expect to find turnover and absenteeism giving us useful indices of organizational integration. In the Tremont Hotel, turnover and absenteeism did fluctuate widely and thus could have provided very valuable indices of integration.

APPLYING THE THEORY IN ACTION

(The theory indicates that sentiments of satisfaction or dissatisfaction with the organization, the conditions at work, and the leadership of the organization can most readily be affected by operating upon activities and interactions. We assume also that one of the most effective ways to change activities and interactions is through making environmental changes.)

In Chapter 12 we have examined certain examples of changes in work flow and technology in the hotel's food service operations and of changes in organization structure and distribution of tasks in the Housekeeping Department. In these cases, the changes were self-reinforcing for the participants. That is, the changes were so effective in reducing friction that the participants did not need to be told by their superiors that the changes were a good thing. The association of the project with this marked tension reduction naturally tended to build greater acceptance both of project personnel and of the project's way of working through problems.

It is not always possible to achieve the desired changes in activities, interactions, and sentiments through reshaping the environment. Some of our most crucial interventions were directly into the interactional system itself. To illustrate, let us review in schematic form the early history of intervention in the Coffee Shop.

1. *The pre-existing situation.* The waitresses were suffering under heavy downward pressures and inadequate working conditions. While favorably inclined toward their immediate supervisor, they had very unfavorable reactions toward Kraus and had lost hope of being able to initiate any changes up the line of authority.

2. *The interviewing program.* Edith Lentz provided a temporary release of pressure by encouraging the girls to talk their problems out with her.

3. *Insulation of department from downward pressure.* No constructive program would have been possible if Kraus had continued his crackdowns here. In order to secure a chance at organizational therapy, we—and Smith—managed to block Kraus off from this department temporarily.

4. *Providing a substitute channel for initiating activity upward.* From waitresses to Lentz to Wiley to Whyte to Smith, we carried the problem of the water spigot from the bottom to the top of the organization, and Smith responded by ordering the change made. This apparently trivial physical change came to have great symbolic significance for the waitresses and their supervisor. It connected speaking up on their problems with getting results on those problems. But this only reinforced the value of talking to Miss Lentz. Upward initiation had still to be built into the system.

5. *Development of group meetings.* Now we were building upward initiation into the system. This won quick acceptance within the department, but a further step was necessary to secure its effectiveness even within the department.

6. *The symbols of top level recognition.* These came in two forms. Wiley developed turnover figures, and Smith publicly stated that henceforward these would be important symbols of performance; he also endorsed the thesis that increasing upward initiation would decrease turnover. The Whyte account in a department head meeting of the success of Miss Paris with group meetings, combined with Smith's strong endorsement of this point of view, served to symbolize—and not only for Miss Paris —that a new pattern of supervisory leadership would now be rewarded.

As has been pointed out earlier, Kraus was not immediately integrated into this new pattern of relations—nor was he ever thoroughly integrated. The new pattern developed around him, and he eventually adjusted to it as best he could.

In retelling the Coffee Shop story, we have concentrated on the reshaping of activities and interactions up and down the hierarchy of authority. It is important to emphasize that our intervention was not limited to these hierarchical relations. In this case, as in others, Wiley worked on work flow and inter-departmental relations (waitress-checker, kitchen-dining room).

A COMPARATIVE VIEW OF ACTION RESEARCH

So far we have viewed this case in isolation from the literature of action research in organizations. Let us now take a comparative view.

I shall not attempt to determine what is the *best* way to do action research in organizations, much less to argue that our efforts represent this best way. Organizations differ widely both in the problems they face and in the way they operate, so we can hardly expect to find one universally effective strategy. Nevertheless, we can learn more about action research if we examine these several projects, each in relation to its own setting and also in relation to the Tremont project.

Elliott Jaques, a psychiatrist and social anthropologist, reports[4] on an action-research program in Glacier Metals in England, a large factory employing approximately 1,200 workers. Jaques headed a team of eight research people. Six were student trainees and one was a professionally trained person.

In line with the policies of the Tavistock Institute of Human Relations, the research team insisted that work would not begin until the project had had acceptance from all significant segments of the organization: management, workers through the Works Council, and union leadership. There was several months delay while local union leadership was communicating with higher levels of the union. It was arranged that the project be

---

[4] Elliott Jaques, *Changing Culture of a Factory* (New York: The Dryden Press, Inc., 1952).

responsible to the Works Council, composed of worker and management people representing the factory as a whole.

A large part of the effort of the action-research program was concentrated upon certain key groups within the factory which had frequent meetings: Works Council, division managers' meeting, service department, works committee, and superintendent's committee. The research team provided certain information and analyses in discussion with these groups, but only under certain strict limitations as to what could be communicated. These restrictions were indicated on a notice posted on the factory bulletin boards, in these words: [5]

> It is not the intention of the project that the research team should gather secret information from one person or group about another. The only material that will be of real value is information that is public and can be reported.
>
> . . . no matter will be discussed unless representatives of the group are present or have agreed to the topic being raised.

The action aspects of the project were introduced primarily through Jaques' observation of, and interpretation of, the meetings he sat in on. That is, he refrained from offering concrete advice but, from time to time, contributed his own interpretation of the way the group was attacking a problem in question and how the group functioning might be helping or hindering the group in its search for solutions.

Let us first look at what the Glacier and Tremont projects have in common. In both cases, there was a process of prolonged intervention. Jaques reports upon two years and nine months of effort. The Tremont project lasted only 12 months in its original form, but we have limited data on intervention and changes initiated by Wiley over a period of two years following termination of the formal project. In each project, the team worked out a variety of problems, not limiting itself just to the functioning of the hierarchy of authority, and, in each case, some far-reaching changes were brought about. The projects were similar

[5] *Ibid*, pp. 13–14.

also in the research methodology used, chief reliance being placed in both cases upon observation and interviewing.

There are also far-reaching differences. At Glacier, the responsibility for the project was firmly placed with groups and particularly with the Works Council. At the Tremont, we had a primary responsibility to Smith. Related to this basic difference, the Glacier project involved consultation of project personnel with groups, while the Tremont project involved primarily consultation of Wiley and Whyte with key individuals. Finding no groups established and functioning on a regular basis, we did seek to promote group meetings and develop a more effective group process, but we consulted with the supervisor who was, in effect, the chairman of each group.

Our intervention was also more active, especially in the early stages of the project. That is, while the Glacier team limited itself to consultation and interpretation, we at times urged that particular steps be taken. Note, however, that our aim was to de-emphasize this sort of initiative in the hope that the key individuals and groups would develop their own problem-solving ability, and, indeed, specific concrete advice was offered less and less as the project went on.

The Tremont project had as a specific objective the establishment of a new role for the personnel man, whereas no such role establishment was explicitly undertaken at Glacier. Nonetheless, there is evidence that the role of the group observer and research interpreter did become crystallized as part of the company structure, for Jaques has continued to work with Glacier, having later gone on the regular payroll of the company.

In the Glacier project, there was an explicit understanding at the outset that nothing would be published except that which had the concurrence of the groups chiefly involved. At Tremont, we made no such commitment, but we assumed the same responsibility to protect the individuals in the organization, and this resulted in a long delay in publication.

How can we account for these differences in strategy and tactics?

One type of answer traces to the educational backgrounds of

the chief investigators. Jaques states quite explicitly: [6] "The model for this kind of research was taken from clinical medicine." We cannot think of any such clear model in the Tremont project, but our own background led us to a more predominant emphasis upon structure and human interaction than was the case with Jaques. However, these are matters of intellectual history and have no bearing upon the relationship between a particular strategy and the nature of the organization upon which it is tried out.

I would argue that our strategy was reasonably well adapted to the Tremont case, that the Jaques strategy was well adapted to the Glacier case, and that neither strategy would have worked well at all in the other organization.

Jaques was dealing with an organization with a well-established structure and distribution of labor, and one which had a stable and rationalized set of personnel policies. Groups played a very important role in the management of the organization. Furthermore, the Glacier people individually and collectively gave the impression of having a well-established way of working through their problems. Their need was for research observers and interpreters to help them to make these established ways of doing things work better. In the long run, the research did lead to some important changes, but the guiding assumption at the outset was that the observer-interpreter could contribute best in assuming a relatively passive role.

The Tremont situation was drastically different. Policies and procedures were in a state of confusion. There were no existing groups to which the research could have been related at the outset. Furthermore, there were no established ways of solving human problems that seemed to be working to anyone's satisfaction. It was hoped—and feared—by various members of the organization that the project would introduce far-reaching changes.

If we had required some sort of joint sponsorship by management and worker and union representatives before starting at the Tremont, the project would never have been launched. On the other hand, the approach we took with the Tremont organi-

---

[6] *Ibid.*, pp. 15–16.

zation would most certainly have been rejected by all concerned at Glacier.

While Cyril Sofer was, like Jaques, a member of the Tavistock Institute of Human Relations, he reports [7] on action-research experiences rather different from those reported by Jaques. Instead of going into the three organizations in which he reports as a member of a research-action team, he went in by himself as a researcher-consultant. At some points in his efforts with these organizations, other members of the Tavistock group were involved, either in research or in clinical testing and consulting, but these activities were distinctly supplementary and limited both as to their purposes and their duration. Sofer brought in his associates to meet three needs: to provide coverage of problems he did not have time to handle by himself, to provide a professional service that he was not qualified to give (such as occupational counseling), or to keep separate the role of researcher-consultant to the organization from that of psychologist-consultant to individuals. In some cases, he recommended that executives and potential future executives avail themselves of counseling services in order to help make up their minds as to their own career plans, but he deliberately avoided knowing what the psychological consultant recommended in order to maintain the standard of professional ethics he accepted for his role of researcher-consultant to the organization.

Sofer takes us through three case studies: one in an industrial setting, one in a medical setting, and the third in an educational setting. In each case he tells with great candor and perceptiveness how he proceeded to approach the problem and the people involved in it. We see him moving step by step, defining and redefining a problem, gathering his data, and moving the organization toward action.

These might be called clinical studies, for we see each case primarily as it appeared to the researcher-consultant. It was not Sofer's purpose in this book, nor would his methods have made it possible, to present the research analysis of cases which is

---

[7] Cyril Sofer, *The Organization from Within* (Chicago: Quadrangle Books, Inc., 1962).

possible in the Glacier and Tremont situations, because those projects were established with a much heavier emphasis upon the research function. Nor did Sofer aim to introduce new roles into the organization as was planned in the Tremont case and as eventually developed in the Glacier case. Sofer's aim was to help each organization meet its existing problems and in the process help the organization to become more effective in its problem-solving efforts. The evidence presented suggests that this task was accomplished with a great deal of skill.

Sofer gives particular attention to what he calls the "regularities and principles in social consultancy," and it is here that his book is particularly valuable. While no point-for-point comparison will be attempted here, readers will no doubt find that Sofer has developed more systematically than we did in the Tremont case some of the principles of consultancy and has also added other points that we did not recognize but which may be applied with profit to future action-research efforts.

The Survey Research Center at the University of Michigan is well known for its work in organizational research, and the program has constantly been concerned with problems of applying research knowledge to organizational change. I shall comment on two significant action-research projects, reported in three sources.

The Center has been particularly concerned with utilizing the feedback process of questionnaire survey findings as a means of changing behavior.[8]

The Center has maintained a continuing relationship with the Detroit Edison Company, carrying out a variety of studies over a period of years. In 1948, Floyd Mann and Rensis Likert decided that in their latest survey program they would try out methods of feedback particularly designed to influence the behavior of managers and supervisors. The procedure worked along these lines: after the data had been gathered and organized for effective presentation, and Center action-research people met

---

[8] See Floyd Mann and Rensis Likert, "The Need for Research on the Communication of Research Results," in Richard N. Adams and Jack J. Preiss, *Human Organization Research* (Homewood, Illinois: The Dorsey Press, 1960), pp. 57–66.

with top management to present results and get the top management people involved in a discussion and interpretation of the findings. Throughout this and subsequent meetings, the aim of the Center people was to refrain from themselves telling management people what the findings meant but only to serve as technical consultants who might be called upon to explain certain points and respond to requests for additional data. The Center people worked closely with personnel men from the company in the discussion process.

After members of top management had thoroughly discussed the findings, the discussion-interpretation process proceeded down the line organization. For each meeting, a management man would call together his immediate subordinates and present them with the results that pertained to their areas of responsibility. In each case, the responsible management official led the discussion but sought to involve his subordinates in the interpretation of the findings. The company personnel people and the Center staff people were involved in these meetings only as resource people. In some divisions, this feedback process was carried down to the first-line supervisory level and in a few cases even to the worker level.

In their first report on this approach to action research, Mann and Likert attributed no concrete results to the feedback procedure. A later report by Floyd Mann[9] describes an experiment carried out in eight accounting departments in this company. After a general meeting of top management of accounting and all of the supervisors, in which the general findings were presented, four of the department heads (who apparently selected themselves for this purpose) undertook to organize extended programs of feedback meetings over the next 18 months. In two of the remaining departments no further feedback meetings were carried on. Changes in key personnel eliminated the remaining two departments from the design of the experiment.

---

[9] Floyd Mann, "Studying and Creating Change: A Means to Understanding Social Organization" in *Research in Industrial Human Relations*, ed. by Conrad M. Arensberg *et al.* (New York: Harper and Bros., 1957), see especially pp. 159–62.

A survey was conducted in 1950, and another survey, containing many of the same items, was made in 1952, after the feedback programs of the 1950 study had finished. Comparison between the experimental departments and the two control departments showed that the experimental departments had changed significantly more in the direction of more favorable responses to the supervisor, the kind of work they did, and a number of other items, than had the control departments.

Mann's report gives us no information on the process of change that took place in the departments that led to these changes in worker sentiments. Nor does he consider the influence on the experiments of the self-selection by the department heads of the four experimental departments: the possibility that the initiative the men displayed in this case indicated they were more effective managers than the control group people.

A more ambitious experimental effort, following the same general approach, has been reported by Seashore and Bowers.[10] The experiment was carried out in two manufacturing plants, under the same plant manager. Total payroll amounted to 800 people. The plants were part of a larger corporation. They had been organized for many years by an independent union.

The program had its inception when the plant manager became converted to what he called "participation management" as a result of attending a number of conferences where this approach was presented by some of its leading exponents.

After some discussion with Survey Research Center personnel, the plant manager agreed to an experimental program in which some departments were to be changed in the direction of participation management and other departments were to serve as controls. Change was to be brought about mainly in three ways:

1. Training of management personnel in the participation approach, which seemed to mean considerable emphasis upon group discussion techniques.

---

[10] Stanley Seashore and David Bowers, *Changing the Structure and Functioning of an Organization: Report of a Field Experiment* (Monograph 33, Survey Research Center, Institute for Social Research) (Ann Arbor: The University of Michigan, 1963).

2. Feedback of survey research findings, with discussion and interpretation of these findings, particularly by those whose units were being reported upon in a given feedback session.

3. An SRC agent spending several days a week at the plant, observing developments, talking with people involved, and consulting with management people on the changes they were contemplating. (When the first agent left for another job, he was replaced by a new man who undertook to function in the same fashion.)

According to the report, the research design: [11]

> . . . provided for introducing purposeful change with respect to four variables:
> 1. Increase in emphasis on the work group as a functioning unit of organization.
> 2. Increase in the amount of supportive behavior on the part of supervisors.
> 3. Increase in participation by employees in decision-making processes within their area of responsibility.
> 4. Increase in the amount of interaction and influence among work group members.

Variables one and four seem to be a part of the same thing. The idea was that the supervisor should try to treat his subordinates as a group. As this group identification developed, there was expected to be increased interaction among group members and increased responsiveness of the members to influences from each other. For variable two, the supervisor was to behave toward subordinates in an "ego-enhancing manner." Variable three seems to refer, in our own terminology, to increasing the frequency of employee initiation of activities for their superior.

It was recognized that there might be a need for policy change and clarification, and it was hoped that this could be accomplished by getting employees and work groups more involved in discussion of these matters and giving supervisors more delegated authority to make decisions. It was also recognized at the outset that there might be some need for change in organizational

[11] *Ibid.,* p. 18.

structure, but this was seen primarily in terms of modification of work group membership, so that workers would become part of stable groups and thus be able to develop the ties called for in one of the variables.

It was agreed among the researchers, management, and union representatives that Department A would be the experimental department and the other departments would serve as controls. After the second measurement of the experimental variables, a fundamental change in the design of the study took place. Other key management people became interested in the experimental changes and wanted their departments included in the program. The experimenters might have resisted this change more vigorously had they themselves not come to feel that: [12]

> . . . many of the day to day operation problems that came up in the experimental department proved to have aspects that prevented solution within the experimental department itself.

Furthermore, as a result of market changes, the plants were losing money, and the experimenters could hardly justify withholding efforts that might be of help in this crisis situation.

> For these and related reasons, the last vestiges of independence between the originally defined experimental and control departments were lost. The SRC agent began to disperse his time, plantwide, to wherever he seemed to have receptive people and problems with suitable scope with which to work.[13]

The authors also point to a further difficulty in the carrying out of their original plans. They had assumed that they would be dealing with a reasonably stable organization, with a well-defined organization structure and an established and understood set of policies. Into this well-structured situation they would then introduce the changes planned. Instead they found themselves dealing with a situation that resembled what we found at the Hotel Tremont. A good deal of reorganization and clarification of structure, responsibilities, and policies had to be undertaken or else the intended changes could not take place.

---

[12] *Ibid.*, p. 36.
[13] *Ibid.*, p. 36.

What were the results of the experimental program? With exemplary modesty and scientific caution, the authors give us the data and also the limitations that must be kept in mind in examining the data. While the original sharp distinctions between the experimental and control departments broke down, there were nevertheless differences among departments in the intensity of the work of the SRC agent, and the authors present considerable evidence to indicate that the more intensively treated departments did indeed change more in the planned direction than the other departments. At the same time, they recognize that these departments were to some extent self-selected by their managers, so that the favorable changes may reflect differences in managerial ability just as much as differences in the influences introduced by the program.

For purposes of our comparison of different approaches to action research, we may grant that the results indicate that favorable changes were indeed achieved in this case. Let us go on to examine the limitations and possibilities of the approach that was used.

First, let us note the predominant reliance upon the questionnaire method, both for the gathering of research data and for the action program. The questionnaire is a very powerful instrument for the measurement of the subjective states of informants: sentiments, beliefs, and values. It is not a useful instrument for gathering data upon activities and interactions. In other words, it does not provide the basic data we need for studying social processes.[14]

It is therefore no accident that we find the Seashore-Bowers report very sketchy on the behavioral changes that did take place. The SRC agent was indeed in the plants and in contact with the people frequently and over a long period of time, and yet the data he picked up in this way seemed to have been regarded simply as providing some general background about the plants and the nature of their problems. Even the activities and

---

[14] For a fuller statement of these points, see William F. Whyte, "Toward an Integrated Approach to Research in Organizational Behavior," *Proceedings of the Industrial Relations Research Association*, 1963.

interactions of the SRC agent himself are described in only the most general terms, so that the report does not provide us with the kind of account of the interventions of the change agent which we have from Jaques, Sofer, and the Tremont report.

In this action-research program, the emphasis was placed heavily upon measuring the state of the organization before, during, and after the intervention of the SRC agent, so that the researchers could demonstrate whether in fact changes had taken place and could measure these changes. The social process whereby the changes were carried through seems of no interest to the reporters of the project.

Reliance upon the questionnaire method provided a further important limitation to the project. Effective use of the questionnaire requires having a large number of informants in the same organizational position and responding to the same supervisors, the same conditions of work, and so on. This means that the questionnaire in industry has generally been applied to workers, as in this case, and the interpersonal relations investigated with the questionnaire have been those among workers and between workers and their immediate superiors. The method is generally used to investigate man-boss relations and does not seem well adapted for the study of relations arising along the work flow, or between departments, or otherwise among individuals having no hierarchical relationship to each other. There is growing evidence, which we hope is strengthened by our Tremont study, to indicate that the importance of these nonhierarchical relations in organizations has been seriously underestimated by many researchers prominent today in the field, and the research man who proposes to rely exclusively on the questionnaire is almost guaranteeing that he will continue to underestimate the importance of these relations, which do not fit well into his instrument.

What the researchers are overlooking in this project is illustrated by a case that they use only for illustrative purposes. We find the SRC agent reporting on changes made by Mr. Jones, who was in charge of manufacturing in one of the plants.[15]

---

[15] Seashore and Bowers, *op. cit.*, p. 40.

. . . Mr. Jones has undertaken an application of participation management, which is of rather awesome proportions.

Mr. Jones is forming project teams to handle some of the larger orders. Each team includes the men actually running the machines for each of the operations involved, and the team as a unit follows their particular order or project throughout the manufacturing process. These teams cut across the jurisdiction of the several group leaders, foremen, and area supervisors, and are supposed to work with these men as they need to. . . . Mr. Jones explicitly associates this change with our research project . . . it is certainly a large-scale, visible, and vulnerable application of the ideas we have been trying to introduce, and a failure would be very hard on Mr. Jones and on the plant. . . . Mr. Jones has conceived and activated this effort entirely on his own.

The SRC agent seems here to be referring to a far-reaching reorganization of interactions and activities, so as to bring them more in line with the flow of work. Even from the brief description, the principle of reorganizing relations in the horizontal, work-flow dimension seems clear, but this account leaves entirely to the reader's imagination the pre-existing state of organization of interactions and activities in this plant and what the pattern then came to be after the manager introduced his innovations. Our research suggests that this kind of reorganization may be just as important in its effects upon the sentiments of the people involved as changes that take place in hierarchical relations.

It is curious that the SRC agent describes Mr. Jones's intervention as "an application of participation management" although he also is frank to say that Mr. Jones was acting "entirely on his own" and took the researchers by surprise. How then can we say that this was "an application of participation management"? We may well credit Mr. Jones's reorganization to the action-research program, because it may be argued that the program had the effect of "unfreezing" the organization and stimulating managers to try doing things in different ways. But this is not the same thing as establishing a theoretical connection be-

tween Jones's intervention and the theory of participation management. At the start of the book when the authors sought to
tell what the theory of participation management meant, they
made no mention at all of work flow or other horizontal sets of
relations. The Jones's intervention can only be included under
"participation management" if we give participation management credit for every type of supervisory action that does not
involve the autocratic exercise of authority.

If we broaden the term to include so many meanings, then it
has come to be really meaningless. Indeed, this seems to us one
of the problems of organizational theory at the present time. In
the literature addressed to management, "participation management"—or some analagous term—has come to be by far the most
popular theory of management, even though the proponents of
the theory have been extraordinarily vague as to the types of
behavior that are to be covered by this theory.

With these conclusions, I do not mean to dismiss the questionnaire survey as an instrument for social research. I am currently using it in several research projects. Were I to start another
action-research project in an organization, I would hope to make
questionnaire surveys part of the program.

The questionnaire has great advantages for such a type of
study. The responses are anonymous, so we can deal with a
large body of data and thus avoid some delicate problems of
confidentiality. They also give the impression of being very concrete; we can present the data in percentage form and then make
comparisons that are easy to communicate to people. Furthermore, they seem to be much more impersonal than the interpretations given by the action-research man himself. Data can
be presented in such a way that they seem to speak for themselves much more than is the case where the research man must
seek to describe and interpret the data gained from interviewing
and observation.

Should we then have used questionnaires at the Tremont? In
order to make the most of these assets, we would have had to
apply the questionnaire throughout the hotel at the beginning of
our work so as to establish a base line for later measurements.

Given the very tense situation existing at the time we began, this would have aroused anxieties that would have been most difficult for us to deal with. Furthermore, it would have focused attention upon us in such a way that it would have been very difficult to proceed in a quiet and gradual fashion. As it was, our introduction was unfortunately theatrical, but after this beginning, with Edith Lentz concentrating in the Coffee Shop, we were able to let the organization get used to us as we went to work on a small scale. Furthermore, limiting our work first to one department, we had mainly to deal with the anxieties and expectations stirred up in that department, until we were ready to provide some general feedback of that department's results, at which point we could move on to the next step. Had we begun with a hotel-wide questionnaire, it would have taken some weeks for us to process and analyze the data, and we would then have been expected first to provide a general feedback, not only for the hotel as a whole, but also at least for some of the major divisions of the hotel's operations. We assume this would have stirred anxieties and controversies throughout the hotel, and yet it would not have been possible for us to deal with more than a small sector of the social system at one time.

Nevertheless, I am inclined to believe that in organizational situations where a reasonable degree of stability is to be anticipated—even where conflict is present—the action-research team can make effective use of questionnaire surveys. In fact, the questionnaire potentially offers us measurement through time of changes in sentiments in a much more systematic way than anything we were able to obtain in the Tremont Hotel through our methods of observation and interviewing.

Let us turn now to Chris Argyris who has been at once one of the most productive and most controversial of action-research people.

Argyris has been one of the chief targets for attack by a number of us who have taken the environmentalist side of the argument that may popularly be styled "conversionists versus environmentalists." In this oversimplified form, the issue is between those who place primary emphasis upon changing work environment to produce behavior changes and those who place primary emphasis upon changing the values, beliefs, and interpersonal perceptions of members of an organization.

A close reading of some of Argyris's writings suggests that his position has sometimes been caricatured. Perhaps he is a ready victim for this kind of interpretation because in recent years he has worked intensively on problems of changing interpersonal relations through research feedback and through intensive training in group discussion situations—to be described later.

In the book which will provide the basis of the present discussion,[16] Argyris makes quite explicit the views he holds regarding "the integration of the individual and the organization." [17]

> The lower one goes down the chain of command, the more the job and work environment control the individual's behavior; the more important it becomes to change the psychosocio-technical environment. For example, changes in technology, job design, incentive systems, budgeting activities, salary systems, and training activities.
>
> The higher one goes up the chain of command, the more the individual has control over his work environment and the more important it becomes to change the interpersonal (and then the policy) environment. Examples of the former are the rivalry, defensiveness within the organization. Examples of the latter are policies in the service of human growth and commitment such as decentralization.

Those advocating group discussion approaches to changing of interpersonal relations have often been criticized for the heavy emphasis they place upon the emotional aspects of human relations, and here again Argyris disassociates himself from this extreme emphasis: [18]

> . . . laboratory training in the past has neglected and unduly de-emphasized the importance of intellective competence to the development of interpersonal competence.

---

[16] *Interpersonal Competence and Organizational Effectiveness* (Homewood, Illinois: Irwin-Dorsey Press, 1962).

[17] *Ibid.*, pp. 3–4.

[18] *Ibid.*, p. 275.

What then is Argyris trying to do? In recent years he has been focusing primarily upon problems of communication and interpersonal relations at high levels in organizations. The concentration on high levels is explained by Argyris's belief that only the top officials have the leverage upon the organization to bring about the kind of far-reaching changes that he has in mind.

Argyris argues that most hierarchical organizations operate so as to limit communication among members of management to technical, rational considerations. The expression of emotion in committee or other business meetings is discouraged. When the formal leader of the discussion finds an individual becoming emotional, it is thought that he should change the subject or take other actions which would prevent the open examination of feelings in the group situation. When this kind of communication norm prevails, the subordinate may find himself seriously upset by proposals for action from his organizational superior to which he feels he is prevented from making any effective reply. Since to express how he feels would seem to reveal him as a person incapable of controlling himself adequately, he can only try to phrase objections in technical, rational terms which may have no relationship to the real problem as he sees it. When communication proceeds in this fashion, according to Argyris, superiors universally receive assent from subordinates for actions they propose, only to find out later that the actions have not been carried out as they had hoped. This leads them to "sell" their own point of view even harder next time, thus still further stifling the possibility of feedback which would reveal to them more of the nature of the interpersonal problems with which they are dealing.

The Argyris prescription for this condition is not a substitution of emotionalism for technical, rational discussion. He advocates what he calls "openness" or "authenticity," which is his particular combination of rational *and* emotional communication. Openness does not mean that each individual should express whatever is on his mind regardless of any concern for the feelings of others. The aim is to create a situation in which the members of an organization who are working closely together can each express how they feel about problems in their relationships in such a manner as to help those with whom they are communicating to express themselves in a similar open manner. The theory is that the emotional problems within the group do not simply disappear when they are not faced by members of the group; rather they tend to obstruct the carrying out of the rational plans of the members. The theory holds further that the technical problems can be more effectively resolved if emotional problems are not suppressed but are dealt with along with a development of rational plans.

Argyris believes that the barriers to his desired authenticity stem in part from such environmental forces as the organization structure, the budget and other control systems, the technology, and so on. He therefore does not see a change in interpersonal relations and perceptions at the top level as a solution to the basic human problems of organizations. He rather looks to these interpersonal changes as providing the necessary first step toward the facing of the structural changes that need to be carried through.

Let us see how these ideas are put into practice in the case examined for us by Argyris.[19] The project began at the point where he got the president of a large division of a large company interested in his ideas and willing to carry on a sort of experimental program. Argyris began work by seeking to diagnose the existing interpersonal situation through sitting in on a number of meetings of the top management group and interviewing the members individually. To a somewhat lesser extent, he also observed and interviewed management men a level farther down, whom he subsequently took as a control group in his experimental program. These observations and the attendant diagnosis Argyris fed back in extended discussions with the top management group.

This led the president and his immediate subordinates to participate in the isolated setting of Arden House in an intensive seven-day laboratory discussion program, led by Argyris and an associate. Eleven men participated in the program, which consisted largely of two types of discussion groups. There was the T-group, as it is commonly known in the training literature, in which the members were expected to learn something about their

---

[19] Argyris, op. cit.

problems of perception and relationships by the direct examination of the process of discussion that went on within the group. There was also another type of discussion in which there was an explicit focus on some problem the members faced within their industrial organization. As the days went on, Argyris observed, there came to be less and less distinction between these two types.

Argyris and his associate did not serve as discussion leaders in the traditional sense, nor did they assume the extremely passive role sometimes adopted by T-group leaders. Argyris argues that if he aims to help people to express themselves openly, he has to express how he sees things also; otherwise he would not be true to the model of openness he is trying to promote.

It is impossible in a few sentences to do full justice to the role Argyris played in relation to other T-group training roles. For a full exposition, readers are referred to his book.

Argyris provides us with a detailed report of the discussion meetings, which gives some idea of the way the members changed in their patterns of communicating with each other within the laboratory setting. Did these changes carry over into the job situation? Within the first two weeks after the end of the laboratory period, Argyris re-entered the division to interview members of the experimental group regarding their experiences in trying to apply their laboratory learning to the job situation. Argyris sat in on meetings once again to see whether he observed any differences from the way they had been conducted before the start of the change program. He also interviewed the subordinates of the experimental group who had not attended the laboratory and some of their peers who also had not been in attendance to try to check on any changes that had taken place in the behavior of members of the experimental group. Six months later, he again conducted interviews with members of the experimental group, and nine months after the end of the laboratory session he returned for an extended group discussion with members of this group. These observations and interviews were supplemented by responses to more structured questions regarding the way a leader and group member should behave. These measures were made before and after the training experience.

Argyris readily admits the difficulty of evaluating the extent of the changes that did come about. There seems no question that the members of the experimental group felt that the experience was exceedingly valuable and were able to cite a number of situations that they had handled differently than they would have before, as a result of their training experience. Did the subordinates perceive these differences? The answer is not clear cut. Certain differences certainly were perceived, but there was some reaction to the effect that the differences were noted at first and that then there seemed to be a fade-out effect. In spite of this possible fade-out, there seemed to be a good deal of recognition that changes had taken place, and yet, as might have been expected, the subordinates were not entirely comfortable with these changes. In fact, they found it difficult when they went in to see a superior about a problem to have the problem turned back to them for solution instead of getting a crisp instruction or order from the boss as had happened before the training.

Argyris makes it clear that the laboratory experience did not enable the training group simply to transfer the atmosphere of openness to the work situation in dealing with subordinates who had not gone through the training experience. He argues that it may be necessary, in order to carry out change to the fullest extent, to have a series of training meetings at successively lower levels.

There was a further limitation in the effectiveness of the divisional management in putting the new communications program into effect: relations with corporate management. Division management people continued to be on the receiving end of the same kinds of pressures that they had received in the past, and to some extent they reacted as before, passing these pressures down the line, even as they became more aware of the effects of this behavior. We see here a further illustration of the interrelatedness of parts of the social system. It is not only a problem of effecting changes in one part of the system, as Argyris demonstrates was done here, but it is also a problem of making this changed pattern viable within the larger system and then reaching out farther to change the pattern in that larger system.

Let us now look at this case in relation to our Tremont study. At the Tremont we placed heavy emphasis upon interventions designed to change the organization structure, the work flow and the pattern of initiation of activities, and we gave no explicit attention to questions of authenticity in interpersonal communication. In the Argyris case, we see the emphasis predominently upon reshaping the direct person-to-person relationships through training experiences designed to increase openness and authenticity, with relatively little attention to environmental changes. To be sure, Argyris does grant the importance of these environmental forces at the outset, and, in his concluding chapter, he gives brief examples of the way members of this top management group were beginning to work out new procedures in handling the budget and to make other changes in the environmental conditions of interpersonal relations. The nature of these changes is not specified in any detail.

Could we have used the Argyris approach to advantage in the Tremont situation? First, it should be noted that our action-research project took place before the founding of the National Training Laboratory for Group Development, which first established work along these lines on a firm foundation and still longer before Chris Argyris himself started his action-research efforts. We therefore did not have the choice of approaches available to us then that would be available now. Nevertheless, let us look again at the Tremont to see whether, in like studies in the future, the Argyris approach might be used.

In the light of this re-examination of the Tremont experience, we must note one key point of the structure that we could not reach with our environmental strategy: Smith himself. We could reshape the environment to which his subordinates were responding, but we had no such powers over him. Perhaps it would have been impossible to lure him into any human relations group training experience, either with his subordinates or in a regular training laboratory made up of members of various organizations. By the time we worked with him, the man who had started as a dishwasher was already worth several million dollars and was well on his way to a larger fortune. His methods were spectacularly successful by this standard of measurement. He was troubled enough by some of the human problems he faced to support our effort, but it seems doubtful that we could have got the major commitment from him to engage in a painful re-examination of his interpersonal relations and perceptions in a laboratory situation. Nevertheless, his case may well be illustrative of a great many problems in organizations. We may find that, for some of the major changes we would like to bring about, we have to introduce changes in the behavior of a key individual. If we cannot restructure the environment around him on his job, the only possible approach to changing him may be to try to involve him in some kind of human relations training experience.

While the difference in emphasis between Argyris and ourselves is obvious, what of differences in concepts and theory? Here there seems to be no fundamental incompatibility.

With his concern for "openness," Argyris is concerned in part with the creation of interpersonal relations characterized by direct and reciprocal exercise of personal influence, especially between superiors and subordinates. He observes superior "selling" his subordinate on some line of action and subordinate giving his passive assent, only to carry out the actions halfheartedly, if at all. He observes subordinates suppressing their real feelings and failing to come out with the criticisms and suggestions that might move the boss to action.

Observing the same interpersonal events, we would say that superior was attempting to initiate activity changes for subordinate, and we would check on the frequency of these attempts and seek to assess their success in terms of the frequency of subordinate's response along the lines of these influence attempts. Similarly, we would observe that the subordinate seldom attempted to initiate activity for the superior and still more rarely succeeded.

Argyris gives primary emphasis to the *content* of interpersonal communication. We concentrate on quantities and sequences in the organization of interactions and activities. These are alternative ways of describing the same interpersonal events. On the other hand, the two schema are not so completely overlapping that a description in one set of terms can be translated entirely into the other set. Our reports do not give Argyris all the data he would need to assess the "openness" of communication in the system, and his reports often fail to give us the data on interactions and activities that we need for our analysis.

The difference in emphasis has practical as well as theoretical implications. The change agent cannot do everything at once. Should he seek to change organizational behavior through working on the quality of interpersonal communication or through restructuring activities and interactions?

Argyris has demonstrated that his strategy may result in significant changes in the behavior of those going through the training experience. He acknowledges that these changes do not readily filter down through the organization, so that further research-training efforts may be needed at successively lower levels. He also recognizes that the favorable changes in interpersonal relations can be neither maintained nor extended unless they are supported by the sort of environmental changes we have been emphasizing at the Tremont.

Argyris has not yet demonstrated that executives who go through a training experience that reshapes their own interpersonal relations will necessarily go on to change the social, economic, and physical environment of the organization so as to support the kinds of changes in interpersonal relations he has introduced. For this reason I question the emphasis he places upon T-group and related types of training. If we indeed do agree upon the importance of the environment of work, then it seems to me more promising to design interventions that will have a direct impact upon the work environment, rather than seeking to get at that environment through human relations training. By following this environmental route, we will indeed need to do some training as we go along (as we did at the Tremont), and we may find the Argyris approach to training particularly effective at the top levels of the organization. This is not an either-or argument. We do not yet have a study which effectively integrates the environmental emphasis of the Tremont with the interpersonal sensitivity emphasis of Argyris. A project which attempted such integration would offer much to both approaches.

ON THE GENERALIZABILITY OF OUR APPROACH

To what extent can the lessons of our Tremont experience be generalized to other types of organizations?

As I discuss this case with management groups, I find the main grounds for their skepticism in what they consider the peculiar nature of the Tremont Hotel. They view it as a great mass of disorganization, confusion, and conflict. In such a situation, almost anything we did would have been helpful. But could our approach be applied to a "good" organization which was operating in accordance with "sound management principles"? There is certainly some merit in this argument, but let us examine it further. In comparing the Hotel Tremont with a "good organization operating in accordance with sound management principles" are we comparing disorganized conflict with organized cooperation? I doubt it. It would be more accurate to say that we were comparing *disorganized* conflict with *organized* conflict.

I have done research in a number of these good organizations that were following these good principles, and I find the difficulties not in lack of system but in competing and conflicting systems. The organization has systematic, well-organized procedures, and it has specialists to apply these procedures. The problem of the organization is a lack of integration of the various systems and procedures.

We may find, for example, that the personnel department has a very systematically worked-out scheme of job evaluation whereby the jobs are ranked in terms of skill, responsibility, and so on, and are paid accordingly in hourly rates. At the same time, the industrial engineers have developed a piece-rate wage incentive system that introduces major inconsistencies into the job evaluation program. We may find that the skilled maintenance workers who are at the top in hourly rates are now getting little if anything more than certain production workers who happen to have a "loose" piece rate. In two different jobs that are both on piece rates, we are almost as likely to find that the lower hourly rated job is yielding more total earnings through the incentive than the more highly rated job as we are to find it the other way around. Here the problem is not a lack of systematic procedures but the fact that two sets of systematic procedures operated by two different groups lead to differing and sometimes conflicting conclusions, with resulting friction throughout the organization. Such conflicts are explored much more fully in an earlier book.[20]

Consider also the introduction of technological changes. Customarily these are entirely in the hands of the engineers, even though we can readily demonstrate that a technological change may have drastic consequences for human relations in the organization. The traditional approach is for the engineer to introduce the changes and then for the personnel man to try to mop up the resulting difficulties. No attention is given to the necessity of integrating the human and technical aspects of the problem. These questions are further explored at length in my *Men at Work*.[21]

If this analysis is correct, then our main advantage was that the Tremont had not previously developed these specialized systems and procedures so that we were in fact able to take an integrated view of the organization and its problems. When we observed the impact of technology and work flow on human relations, we could deal systematically with that technology and work flow and did not have to leave it to some other group of specialists.

On the other hand, we suffered from one serious disadvantage. Since personnel procedures and policies were in a state of disorganization and there was no one else available in the organization capable of meeting the pressing needs in this area, Wiley necessarily stepped in. We had to make the best of the situation with Wiley in the job as personnel manager.

Suppose we were to undertake a project with the same general objectives in an organization that had a well-established personnel department and personnel program. Should Wiley (or his counterpart) enter this situation as a personnel manager or other personnel executive? I think not. There are two main considerations that argue against this solution.

In the first place, a well-developed personnel department tends

---

[20] William F. Whyte, *Money and Motivation* (New York: Harper & Bros., 1955).
[21] Whyte, *op. cit.*

to be organized around certain established activities (wage and salary administration, training, safety, and so on) which are demanding enough to require the full attention of an executive of such a department and thus would pull him away from establishing the new functions that we were able to build in the Tremont case.

In the second place, most personnel departments are, by practice and tradition, excluded from functions in areas that proved to be of crucial importance to our Tremont program. The planning and analysis of organizational structures is generally located in a department other than personnel. Studies and action in the fields of technology and work flow are allocated to development engineers and industrial engineers. Responsibilities for the pattern of communication and the initiation of activities are generally in the hands of the line executives, with the engineers also involved in innovations that change these patterns. The symbols of rewards and punishments are generally the concern of the line organization, of industrial engineering (incentive systems), and of accounting and cost control (budgets and cost records).

In a company where the distribution of functions and responsibilities has been well established, I assume it would be harder to revise and extend the mandate of the personnel department than it would be to establish a new concept of human relations activities and a new department in which to carry them out.

A design for the building of these human relations activities into a company would be worthless except insofar as it was based upon knowledge of the structure and functioning of that company. I shall therefore not undertake to work out a blueprint in detail. Let us simply consider the essentials of the new roles we would be seeking to establish in the organization.

I now see the task as one of establishing what in effect would be an internal research and consulting department, which would incorporate research activities into a consultation program so as to provide for the application of knowledge gained in research. Depending upon the size of the organization, we can think in terms of a number of teams, each one composed of one research applier or trainer and one or more research men. It is important that the research men be free of all administrative responsibility.

It is also important to emphasize that the interviews the research man conducts must be strictly confidential, for otherwise people will not have the confidence to talk freely with him.

The research applier can use research data and findings in various ways. He will find that discussions of the research may stimulate management people to think about their human problems in new and more productive ways. He could be active in interpreting research results to line and staff people. At least in the early stages, this activity would involve advising on actions, but the research applier might also work, as Wiley did, toward helping management people to make their own interpretations of the research data and to draw their own conclusions for action.

Insofar as training programs grow out of research and are not simply canned programs, training activities on the part of the research applier seem to me compatible with his central role.

Let us now consider what may be incompatible with this role. I am convinced that the research applier must avoid the direct administration of rewards and punishments. Thus he should not be responsible for the placement, promotion, demotion, and discharge of workers, supervisors, or executives. If he does become so involved, members of the organization will look upon him as someone who can bring rewards or punishments, and this will color their behavior toward him and even their interviews with research people. If the research applier is to be of assistance to people in the organization, they must look to him as a resource to which they can freely turn, without any fear that by admitting weaknesses they might jeopardize their positions.

This is not to say that line executives may not need specialized assistance in the fields of selection, placement, promotion, demotion, and discharge. It is simply to argue that the techniques of analysis and the responsibilities for recommendations on these problems should be lodged elsewhere in the organization, so that the research applier can be regarded as someone who helps people to improve their performance and not as one who passes judgment on that performance.

While the research applier should keep clear of the administration of rewards and punishments, he may, indeed should, seek to influence the criteria that executives use in arriving at the decisions and also to influence the display of symbols in the organization that indicate to people the types of behavior that will be rewarded and the types that will lead the punishment. Once these symbols are established, the research applier can step in to help people direct their activities in terms of this symbol system.

In our work in the Tremont Hotel, it was relatively simple for Wiley and Miss Lentz to provide an approach that would integrate industrial engineering, organization structure planning, and other specialties. They simply combined these activities in their own persons.

Does this suggest that in a large organization with well-developed specialist departments, the consulting organization should simply take over the work of all of the specialists? Clearly this would be undesirable. In analyzing the problems of the checkers and waiters and waitresses, Edith Lentz applied research methods from industrial engineering, but the problems of space and work flow were so obvious that a brief exercise of observation and mapping was all that was needed to provide keys to the solution of the problems. On problems of larger scale and greater complexity, the responsible person would need specialized training in industrial engineering. Furthermore, if the human relations research man is to take over these responsibilities, he will not have time for his more central responsibilities.

The research man needs to focus his attention not only on line executives, supervisors, and workers. He needs to recognize also that industrial engineers, accountants, organization planners, and other specialists are not simply machines that produce technical solutions. They too are people who play an important role in the social system, and he needs to study them and seek to understand them just as he does other individuals and groups in the organization. In a large and developed organization, the research applier needs to learn to work with specialists as well as with line executives.

If one man or one department cannot do it all, then clearly we need to think in terms of working teams, in which the research applier will be working on human problems in collaboration with industrial engineers, accountants, organizational planners, or such other specialists as may be required for the problem in hand. Just how these teams should be organized and fitted into the structure of the company cannot be usefully stated in the abstract. There is much to be said for the integration of functions at the level of the team members working together on problems. If the functions of industrial engineering, organizational planning, and so on are carried out in isolation from each other and must be coordinated at a high level, all sorts of intergroup conflicts and rigidities will develop. On the other hand, it is clear that the consulting on the research application function must be tied into the organization structure at a very high level if these new activities are to get the recognition they require and to establish a position that will attract able men to them.

The approach presented in this book calls for radical changes in management structure, policies, and procedures. The possibilities and limitations of this approach cannot be explored further until some management people are willing to apply to organizational behavior the same daring and creativity they now apply in research and development for new products and new manufacturing methods.

Appendix A

SAMPLE OF AN EMPLOYEE INTERVIEW [1]

Agnes, maid on 11th floor. Worked for Tremont 12 years; single, age probably about 45.

I had to ask Agnes her name and introduce myself, because somehow we had never met. When she said she worked here for 12 years, I was amazed.

> LENTZ: I'm going around talking to the girls, trying to get the maid's point of view.
> AGNES: Well, there are lots of suggestions I could make for improvements (*timidly*).
> LENTZ: That's good news, I'd like to hear them.

We worked together and Agnes talked, shyly at first but with growing confidence. At the last she was going full blast, speaking with vehemence and almost tearfully at times. Later I spoke to Miss Dickson about her and she told me that Agnes is a very intelligent girl and that she often wondered how she got into maid's work in the first place.

> AGNES: For one thing, they might do something about the shelves for glasses. We have usually one shelf for glasses and bottles and often it is up so high that it is all I can do to reach it. I don't know what the shorter girls do! And one shelf isn't

[1] Interview #232 (Oct. 30, 1945). By E. L. H.

enough, the bottles get parked all over the floor and the first thing you know, we can hardly get into the closet. We use more glasses all the time. Don't you think that would be an easy thing to fix?

LENTZ: Seems so, doesn't it?

AGNES: That's my idea. Maybe it's not such a good one, but that's my suggestion.

LENTZ: It sounds like a practical one, and I'm glad to get your idea.

AGNES: Do you think we should have to eat in our lockers? Since Mr. Smith got here, we haven't had a lunchroom at all. We used to meet in the lunchroom downstairs and all the girls could get together and talk and meet their friends. Now I don't even know if somebody's sick. They don't want us to visit on the floor, we get scolded for that. Well, a person wants to see her friends once in a while, can you blame us for that? Oh, I was saying, about the lunchroom, I don't like to eat in that locker room. It isn't sanitary. People are forever changing their clothes and things are flying around—I don't think it's sanitary at all. I'd rather eat in my locker, but that isn't very attractive either. There isn't any way to get warm food. My stomach has been upset too much lately and the doctor said I should try to get more vegetables at noon. How can I go out to get hot vegetables? We only have a half hour, and all the restaurants are so crowded and you have to wait—I just can't see how I'd do it, unless I threw the stuff down and what kind of a way is that to eat?

I never heard of a hotel where they didn't arrange for some place for the employees to eat. When I tell my friends that I work in a hotel and can't even buy a cup of coffee, they can't believe it. They think I'm crazy to stay here. Well, I don't believe in changing jobs, either. Every place has its drawbacks doesn't it? I can't see moving around, the way some people do. Far as that goes, I don't have to stay here either. I can quit any time I want to, but I don't see the sense. Every place has its drawbacks (pause).

Lorraine [the floor supervisor] says we shouldn't visit on the floor. Well, I can see that, it wouldn't do for us to spend our time talking to one another. We have too much work to do. You can't get your work done and stand around talking too. But on the other hand, I don't see why this place should be run like a prison either, do you? Why shouldn't I stop to say hello to the other girls on the floor? What's wrong with that? It's just human to want to see your friends to say good morning. I don't know, this is a funny place. You are supposed to work alone all day and eat alone, it isn't human. I can see her point too, she wants the work done (*pause*). Well, that's all the suggestions I can think of. Do you like this work?

LENTZ: Oh, it's a lot of fun, Agnes. I like to talk to people and get their slant on things. One thing I'm supposed to get an understanding of is why we have so much trouble getting good girls and keeping them. It is discouraging when they stay a day or so and then quit.

AGNES (*filling up with tears, speaking with great earnestness*): Lorraine brings the girls to me for their training and I think that's wrong. How can I train them and do my work too? They should have somebody special to train the girls. Now take yesterday, that new girl Mabel was turned over to me. Well, I worked with her for an hour or more, well, two hours altogether at least. It takes time! I have to show the girl where the linen closet is, where the soiled linen chute is, where she can get supplies, how she is to do this and that. It takes time to do that and do it right! Then I still have my 16 rooms to do, they don't make any provision for that at all, I'm just as responsible that day as any other for my own work. I don't mind training the girls. In fact, I'd like it if they made some arrangement that would take care of my rooms that day. But I can't do both jobs without getting behind in my own work.

LENTZ: How do they arrange it now, Agnes? Like yesterday, for instance, how many rooms did the girl work with you?

AGNES: She worked with me for four rooms. Then they counted that as two for her and two for me. I still had 14 other rooms to do by myself. They didn't give me any credit for the time I spent showing her around and I was way behind. Now that girl looked like a fine maid, to me. She didn't have hotel experience but she did work in a club for a year and she knew the type of work. I put a lot of pains into training her and now I hear she quit already. It is so discouraging, they all quit after a day or so. What use is it for me to take pains? After awhile you get disgusted. You don't want to show them around, you just want to give them the most important things and then turn them loose. That isn't right either, they should be given every help at the beginning.

I don't know *why* Lorraine gives them all to me. It seems to me she gives more to this floor than any other.

LENTZ: Maybe she thinks it's a compliment.

AGNES: Huh, I doubt it. But don't you think there should be one person to train new girls? I don't know who exactly, maybe you, maybe an inspectoress, but some person who would be responsible, not a maid. It just isn't right to ask a maid to do it.

You know Mrs. Jenkins used to be Housekeeper here and she held meetings for us. Get togethers, they were, and we would make suggestions and she would say how she wanted things done. Once we met in a regular guest's room and she showed us just how everything should be taken care of. I thought that was a good idea. Why don't they have something like that for new girls? Just one room or them to practice in. Then another thing, my sister works for the department store and they have a regular training room for new girls where they learn how to take care of customers. Why don't we have something like that? After all, a maid is important. She meets the customers and when they talk to her, she should talk back politely. Well, new girls should be told about that, don't you think so? We don't have time to do that, either. New girls are lucky if they get shown the important things. If we had one girl responsible for training them, I think she should tell them how to talk to people, too (*pause*).

You know, one reason girls quit is Lorraine (*spoken in a low, hurried tone*). She criticizes them and they get peeved and quit. Maybe we don't train them as thoroughly as we could. Then she goes into their rooms and sees something wrong and speaks to them about it. They don't like that. If they are trying to do things right, it hurts their feelings to be corrected for something when they didn't know they were doing it wrong. A girl blamed me for something the other day. She told them that I had instructed her not to bother about a certain thing. Well, that was silly. Why should I ever say such a thing as that? But she blamed me. It goes back to the same thing, we can't train them right, not as they should be trained, and then we get the blame if they aren't perfect (*pause*).

LENTZ: You were saying that Mrs. Jenkins used to have meetings for the girls. Did they like that?

AGNES: I did, I can tell you that. I don't know how the other girls felt, but I thought it was a good idea. People should have a chance to speak up and give their viewpoint. I thought those get-togethers were a fine idea. Since Mr. Smith came in, we haven't had anything like that. Not since Mr. Kane took over.

LENTZ: How about when Mrs. Grellis was in charge?

AGNES: She had a couple, I think. Well, they should, don't you think so? And another thing Mr. Flood who used to be manager here used to give the employees a party at Christmastime. I thought that was a good thing. My sister works at the department store and they have parties every once in a while. The way I see it, after a person works at a place for years, they have it coming to them. It is a sign of appreciation. That's the way I looked at it, anyway. It was as if Mr. Flood was saying, "We know you do a good job and we want to thank you for it." We haven't had anything like that since Mr. Smith got here. They never do anything for us to make us feel as if they care for us one way or another. We just work here, that's all (*pause*).

The way I see it, maids are important people. They don't figure that. To them, we're just maids, clean-up girls. Well, they don't realize that we take care of the guests. We are responsible for their comfort and cleanliness and if we fall down on the job, it's just too bad, now isn't it? They should tell that to the new girls, too. Maybe if the new girls felt that the job of maid was important, they would stay on better than they do. Nobody wants to be "just a maid."

Agnes scrubbed away at her bathroom floor, then spoke up again.

You know I think this 12th floor business isn't so good. The girl on the 11th floor has to pick up those 12th floor rooms. I have been up there three times today and only got one room made up. Three trips! That takes time. I'm just a swing girl on here now, but this used to be my floor. I was on this floor for 12 years.

LENTZ: You were? How come you took swing girl shift, Agnes?

AGNES: It wasn't my idea! What happened was, I had Sundays off. See Lorraine used to have Sundays before she was made inspector. Then I got her Sundays. Well, Lorraine, I don't know, she seems to think we should work on our days off whenever she asks us to. I'm glad to work when I can, but sometimes I have plans for the day and then I can't see why I should give them up at the last minute. If she'd ask ahead, I wouldn't mind so much, but coming at the last minute, well, sometimes people expect me to meet them places and then what can I do? The last time this happened was the Sunday after the 4th of July. I had plans made for a trip in the country and Lorraine asked me to work. I told her I just couldn't, and I couldn't either. I felt I was entitled to my day off, same as anybody else. That made her mad, I guess, because after that she said I couldn't have Sundays any more unless I did the swing shift. She thought I wouldn't take it, maybe, I don't know. But I did. It isn't as bad as I thought it would be. I'm getting used to it now. But after 12 years on one floor—you know, I knew every crack in the walls. It was hard! Now why should a swing girl have Sundays off any more than a regular girl, can you tell me? Does it make sense to you? Oh, I don't know, I get sick of this job sometimes. But then every job has its drawbacks.

Somewhere along the line Agnes mentioned something to me about the changes that had taken place around the Tremont and I asked her, "What brought that about, the union?"

AGNES: No, the union didn't do that, but it has done plenty.
LENTZ: Has it, Agnes?
AGNES: You bet it has. It got us all the raises we ever got! And seniority rights too. I swear by the union. You know, I was one of the first ones around here to join it.
LENTZ: Is that right? For goodness sake.
AGNES: Sure, I swear by the union. I think a house like this should be 100 percent union.
LENTZ: How come, Agnes?
AGNES: Well, so we get the money we have coming to us. And seniority too. Now for instance, right now it doesn't matter. There is a shortage of help and we don't have promotions, so seniority doesn't mean anything. But it didn't used to be that way. When times were bad, some of the girls would be laid off. Sometimes they would be sent home after they came in to work. Well, it wasn't right if an old girl was sent home while a new one worked, was it? Those times may come again. Nobody knows, you and

me, we don't know, but maybe they will, maybe they won't. That's what we need a union for. That's the way I see it, anyway. Oh, I swear by the union, you couldn't tell me any different. Well, I told you plenty, didn't I? I spoke my mind free and open.

LENTZ: Yes, you did and I appreciate it, Agnes. I've learned a lot this morning.

AGNES: I don't know that it's any good. My ideas may not be so hot.

LENTZ: You gave me lots to think over and I had a pleasant time, too. Thanks ever so much, and I hope I can talk to you some more another day.

Appendix B

MANAGEMENT MEETING[1]

Called by Smith, led by Whyte.

PRESENT (around long white table): Smith (vice-president and general manager); Kraus (resident manager); Kolaja (chef); Burk (Zebra Room manager); Larry (King Cole Room manager); Miss Paris (Coffee Shop manager); Miss Oliver (Fountain supervisor); Green (auditor); Kane (Housekeeping Department manager); Flanagan, Hume, Shipley, and Nisey (assistant managers); Miss Bragan (switchboard supervisor); and Miss Lentz, Whyte, and Wiley.

The meeting opened with Mr. Smith introducing the new chef and the new Fountain supervisor to the group. The chef expressed his appreciation for his cordial reception and the cooperation shown him by various department heads. Then Mr. Smith turned the meeting over to Dr. Whyte, who presented the following diagram:

A–Head man (Smith)
B–Assistant to head (Kraus)
C–Any other person within the "line" who comes above the work supervisor (assistant managers, etc.)
D–Supervisor or department head
W–Worker

---

[1] Held in Room 118, 2:30 P.M., Oct. 22, 1945. Reported by E. L. H.

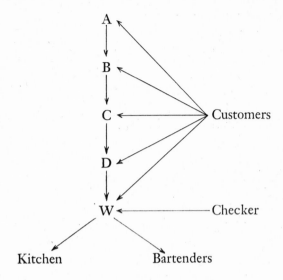

Dr. Whyte explained that the organization of any business would correspond roughly to the above, with the A, B, C standing for higher management, D standing for the supervisor immediately responsible for the work performed, and W standing for the workers. What he had in mind particularly, however, was the organization of restaurants. In his study recently completed for the National Restaurant Association, he found that all restaurants had much the same problems in regard to structure and pressures resulting from it. This diagram on the blackboard did not pertain specifically to the Tremont or to any department in it. It represented a general situation existing in all restaurants.

In a factory or similar organization, the worker has to adjust to his supervisor and to his fellow workers, but there his job ends. In a restaurant, however, the waiter and waitress have also to adjust to customers, checkers, kitchen workers, bartenders, and others who work along with him such as bus help, porters, etc.

The additional pressures coming to a waiter or waitress from the customers and checkers, added to those resulting from the supervisor and top management wanting to have the highest level of efficiency, mean that the waiter has a lot of nerve strain which needs to be worked off in some fashion. The usual way this happens is for him to express his feelings in the kitchen. A waiter may use words to let off steam. A waitress may use tears. In either case, the cooks, pantry workers, bartenders are the ones who catch the pressure from the waiter or waitress. Then they in turn have to push the heat onto somebody else and so it travels throughout the organization.

Sometimes this pressure is particularly hard to bear because a worker feels the supervisor is not working beside him in a helpful way but is actually bringing more pressure to bear and thus adding to his burdens. In order for a worker to function successfully he must work in an ATMOSPHERE OF APPROVAL. This doesn't mean that his mistakes should not be called to his attention or that discipline should be relaxed. It means simply that the worker must feel that despite his mistakes and the supervisor's corrections, the supervisor believes in him as a worker and as a person. The supervisor must get across to the waiter or waitress that he is on their side. In other words, they must have recognition for doing a competent piece of work if they are to be successful employees.

How can this problem of granting sufficient recognition be solved? Dr. Whyte suggested two techniques which he has seen used effectively. One is for the supervisor to interview the worker. By listening to his suggestions and complaints, communication is stimulated all along the line. The supervisor can get the worker's point of view and express it to his immediate superior, and eventually it will reach top management. Thus the worker feels his ideas are being given proper attention and respect. The second technique Dr. Whyte had seen used is that of the group meeting. He told of his experiences at the Maramor restaurant where he sat in on such a meeting and watched the waitresses as a good half of them participated by bringing forth ideas and suggestions.

[At this point I gazed around the room, noting facial expressions. Mr. Kraus looked sleepy. He was blinking and his facial muscles sagged wearily. Mr. Kane looked distinctly bored. The people giving deepest attention were Mr. Smith, Larry, Miss

Paris, and the chef; in other words, those who were responsible for food departments. The others were listening impassively.]

Dr. Whyte stressed the importance of Mr. C. If D takes a good suggestion which a worker has given to him, and tells C of it and then C doesn't act on it or give it adequate attention, D is placed in an impossible position. He is no longer able to encourage his workers to bring suggestions to him, since they will gradually become aware that he cannot do anything about them. Communication must be operating at all levels.

[At this point Mr. Kraus and Miss Oliver, his assistant, exchanged long glances. Oliver smiled and continued to have a half smile on her face for some time. Kraus would whisper something to her and she'd nod. Her face was somewhat cynical, I thought, but K's remained enigmatic.]

Dr. Whyte went on to speak of a "system of human relations" existing in a hotel which took in everyone from top to bottom. No one section of it could be isolated for inspection. The only intelligent way to regard it is as a whole. This is true of all such organizations, not only the Tremont. The attitude of people all up and down the organizational line must be taken into consideration.

At this point, Dr. Whyte apologized for talking so long and threw the meeting open to discussion.

SMITH: I guess all of us would like to alibi or otherwise defend our positions, at this point. As Mr. A, I'd like to make myself clear in this respect. In a sense, we are in a worse position now than we were in July if our employees are saying, "Well, they did a lot of talking, but what have they done about all these things they talked about?" I have deliberately stayed away from group meetings in the hotel because it seemed to me that Mr. A, B, and C do all the talking and Mr. W doesn't get a chance. I find, however, that even when I'm not there, Mr. B and C are presenting my viewpoints and saying that certain things were what I wanted done. The pressure, in other words, has all been downward when what we wanted was some upward pressure.
Now some suggestions have been made by employees and they have been ignored or brushed aside. This makes the situation even

worse. For instance, in the Coffee Shop I'm not told that the waitresses have been asking for a water faucet for months now and I'm just hearing about it. Each time they asked for it they were told that we are to build a new Coffee Shop and don't want to spend money on the old one. Well, that was true a year ago, I was saying that myself. But now I realize that certain things must be done at once to relieve the pressure down there. Our business has increased so greatly that certain adjustments are absolutely necessary if the work is to be done efficiently. This faucet business just goes to show the runaround people get when they have ideas to offer. I want to know what people are thinking about and what they want done.

GREEN: Since I brought this up at the last meeting. I might as well make a report on how Mr. Smith is doing (*laughter*). You may remember that it was suggested that Mr. Smith speak to employees as he walks through the building. Well, he's doing very well, and it has made a real difference, too. In fact, I received a memo from him myself, commending me for a piece of work I did and I was so proud that I couldn't talk to anybody for a couple of days (SMITH *beams*).

SMITH: Speaking of things I was to do, I've been working on an organization chart. I knew somebody like the chef here would benefit by having a chart showing them just what positions the various people around here fill and who they should go to when they need something done. But business has been changing and growing so fast that I no sooner get something figured out than I have to rearrange the work again. I realize that having this on paper would prevent a lot of false moves and I still mean to get it done at the first possible moment. Incidently I asked each of you at the last meeting to give me a sheet of paper showing the organization of your department and up to now I've only received three of them. The personnel office and Mr. Kane got theirs in to me, and the old chef got his in.

Not to speak of the departed, but sometime I want to show you that chart of the chef's. You would get a good laugh out of it. He showed himself in the middle with spokes going out in all directions from his office. (*General laughter and comments of*, "Well that's where he was most of the time.")

KANE: The question, as I see it, is how can we take off those pressures that Dr. Whyte has been talking about.

SMITH: It seems to me that if Mr. Wiley relieves the pressure. it will only serve to increase pressure in the long run because Mr. D will tend to resent the interference and will take it out on the worker for going over his head. That would be the tendency, wouldn't it?

WHYTE: Suppose Mr. W makes a suggestion to you and you can't get action on it, what then?

KRAUS: One thing about this place, 99 percent of the suggestions made by employees are acted upon. None are ignored completely. We always give them consideration.

SMITH: Skillful handling is necessary in cases where bum ideas are brought up. The supervisor certainly shouldn't say, "That's a bum idea" but maybe the same thing can be done by letting the other people in the group challenge it. In other words, if one employee makes a suggestion, get the others to comment on it and if it is a bad suggestion, they can spike it there and then. By the time an idea is passed along to Mr. B and Mr. A, it should not be the idea of one person but the consensus of the whole group.

WHYTE: You understand, this is not a common practice in industry. These ideas are being worked out in various places and we have utmost confidence in them. The problem is, how can we get started on this? Once the pattern is set up, it should be easy to proceed, but how do we start?

KRAUS: What would happen if Mr. W went straight to Mr. A or B? What should Mr. B do in a case like that?

WHYTE: Now what about a case like that? Do you think the first thing is to ask the employee whether he has spoken to his supervisor? I have seen management people handle it this way. They ask the employee that question and if the worker says he hasn't spoken to the supervisor, the manager will tell him, "Well, don't talk to me about it, go see your supervisor first."

What's wrong with that approach? Isn't it possible that the employee has considered talking to his supervisor and feels that he wouldn't get any satisfaction there? Shooting him back to his own department that way will just block off further communication, wouldn't it? The only thing that could happen which would restore communication in such a situation would be if a union, I might say an active union, steps in and in that case they would go right to top management, we all know that.

Now there are several other ways to deal with a thing like this.

One way is to talk to the employee and let him blow steam off. Then when he is finished and has it all off his chest, then ask him whether he has seen his supervisor, and if he hasn't, suggest that he do so. Tell him if he doesn't get satisfaction, to come see you again. Meanwhile you might manage to speak to the supervisor about the matter. Don't just hop on him, of course, but simply present the problem and suggest that he get together with the employee and see what can be done to straighten it out. Now suppose they can't work out something? Then perhaps Mr. A or B will have to make a solution, but in this situation it is important for Mr. A or B not to hand out the solution themselves, but to give it to the supervisor or Mr. D, and let him officially have the job of handling down the the verdict.

Another way I have seen worked successfully is to have A or B call in the worker (Mr. W) and supervisor (Mr. D) and have them sit down and talk it over. Mr. D in that case would have to have prior assurance that any decision he makes will be backed up by Mr. A or B. After the employee leaves, Mr. A might talk further with Mr. D and if he thinks the solution isn't a very good one, he could then suggest that the supervisor think it over some more. He might let the supervisor know that in his opinion, trouble will continue until a fairer decision is reached. That leaves the supervisor free to go to the worker and say he has been thinking it over and has changed his mind. This way, Mr. A or B, whoever is handling the case, is able to encourage upward communication and at the same time uphold the position of their supervisor. Now this way of handling the problem takes a lot of skill and I don't recommend it as a wholesale procedure. Mr. A or B has to be able to prevent excitement when Mr. D and Mr. W get together in his office and that's a tough job for anybody. Unless you feel you can control such a situation, it might be better to try one of the other techniques.

SMITH: All this goes back to the fact that you need these meetings. If you have them often enough, the employees can talk up and get things off their chest there and then. It means that A, B, and D have to keep quiet at these meetings to give the workers a chance.

That reminds me of the kitchen meeting that took place after Joe left. I noticed that Mr. Kraus, Mr. Wiley, and myself did all the talking. The employees didn't have a chance. I don't know what we can do about it, maybe we should hold smaller meetings. Now Mr. Flanagan hasn't had a meeting of his employees for several months and yet the front office has a great many problems that need to be thought out.

KANE: Isn't that true throughout the house? Not only of the front office, I mean. For instance, I overheard a maid and a houseman having a private meeting of their own in an upstairs corridor the other day. I just wondered how long it has been since they had a chance to express their ideas in a meeting.

SMITH: That's right. And speaking of unions, Kane's department was almost to the exploding point not so long ago. We held a meeting and talked it over with the result that all they could complain about was the shortage of bath towels. All the time we had plenty of towels, they were just being held in the storeroom. Now it shouldn't be necessary to go through all of that mess in order to get a need expressed. What the whole organization needs, it seems to me, are more frequent and short meetings.

WHYTE: One of the things I've been working on lately is union-management relations. I've been talking to business agents and they bring out that same fact that Mr. Smith just stated. They say that many things which come to them could have been handled by the immediate supervisor and settled in a few minutes; little things, which become great issues when they aren't dealt with right away. That is the case with most of the grievances which they are called upon to settle. I have heard of a whole factory walking out on strike and the root of the matter was that certain coat racks had been removed over the employees' protests.

In a case like that, the business agent of the union has to step in and battle for something which he doesn't really want to fight about, something he feels should have been settled right on the spot with no fuss or bother.

SHIPLEY: A year or a year and a half ago, somebody from the outside stepped into our kitchen and settled a dispute for us when none of the people working in the kitchen could see a solution. Sometimes an outsider can see things clearer than the people who work with a problem day after day.

SMITH: Don't you think that depends on the department and its head? Sometimes that might be true, sometimes not.

SHIPLEY: An outsider can always bring in new ideas and practical suggestions.

NISEY: Mr. Wiley might find out more at those meetings without Mr. A or Mr. B present. Maybe the employees are afraid to talk up in front of Mr. A or B.

SHIPLEY: Same thing goes from Mr. D, doesn't it? Take the Coffee Shop, for instance. Maybe those girls would talk up sooner without their supervisors present. How would it do for Mr. Wiley or Miss Lentz to run those meetings?

SMITH: Mr. Wiley and Miss Lentz are just interested observers. It isn't their job to run the meetings but to help the supervisor run them.

KRAUS (to OLIVER in stage whisper): Professors!

SHIPLEY: Well, couldn't they just record the suggestions, and then those which are good could be put into use.

SMITH: How would you feel if Mr. Wiley conducted a meeting in your department? You wouldn't feel so good. If department heads know their own business, they should be able to run the meetings.

SHIPLEY: A lot of the trouble around here is that no matter what a person asked for, we have to tell them they can't have it until after the hotel is rebuilt.

SMITH: Well, there's some truth in that. And that reminds me, I want to tell you something about the improvements and changes we are planning to make around here, so you can understand some of the stuff you are reading in the papers. [He then proceeded to tell in detail about certain changes, most of them affecting the kitchen and dining rooms, and the lobby. Mr. Kane continued to nod sleepily as Mr. Smith talked.]

I realize that we often have stalled people off on making improvements on the ground that we were going to rebuild, but now we realize that some things cannot be delayed any longer without serious loss of efficiency. Our business has grown so large that we can't accommodate people without making some adjustments. For example, our business so far this month is 35 percent larger than in August; August's business was 35 percent better than January's; January's was 35 percent better than the January before. The kitchen is so jammed up that they can't do a good job down there any more. We hope to start on the new kitchen and Coffee Shop in March. I suggest that in the various catering departments, people think in terms of permanent things and temporary things.

GREEN: Looks to me like what we are all driving at is the need for cooperation and coordination.

WHYTE: This remodeling program opens just the kind of topic around which to start employee meetings. If we can get the employees themselves to take an interest in it and say what things they would like to see changed or improved, that might be a way to begin our program.

I'd like to say here that I've been hoping Miss Paris would tell us about her meetings, but she's too bashful to tell you of the good job she's doing there. She has been holding group meetings for several weeks now and from our observations, it appears she has been doing a good job there.

SMITH: The thing to be stressed is that an expanded hotel means a chance for all of us to expand with it. Now Larry, for instance, will have a King Cole about twice as big as the present one. That means he'll have twice as big a job, doesn't it? And not only a bigger salary but more assistance to help him too, thus making his management better and easier. Tell your employees about this, because an expanded hotel means more jobs and we hope to move old employees up and put the new ones on the bottom jobs.

BRAGAN: Will we get a new switchboard, Mr. Smith? You didn't mention any improvement for us. We have the oldest switchboard in the region.

SMITH: We'll take care of the switchboard, don't worry about that.

SHIPLEY: Do we have the oldest telephone supervisor in the region? (*Jokes about* ANN's *age and her taking it well.*)

KRAUS: I've been sending memos around telling supervisors to have roll call meetings of their dining room employees, how many have done it? Larry, how about you? Now I want you to have one every day and not every other day.

LARRY: Well, it isn't as easy as that. We have to consider the time.

SMITH: You'll have to sit down and figure out how many meetings are necessary. There should be a conference between Mr. Kraus and the department head, it shouldn't be decided by one person. We don't want meetings just for the sake of having meetings. We want to accomplish something. Meetings should be planned ahead and you should know just what ground you want covered and what you plan to say. Another thing, there is a difference between roll calls and meetings. Maybe we need roll calls every day and meetings once a week. That's something we must figure out.

Now last Saturday is a case which will illustrate our difficulty. We decided to open all the bars and restaurants early because of Homecoming Week and memos were supposed to go out to everybody. At the last minute it turned out that the accounting office was never notified and no checkers or cashiers were on the job.

KRAUS: I sent memos to all of them, Accounting too. It was the checkers' own fault, I let them know ahead of time.

GREEN: I want to defend the checkers on that score. Those girls were told the bars were to open "early." Now how were they to know what early meant? They were on the job a little after 11 but nobody knew they were supposed to be there before that.

WHYTE (*interrupting*): Before this meeting breaks up, I want to state again just what Mr. Wiley and Miss Lentz's jobs are. Mr. Wiley is supposed to help you stimulate upward communication and he will be glad to consult with you on plans for group meetings or any other technique that might aid toward that end. I don't think it would be a good idea for him to set up a new channel of communication by having the employees come to him with their suggestions. That way the supervisor would not know what was going on in his own department. What we want to do is to send ideas right up the line from Mr. W up to Mr. A by way of Mr. B, C, D, and down the line the same way. Miss Lentz will help by interviewing the workers separately to get them interested and encouraged in expressing their ideas. If it seems wise, perhaps Mr. Wiley or Miss Lentz or Miss Dickson can sit in on a group meeting and give suggestions for making them more effective.

WILEY: I think we all realize that different departments have different problems. We don't mean to prescribe one cut-and-dried formula for curing all of our ills. Maybe some departments will want a meeting once a week, another may want them oftener, another less often. Maybe some not at all. We must consider each problem separately and work together on its solution. Our job is to oil, to lubricate the line organization.

WHYTE: Miss Lentz may be able to fit in another way, too. If you feel your group meetings aren't clicking, the employees might not want to tell you how they feel about it but they might tell Miss Lentz. She can follow up on group meetings and let you know how the employees are reacting. Then she can tell Mr. Wiley her impressions and he can tell the supervisor, who can take suitable action. Mr. Wiley would not tell Mr. A or B, but would go straight to the supervisor with such information and help him plan future meetings with these facts in mind.

KRAUS: About these group meetings, should Mr. A or Mr. B be present or not?

WHYTE: Well, I don't know, suppose we think about that? I should think that usually it might be well to limit the meetings to Mr. D and Mr. W. But occasionally it might be a good idea to have Mr. A or Mr. B present, especially when they have something nice to say to the group, some request to grant. It's my feeling that usually it is better if the top management consults the supervisor and gives him their suggestions and criticisms rather than to speak directly to the rank and file employees.

KRAUS: Usually I participate in all the meetings.

WHYTE: Umhmm. Well, occasionally it is an excellent idea to give the employees a chance to talk to you in a group that way, but ordinarily it could get to be quite a burden if you had to take charge of all the group meetings. Another thing I want to point out here is that this atmosphere of approval should extend all up and down the line organization. Mr. D needs to feel his superiors have confidence in him just as much as Mr. W does.

KRAUS: What if you don't have any confidence in Mr. D? (*Ripples of laughter throughout the group.* KRAUS *flushes.*)

WHYTE: Well, there again the employee, whether he is Mr. W or Mr. D needs to feel that if he needs correction, he gets it. But at the same time it is absolutely necessary for him to feel the moral support of his superior if he is to turn in a good job. If he feels Mr. B doesn't have confidence in him, then he will fail even more tragically than before. If an employee is worth keeping on the payroll at all, he should feel the supervisor thinks him capable of doing an acceptable job.

SMITH: This meeting is getting too long, but before we break up I want to announce that Miss Dickson has been promoted to the position of Assistant Personnel Manager. We hope that position will not only make the personnel office run better but will help you people in getting what you want, too. Well, this meeting has held on too long but it would help if you got here on time. We will have another meeting in this room one week from today. That will be all.

Appendix C

WILEY SHOWDOWN WITH MR. KRAUS[1]

I had an interview with the chef which confirmed my theory that Mr. Kraus was bypassing me consciously with the intention of tearing the personnel department apart. I knew even more definitely than before that Mr. Kraus's relations with Miss Dickson had to be cut off if the well-being of the department was to be protected. Mr. Smith was leaving for an extended vacation the next day so I felt that just in case something should go wrong, I had better tackle Mr. Kraus while Smith was still around. I talked it over with Miss Dickson, first getting her ideas and then agreeing that the present situation put both of us in a difficult position. I then called Mr. Kraus, stating that if he had a few minutes, I'd like to talk to him. He replied briefly and gruffly,"OK," so I went up.

I went into Mr. Kraus's office about 2:30 and laid the turnover chart on his desk.

> WILEY: I would suggest that you don't jump on the department heads because they have a high turnover. In the first place they don't entirely understand why they have a high turnover and it's our problem to work with them. You know, sugar draws more flies than vinegar. I think our responsibility is to help these people, not to ride them.

He didn't respond to this directly but looked rather puzzled.

---

[1] Feb. 13, 1946. Reported by M. W.

Perhaps I hit him with it so fast that he didn't realize what was going on for I would have expected him to ruffle his feathers and take a stand on it. He picked up the chart and asked me what was the matter with the King Cole.

WILEY: It's in a turmoil down there. Both that room and the Zebra. I don't believe we handled this transfer as effectively as we could have.

KRAUS (*going on the defensive*): Why I talked to the union about it and I had George and Larry in here in my office.

WILEY: I think I should have been informed of what was going on.

KRAUS: What's that got to do with you?

WILEY: Anything that has to do with the employees has to do with the personnel office. If I had known about this I could have made it much easier.

KRAUS: George and Larry knew about it for a month.

WILEY: They were pretty quiet about it, then. Something like this will always upset people. The best we can do is to ease it.

KRAUS: Any first-class dining room always has men. You never saw a mixed crew, we did that only because of the war emergency. We must get men back in there.

WILEY: I agree with you that we must keep up the standards. On the other hand we could have made those transfers much simpler. Those girls from the Zebra went into the King Cole considering it a demotion.

KRAUS: Why should they? They get the same money.

WILEY: Which of the two rooms do you think is the nicer? Which do we brag most about, which do we have entertainment in and the finest service?

KRAUS: Why naturally in the Zebra.

WILEY: Well the waiters and waitresses feel the same way we do. They feel that they are going to a lower status room and they consider it a demotion. Right now the rest of the girls in the Zebra Room are all upset. They wonder when we are going to start on them.

KRAUS: I'm perfectly satisfied with that, it's all right to leave girls on during lunch hour.

WILEY: Then we had better let them know so they can have something to rely on. Right now they are anxious.

KRAUS: It's all right with me if you go and tell them.
WILEY: All right. I'll do that.

Mr. Kraus then went on to the other departments listed on the turnover chart, casually remarking when he came to one where the turnover is high that they have gone up. He asked me what was the matter with the kitchen.

WILEY: The kitchen turnover has gone down this month.
KRAUS: What's the matter with the Fountain, that's gone up.
WILEY: I think we have to do some training with the night supervisor. We had the Fountain going along very nicely but we were without a night supervisor for awhile which left things in a turmoil. Now I think we have some work to do with this new supervisor but I believe we can take care of that all right.
KRAUS: Who is this night supervisor, do I know her?
WILEY: She's the little short dark girl with the glasses, back by the sandwich board nights.
KRAUS: Oh yes, she doesn't look very good does she?
WILEY: Yes I think she could improve her appearance but we should be able to fix that up. I'll work on it through Miss Casey.
KRAUS (going back to the Zebra and King Cole situation): How come I don't see any new faces in the Zebra Room?
WILEY: No, you haven't noticed any yet but it will show up. You can see plenty of new faces in the King Cole. (KRAUS paused, appearing to think a moment, then nodded his head.)
WILEY: I was talking with Mr. Smith. If you remember some time ago Miss Lentz was interviewing people in the food checker and cashier department. We found a lot of interesting things. I know you are very much interested in this department and because of your knowledge and your position I suggested to Mr. Smith that you and I work with the auditor to improve the place down there. I know you have already been thinking about re-arranging the work load and that's the type of thing we want to get to doing. [KRAUS seemed somewhat interested, perhaps enthused, about this.]
KRAUS: I'll be very glad to work with you on this. We will get Mr. Adams in to talk the first of next week.
WILEY: That's fine. Now there's another thing I would like to talk to you about. From now on I would like to have all your

contacts with the personnel office come through me. [KRAUS *reared back and was as mad as I have ever seen him. He almost exploded.*]

KRAUS (*loudly*): If Miss Dickson wants to come in here, she can come in here and talk to me any God damn time she pleases!

WILEY: I'm talking about business that has to do with the personnel office. I believe you should, and I want you, to go through me on business matters. You know that if you have anything to say about the Zebra Room you wouldn't go to a waitress. You're too big for that. You would go to George. It's the same situation with the personnel office. I want you to come to me, I'm responsible for that department and I want to know what's going on.

KRAUS: What are you talking about? Give me an example.

WILEY: I could give you a thousand examples but just to give you something that happened today you called Miss Dickson about Lou Tawney's wage raise.

KRAUS: You found out about that! (*By now the room was blue with electricity and tension.*)

WILEY: Yes but I found out about it through the back door.

KRAUS: Back door! What do you mean?

WILEY: I mean that you should have come to me directly with these things.

KRAUS: What about the Zebra Room, what have I done down there?

WILEY: I merely say that as an illustration. I could have just as well cited the King Cole, the Coffee Shop, accounting office.

KRAUS: I get along with everybody.

WILEY: Seems to me that your and my relations could be improved.

KRAUS: If for no other reason, I'm older than you are.

WILEY: If you mean do I respect you, I would like to say with no flattery or blarney that I believe you are one of the most intelligent men I have ever met. (KRAUS's *face lighted up.*)

On the other hand I respect my own intelligence too. And I think I know my business and I'm not the kind of fellow that can be pushed around.

KRAUS: You don't work with me. You never come in here.

WILEY: You have been working through Miss Dickson, I haven't felt that I was welcomed.

KRAUS (*vehemently*): My door is always open. I'm going to be here a lot longer than anybody else.

WILEY: Well I might say that I don't feel my position is in-secure, but that is neither here nor there. [MR. KRAUS *now became even angrier than before.*]

KRAUS: You don't work with me.

WILEY: I don't believe anyone is perfect and I'm willing to admit that I have made some mistakes. If you will point them out to me and I have been wrong, I'll be glad to do something about it. What was it that you have in mind?

KRAUS (*fumbling around for quite some time, not able to think of anything specific*): What about the King Cole turnover? I should know about those things. I didn't know a thing about it. I was out riding with Mr. Smith to a funeral and he turned to me and said, "What's the matter with the King Cole, why are all those people leaving?" He holds me responsible for that.

WILEY: Yes, and he holds me responsible for it. But as far as getting those figures, just as I told you before I can give you no more than my word but I can tell you that I am always honest with you. Mr. Smith didn't get those King Cole turnover figures from me and you will have to believe me on that. [KRAUS *seemed to calm down, then he reared up again as he thought of another grievance.*]

KRAUS: What do you mean by having Miss Dickson come in here and talk with me and then asking her to write up what I say? If you want to know what I think, you can come in here and talk with me yourself.

WILEY: I will come in and talk with you, but again I have no more to offer than my word and I can say again just as honestly that I have never asked Miss Dickson to come in and talk to you and write up the interview.

KRAUS: I told Dr. Whyte about this, but I asked him not to mention it to you. I said that we might just as well let it go.

WILEY: Dr. Whyte didn't mention it to me but I don't believe we should let it go. This is bothering you and I want to get it straightened out.

KRAUS: Well maybe you didn't tell her, maybe Miss Lentz did.

WILEY: I'm not in a position to say definitely that Miss Lentz didn't tell her. I don't believe she did. However I'm responsible for that department and I'll ask Miss Lentz if she did and explain to her that we will not ask Miss Dickson to come talk to you and write interviews on it.

KRAUS (*calming down*): What would you think if when you came into my office I started pulling all the papers off my desk so you couldn't see them? That's what Miss Lentz did to me. And I don't like that. I don't want to see those papers. All she would have to say is, "This is confidential" and I wouldn't pay any attention to it.

WILEY: Those papers are very confidential. I think you surprised Miss Lentz. She didn't see you coming in and didn't have a chance to pull her thoughts together. You see we have to be sure that nobody sees those interviews. Let me tell you why. In the first place we explain to the employees that everything they say is held in confidence. We do this because we know that if you, Mr. Smith, or even Mr. Jones were to see what the employees tell us, and the employees found it out, they would quit talking to us. Those things that the employees tell us enable us to help you do a better job by letting you know how they feel and bringing you the good suggestions they have to offer.

KRAUS (*much more relaxed, and lighting a cigarette*): Well I get along well with everybody. I will go halfway with all of them.

WILEY: I'll go more than halfway, I'll even go 75 percent.

KRAUS: Yes I'll go 75 percent too. I'll go 75 percent with you. In this turnover chart why don't you break the departments down closer? In the kitchen separate the cooks from the dishwashers, for instance.

WILEY: Yes, that's a very valuable suggestion. I like that. We will do that right away, this is a good time to do it at the first of the year. Then we can carry it through for the rest of the months. I like that idea a whole lot. Thank you. We will do that right away. Now I have a lot of things I want to talk to you about the food checkers and cashiers. I'm sure if we get together we can bring a lot of good out of it. There has been a high turnover there and there's a pretty good chance we can do something about it. You and I will talk it over and then we will get together with Mr. Adams. Then we will have a meeting of the food checkers and cashiers to get their ideas again.

You see we have to bring the employees in on these things. It makes them feel they are a part of it, but it doesn't stop there. They are the ones who do the work and we get some good ideas from talking to them.

I also have a lot of material that I have been working on con-

cerning training. I want to work with you on that. I think you
and I can do a good job on it. But we'll get to that right after we
get the cashiers and checkers started. [*It seemed to me that he was
quite enthused about this.*]

KRAUS (*extending his hand*): I'm glad you came in. I think we
have got this straightened out now.

WILEY (*shaking hands*): Yes, I'm sure we have too. (*Turning
to leave*) Well, I'll be seeing you.

Appendix D

WILEY DISCUSSION WITH MR. SMITH[1]

Sample of a brief contact interview with Mr. Smith, held several days after his return from South America. This was the second interview between the two men. Notice that he asks again about Kraus's actions during his absence, although Wiley had reported to him at length the day before.

Mr. Smith at Breakfast

I had an appointment with Mr. Smith for breakfast at 9:00 in the Coffee Shop. He was late and didn't get in until about 9:45.

WILEY (*cheerily*): Good morning, Mr. Smith, how are you?

SMITH (*a little embarrassed*): I'm all right, I'm late though. Well, tell me about Mr. Kraus while I was gone.

WILEY: He really tried hard. On the whole I'd say he did a good job.

SMITH: How about him and the chef?

WILEY: They got along well on the surface. Underneath, I have a feeling, there is still a resentment. It will take time for that to work itself off.

SMITH: There's Mr. Green [auditor], too. I talked to him last night. Things have to change here. I have been thinking it over. You have a lot of time to think while you are riding on an airplane for 18,000 miles. I'm going to quit blinking at these problems. I have told Mr. Kraus he was holding up what we have been trying to do with employee relations. He couldn't see it. He said he

---

[1] April 10, 1946. Reported by M. W.

didn't do anything. I told him that that was just it, he hasn't accepted what we have been trying to do and that's held us back. That remark in yesterday's meeting was typical of him. Remember when he told Collins about the sugar.

[In yesterday's supervisory meeting Mr. Smith said, "Mr. Collins was at the table with me and he called my attention to the fact that we are going to great lengths to save sugar on fine pastries but we have little leaks. The guests are using far too much in their coffee especially at the Fountain." Mr. Kraus then spoke up and said, "You could have said something to me about that, Mr. Collins."]

SMITH (*continues*): That about put me under. I can't understand that man.

WILEY: I think he has come a long way. There has been a big change in him from the way I remember him when we first came in here. There is no question but what he still needs a lot of training and it will take time. I surely wouldn't want to guarantee results. It seems like a pretty difficult thing to do in a proposition like this. I feel confident that we could bring him around. How long it will take, I don't know.

SMITH: Still we have been held up for a long time. If we are ever going to get any place in this organization, we have got to take a hold on it. I'm through with just sitting back and hoping things will happen. I did an awful lot of thinking. We're going to straighten things out even if it means someone has to leave. I'm going to talk to all of those fellows.

How's Housekeeping?

WILEY: Well, it seems to me we have got to look toward clarifying those jobs and reorganizing the work load, so that everyone knows just exactly what is expected of him.

SMITH: I was thinking about reorganization yesterday when I mentioned that about the maids not doing bathrooms. Well, you get me some job descriptions on that.

WILEY: I have the job descriptions and the work-flow charts. It's a case of our studying them over.

SMITH: Well, you keep working on it.

WILEY: I thought you might be very interested in knowing that Miss Lentz is nearly through with the front office. We found pretty much that Mr. Hume is a good organizer. The morale is going up a lot.

SMITH: Yes, I suspected that. You can see quite a lot of change just by sitting down in there.

WILEY: There was something I wanted to ask you about. At a Housekeeping meeting while you were gone, they asked if they could have hot coffee. Then the laundry employees appointed a special representative to come ask me if they could have hot coffee.

SMITH: I don't know. Some of those things get out of hand. If you gave them hot coffee it means we have to give 500 people coffee at noon and the first thing you know they want soup and then it's sandwiches.

WILEY: Yes, perhaps that could happen. On the other hand I can see their viewpoint. They don't have anything hot in their stomachs at noon and eating facilities are pretty bad all through the house. I have gotten this attitude all over the place. Some of the employees complain that they have to support children and can't afford to buy Fountain food. And they only have a half hour for lunch and that means they can't afford to pay 10¢ a bottle for milk so they go across the street to Walgreen's. To get in and out of their uniforms and eat in a half hour is quite a job.

SMITH: Well, we have got the employees' cafeteria in our plans but if you think best, perhaps we could convert the old sea food room.

WILEY: That's a great idea. I think if the building program is either refused or if the cafeteria is quite a ways off in the future, we might do that, it would be a great move. It would do a lot for the morale and I would predict that it would do a lot to solve our eating problem.

(SMITH *rises and I walk along beside him, talking.*)

WILEY: There was one other thing I wanted to talk to you about and that was a place for me to work. I really don't have any place for working since Mr. Collins has come in. I do all my writing on a corner of someone's desk and I file things in my pocket. I have got things down in the personnel office and some upstairs in Mr. Collins' office and some at home. That's a pretty difficult thing when you want to get organizational work done.

SMITH: Well, this is off the record but I have been thinking about moving Mr. Nisey down with Mr. Kraus and moving Collins into Nisey's office. I haven't done anything about it because I would like to have it come from those two men. I'm beginning to learn that you can't stuff anything down their throats. I'd like to have them suggest it.

WILEY: Yes, I'm sure you will get better acceptance if it comes from them.

SMITH: Well, you're doing a good job. Keep it up. (SMITH *enters his office and I go my way.*)

Appendix E

KING COLE: MANAGEMENT DISCUS-
SIONS OF PROBLEMS AND PLANS[1]

I have been in Mr. Smith's office this morning and we had a short talk. I was interested in finding out what he had done with regard to Larry, for in our last conversation Mr. Smith said something would have to be done about him; so I asked him if he had had a chance to talk to him yet. Smith replied that he would like to have Mr. Kraus, Larry, and myself come up to his office this afternoon, and he left it up to me to arrange the meeting.

We went into the office this afternoon about 2:30 and Mr. Smith was reading over some correspondence. After some delay, Mr. Smith raised his head.

SMITH: Well, go ahead, Mr. Wiley.

This was unexpected. I wasn't particularly anxious to give the impression that I was responsible for the meeting's being called.

WILEY: Mr. Smith was asking me this morning about the turnover in the King Cole. He has been concerned about it the last three months, so I suggested that we all get together and see if we could find a way for decreasing that turnover.

SMITH: Did you know, Larry, you have the highest turnover of all the dining rooms?

LARRY: I can account for everyone of those people, Mr. Smith.

---
[1] May 14, 1946. Reported by M. W.

254

Mr. Wiley, do you have some of those little cards that I make out?

WILEY: Do you mean the finals? No, we sent those up to the accounting office.

LARRY: Could you get me those cards right now? I could tell you why every person left.

SMITH (*interrupting him*): I don't think we care so much what each one of those people said was the reason they left. What we want to know is the underlying cause. People will give any kind of a reason for leaving, not necessarily the right one. Maybe we can get at the base of the trouble.

LARRY: Well the other day I had a boy that came in after working one day and he went right up to the bar and got drunk. Now you don't want a boy like that, do you Mr. Smith? You don't like them drinking on the job, do you?

SMITH: No.

LARRY: Well, there you are! You see I had to let him go.

SMITH: But Larry, that's an individual case. Is there anything we can do to try to straighten out things so they will want to stay?

LARRY: Well then I had a fellow who came in here and thought he was going to get his meals. Just as soon as he found out he didn't, he walked off the job. Now what could I do about a fellow like that?

SMITH: We are still talking about cases, Larry! What can we do about improving the Room? All of the other dining rooms are improving every day and you surely want the King Cole to keep moving ahead too, don't you?

LARRY: Well I suggest that the personnel office instruct these people when they come on the job.

SMITH: That's not the job of the personnel office. Do you think that the personnel office could tell every employee in the hotel how to do their job? Tell the busboys, waitresses, maids, housemen? They can't do that, Larry!

LARRY: Well it seems to me that we should train our people better.

SMITH: All right. Fine. Now that's something, what do you think we should do?

LARRY: When somebody comes in here, they should be told that they don't get their meals.

WILEY: Well I agree with you, Larry. People should be told that they don't get their meals if they aren't entitled to them. They should also be told about vacations, the locker room location and where the time clock is, a number of things like that. They should know they have to join the union in 15 days, and so forth, but we do that now. As a matter of fact Miss Dickson said when she read that final that that boy had been told three times that he didn't get his meals. I think that both the personnel office and the department heads have a responsibility to get new people on the job correctly. You were talking to me the other day about training busboys. I think that was a very good suggestion. How have you been coming along with that? [Larry had told me he was having the captains set up a training program for his new busboys.]

LARRY: Well I don't have time to sit down with those busboys.

SMITH: Then maybe we are giving you too much to do, Larry.

LARRY: Oh no, Mr. Smith, you are very nice to me. You are a very kind man.

SMITH: Well, you said you didn't have time.

LARRY: No, I didn't mean that, Mr. Smith. What I would like to do is go over all those pink cards and I could tell you why every one of those people left.

SMITH: Those people are gone. Can we do anything to keep the people we have now? You had eight busboys last month; you had 400 percent turnover there. Now we should be able to at least keep one of these boys we have now. If we were having trouble all over the hotel with busboys, I would think it was something in the economy but the Coffee Shop doesn't lose busboys. Now how do you explain that?

LARRY: Well, Mr. Smith if you think it's my fault—

SMITH: No, I'm not criticizing you, Larry. None of us here are criticizing you. We are working for improvements.

LARRY: It sounds like I'm on the spot.

SMITH (*becoming a little agitated*): We aren't getting any-place! I thought perhaps we might find something we could do, some way to help you down there.

LARRY: Those boys all left because they weren't doing the kind of job you want down there, Mr. Smith. Now do you want me to cut down my standards? I know you don't. You want a fine room, a well-run room.

SMITH: Mr. Thor [captain] was telling me you had some kind of trouble with your tips for busboys. Is that straightened out now?

LARRY: Oh yes, Mr. Smith. That's all taken care of. I let them take care of that themselves. I didn't have anything to do with that. I figured that was their business.

KRAUS: Didn't you have a paper for them to sign, saying they wanted to pay 75¢ or didn't want to pay 75¢?

LARRY: Oh I didn't use that.

KRAUS: I thought I saw it down there for the waiters and waitresses to sign.

LARRY: Yes, but they didn't sign it so I didn't pay any attention to it.

SMITH: If you put a paper down there for them to sign, you had something to do with it.

LARRY: Oh no, Mr. Smith, you are misinformed, you are misinformed.

SMITH: I'm not misinformed at all, nobody informed me of anything about it. I know if you had a paper down there for the employees to sign, you had something to do with it.

KRAUS: Didn't you tell them at a meeting that you thought you would like them to pay 75¢ a night to the busboys? You thought it would be a good idea?

LARRY: No, don't say that, you don't mean that. You aren't trying to call me a liar, are you? You just ask Mr. Wiley there, he knows about it. I had a meeting and the waiters and waitresses decided themselves what they wanted to pay. I left it entirely up to them.

SMITH: Well that's all under the bridge anyway. I don't know why I mentioned it. Is there anything we can do to improve the department? (SMITH *seems to be wearing down.*)

WILEY: Larry, some time ago you and I talked about the possibility of having rotating stations. Have you thought any more about that?

LARRY: Well I don't think so, Mr. Wiley. Everything is going very fine in the King Cole. All the girls are very happy. I don't want to change that.

SMITH: You think all the girls are happy with that type of station assignment?

LARRY: Oh yes, they all like that. You see the stations down there are all the same. Not only that but we have certain customers who come in and ask for a particular waitress.

SMITH: Well if all the stations are the same, it wouldn't make very much difference if it was decided to rotate them, would it?

LARRY: Oh yes, it would make a lot of difference, Mr. Smith. Now I can do it if you want to, I will be glad to do it. You are a very smart man, you know a lot about the hotel business, and if you say I should do it, I'll do it, but I don't think you know what you are doing, Mr. Smith.

SMITH: I don't want any favoritism down there, either with the guests or with the employees.

LARRY: We don't do that, Mr. Smith. Whoever told you that misinformed you. They don't know what it's all about, Mr. Smith. Uncle Larry wouldn't do anything like that.

SMITH: Don't tell me there isn't any favoritism! If you have special stations for special girls, then that's favoritism; or if you save special tables for special customers, that's favoritism too. Nobody told me that, I can see it.

LARRY: Well I'll do it if you want it, Mr. Smith. You are a smart man but I don't think you realize the situation. The King Cole you know is the breadbasket for this hotel. We bring in the money.

SMITH: Well I can't see you catering to 10 percent of the guests or even 40 percent of your employees, and the rest of them remaining unhappy. That just isn't good business. All well-run restaurants have rotating stations now.

LARRY: Don't say all of them, Mr. Smith, don't say all of them. Because you can't compare a fine hotel like this with other hotels.

KRAUS: Well how about the Zebra Room? We have rotating stations in there.

LARRY: Oh but I said, oh no, Mr. Kraus, oh no, no. The King Cole is different. The King Cole isn't like any other place. We have an informal room. It's a friendly room. You can advertise that, the Friendly Room. It's just like home. Uncle Larry makes everybody feel at home.

SMITH: Do you make everybody feel at home?

LARRY: Yes, I know everybody who comes in there.

SMITH: Well that's not good. You aren't expanding your business then. You can't be showing favoritism to 50 people and letting 450 people go. You can't please 3 waitresses and leave 12 waitresses dissatisfied. That is just poor business.

KRAUS: Well why don't you try it, Larry? If it doesn't work you don't have to keep it. If it does, well that's fine.

LARRY: Yes but I have to let those girls have the best stations because they do little jobs for me.

SMITH: What little jobs do they do?

LARRY: They handle the time book and the schedules.

SMITH: What does your captain do, then?

LARRY: Our captains aren't any good. I never had a good captain who could take care of it.

KRAUS: Do you ever try doing it yourself?

LARRY: Oh the girls are much neater than I am. I like to have a nice, neat time book so they can read it themselves.

SMITH: Well that's a captain's job. What do your captains do?

LARRY: They usually seat the people. I don't have captains who could handle anything like that. Besides they aren't staying long enough.

SMITH: By God I wouldn't blame them for not staying. I wouldn't stay either, if one of the waitresses had part of my authority and responsibility. It's no wonder they leave.

LARRY: Gentlemen, gentlemen, don't take the work away from those girls. I will do it if you want to, but my suggestion is to leave it as it is.

WILEY: Well I don't see that these things have to happen overnight.

SMITH: No, Larry, I don't want you to just rush down and do that tonight. Take your time and think it over. And more than that, I don't want you to do it unless you feel you believe in it.

LARRY: I believe that we should do it.

SMITH: Are you sure?

LARRY: Yes, if you think so. You are a smart man. I like you, you understand. You know the hotel business. Although I don't think you can really see our problems down in the King Cole if you are staying up here.

KRAUS: Well we aren't getting any place, we're just going in circles.

SMITH: Yes, why don't we leave it this way. I like Mr. Kraus's suggestion. Let's give it a try on the night crew. Don't rush into it. Do it when you think it's right and there is going to be a jar, we know that, but do it the easiest possible way. If you need any help, see Mr. Kraus or Mr. Wiley and they will be glad to help you.

Larry: Mr. Wiley, why don't you come down in the King Cole for a couple of nights and try to find out what our problems are?

WILEY: Well I surely would like to work with you, Larry, although I don't believe it would do much good if I would sit down in the King Cole a couple of nights. I'm afraid I wouldn't get a look at the whole thing. You don't understand the problems that way. If we were going to make a study there, I would want to move in 100 percent, have Miss Lentz come in and make a study of the whole department.

SMITH: That's an idea.

LARRY: I don't think so. How much experience has Miss Lentz had?

WILEY: I believe you'll find she was a waitress.

LARRY: I mean how much experience has she had supervising people?

SMITH (*flushing and becoming very angry*): Miss Lentz has done a wonderful job in the departments that she has studied. We have made a lot of good improvements there and the departments have gotten better every day since. Miss Lentz knows her job. She's done a good job and that's recommendation enough. I don't think we have to discuss that any further.

LARRY: Yes, that's right. Well anytime you want to come in, we will be glad, that will be fine with me.

SMITH (*to* WILEY): What is Miss Lentz working on now?

WILEY: She is in the Service Department. It might be possible to work the two together, although it would go a little slower than usual.

LARRY: Anytime you want to do that, I would be glad to have it but I don't think you will find out anything.

SMITH: What do you want to do, Larry? Build a barrier up around that little room down there?

LARRY: If you do that, I would break it right down, right away. I wouldn't let you do that. You wouldn't do that to me, Mr. Smith. You are too kind a man. Besides we don't dare change anything down in the King Cole. It's got tradition. [Smith himself made this same statement once.] Besides we are making too much money down there. I know if we change it, it would fall off.

SMITH: You mentioned that once before. I don't know if you know it, but I'll tell you what departments have made the best progress. The barber shop is first. Then comes the Fountain and then comes the Zebra Room. And the room service has gone up about two and a half times.

LARRY: Yes, we are getting that straightened out, aren't we? And we will do better, Mr. Smith, we will do even better than we are doing now.

SMITH: That's right. There is still a lot of room for improvement there. But there's a lot of room for improvement in the King Cole. The King Cole has stayed just the same. (*This seems to jar* LARRY.) What we have got to do is make that better and better every day. You have got to be flexible, Larry, you can't stand still.

LARRY: Yes, I know that all right, I know you have to improve. Here, you just look at this a minute. [He pulls out a notebook of some changes he plans to put into effect. From past experience I would imagine that it concerns some criticisms he has of the service the waiters and waitresses have been giving.]

SMITH: Yes, I will read it. I have got a meeting in five minutes so I'm going to have to go. Now you give that a try and see if it works and then let us know how it comes out. Just give it a fair try and if it doesn't work, we haven't lost anything.

(*We depart.*)

Appendix F

KING COLE: LARRY'S REACTIONS TO OUR PROJECT [1]

I went into the King Cole about 10:30 this morning and talked to Larry about the girls on his day shift with whom I had yet to talk. It turned out that they weren't working this week and that was why they hadn't been up to see me. Larry said he'd start sending up his night crew this evening at 5 P.M. (I have to eat between 5 and 6) but I thanked him and said that Betty, his night headwaitress, had suggested 8 P.M. as the best time so I thought I'd start coming in at night to talk to the girls.

> LARRY: Oh, that shouldn't be necessary. Look, why don't you talk to them in a group? I'll have them meet tonight at 4:30 and you talk to them in a group, all right? That's the way we'll do it then.
>
> LENTZ: No, Larry, no—No thank you, but I think it's best to see them one at a time, if you don't mind.
>
> LARRY (*disappointed*): Well, any way you think best—say Miss Lentz, come on over here, will you? I want to talk with you. I want to show you something.

[He led me to the booth farthest back in the King Cole Room. It is the upper left-hand corner, the one everybody has told me is the last to be used for customers. Here we sat until after 12

---

[1] Interview 502, May 24, 1946. By E. L. H.

noon. Larry shooed away everybody who came near, including Philip who wanted to bring Larry his breakfast. He leaned across the table and talked with greatest earnestness.]

LARRY: Now Miss Lentz, I know you are good friends with Mr. Wiley and you work in Personnel, but your work is different again, isn't that right? You are not responsible for that office like he and Miss Dickson is. That's the way I have it figured out, anyway. Now I know you like Mr. Wiley, so do I like Mr. Wiley, but I am very disappointed in him. VERY disappointed, Miss Lentz, and I'll tell you why. Now I know you are a friend of his but you are an intelligent young lady and everybody likes you. All my girls like you very much, they come to me and tell me that. And I know you will be impartial in your judgments. I will show you the plain facts and I feel very sure, very sure indeed that you will give me your impartial judgments.

Now last week Mr. Smith called us all up to his office. He was sitting there and Mr. Wiley was sitting here (*opposite him*) and Mr. Kraus and I were sitting here. Mr. Smith was upset because he seemed to think we had too many people leaving the King Cole. Maybe he thought I was driving them out, maybe he thinks Uncle Larry isn't doing the right thing down here. Well, now that's all right. If he thinks things aren't going right, this is his hotel and he has the right to ask questions. I don't mind that at all, he was absolutely right to ask questions if he doesn't think I'm doing a good job down here. But Mr. Wiley—(*he paused fumbling for words*) well he just sat there and he never explained the facts of the case.

Now Miss Lentz, you are in personnel work, tell me—isn't it the job of the personnel man to know why people leave? Isn't he supposed to have all the facts? If he doesn't have the facts why doesn't he? And if he does have them, why doesn't he present them when questions are asked? Mr. Smith asked about why people were leaving the King Cole Room and he sat there and never said anything. All the heat came on me. I couldn't explain everything, I didn't have the information at my fingertips. Now understand I know why every employee leaves this room. I know each of my employees by name and I make it my business to understand them and to get their viewpoint and when they leave, I know why they leave. Isn't that the right thing? Shouldn't Mr.

Wiley know that too? You tell me, now should he know that?
LENTZ: You think he should be acquainted with all the facts?
LARRY: You tell me, shouldn't he?
LENTZ: Well, ideally, I think he should, Larry. Of course he would never know the facts so completely as the department head.
LARRY: But I send him the cards. Now I admit June was at fault. She makes the final cards out and I told her to put down either "fired" or "quit" but I never meant to have only one word. I criticized her for that. I corrected June when I came back downstairs, I realize Mr. Wiley is right there, there should be a full reason given for why people leave. I told June that. She should know better. I thought she was more intelligent. But why didn't Mr. Wiley come to tell me that, if we didn't have the cards made out right? Why did he let Mr. Smith jump on me for it? He should have spoken up and said that I was doing it wrong, and I would have fixed it long before that. But he didn't say that, he just let things drift until Mr. Smith called me upstairs. Then I got excited, I admit it, and I couldn't remember who all had left and just what reason was behind it. Don't you think Mr. Wiley should have helped me there? He gets the cards, he should have some idea who left and why.

Now look at this, Miss Lentz. I have figured it all out. I came right down and figured it all out from my memory. I remember each and every employee. I can tell you every incident that happened to them, I know my people. That's my job. I have a memory for such things because I practice remembering things, that's part of my job and I do it. Now I have written down here just exactly who left my department and why.

[Larry placed before me a stenographer's notebook with about three pages of notations. These included the names of captains, busboys, and one waitress who had left the King Cole Room. The captains went back to about 1942. Beside the names he had written the reason why they separated from our service. The way the book was placed, the handwriting was upside down to Larry, but he read it aloud and got each word perfect. He went through the entire list, reading the reason and then giving me a fuller explanation about the case. Several of the people had been transferred to the Zebra Room or to Room Service. Two of the men had left the Tremont and then were brought back, "Saved for the House," Larry said, by Larry. Others left to go into service. About a fourth of them left for drinking on the job. The one waitress was a girl over whom Larry and Mr. Wiley had struggled, and Larry told me the complete story of her last blunder in handling customers. She had "insulted" the owner of a rival *café* and he had been forced to let her go. Among the other names were those of two captains who are still working for us.]

LARRY: I'd like you to interview Slim. He's a new man, he's been here since January now and he's doing all right. I want you to talk to him. I'll send him up today. He can tell you whether I treat him all right or not.

LENTZ: I talked to him, Larry. I talked to Slim yesterday, we had a long interview and both of us enjoyed it, I think.

LARRY: He's a nice fellow, isn't he? Now I try to make it as pleasant as possible for these men, Miss Lentz. We have had an awfully hard time getting captains and we aren't out of the woods yet. But this young man came in here and he didn't know anything about this business. All right, I have told Mr. Smith lots of times, I do not expect to get someone who is perfect. He has said to me, "Oh, if only I could get another Larry down there." I said to him, "No, Mr. Smith, there are many Larrys, you can get one easily. You can get many men much better than Larry." Now that's only true, isn't it? [I shake my head, smiling.] Oh yes, it is true, I know that. But I told Mr. Smith I am only too glad to take a young man and train him. I am not too proud to do that, I will build a man for this room. It is a very hard room, believe me. This is a tough job and it is not surprising that men get discouraged. They take so much from the guests and then they are fed up. All at once they cannot take any more. It's a hard job.

Now I try to make it as easy as possible for these fellows. I said to Slim the other day, "Now you take over the time book and learn that work." But he said, "No, Larry, June and Gens do a good job there, much better than I can do. You let them do it." He doesn't want to do it, see? He prefers that the girls keep on doing this work. So I say, OK, if that's how he wants it, that's all right with me. Isn't that fair? Should I do otherwise, you tell me (*pauses while I just smile sympathetically*).

Now take this night captain. He's been with us now for ten

days. I said to him yesterday, "Sam," I said, "Sam, the vacation is over." I said, "Now I told you just to take it easy and look around and see how things are around here, but starting now I will expect you to take over. Now you are the night manager and you run this room the way you think best. You make your own decisions and I'll back you up. You decide how things should be, within reason of course, and I'll back you up. If you think the stations should rotate, OK, rotate them. If you think they should stay stationary, you make them that way. Anything you do is all right. You are Larry on the night shift. I will let you alone. If I decide to come back and see how things are going, you are still the boss, not me. Is that clear?" Now was that fair, Miss Lentz?

This Sam was a captain in the war. He is a drinking man, Miss Lentz. He drinks outside the Tremont, that I know. But that isn't our business, is it? So long as he doesn't drink here, it isn't our business. He worked his way up to being a captain in this way. Now to be a captain takes intelligence. It takes a leadership and skill in handling men. It takes leadership! Now if he can be a captain and lead men, he can run the King Cole, isn't that right? So I told him he is in charge here, in complete charge, and I expect him to run the room from now on, on the night shift.

We called a meeting last night and I told the girls just that. I said, "Now Sam is the Larry at night from now on." So they all know he is the boss.

All right, now you have heard the whole thing, what do you think? Do I do right? Could I do anything different than that? Mr. Smith thinks something is wrong down here or he wouldn't have asked me to come up there. He has been misinformed, Miss Lentz. There is no favoritism here. I raise my right hand to the sky (raising his hand), I raise it to the very sky. I try to do what is right by all my employees. I treat all my chickens alike, that is my way of doing things. [His fat little face was pale and drawn with anxiety.]

LENTZ: Uh huh. You feel you were on the carpet, upstairs?

LARRY: There is no question of that. I was on the spot, and what did Mr. Wiley do about it? I am very disappointed in that man, Miss Lentz. I did everything I could to help you people when you came in here. You are fine young people and I wanted to help you in every way. You are intelligent but you haven't had the experience I have had in 40 years at this business. Well I know that in 40 years I have not learned what you know now, I know that. I am not a proud man; [I murmur something about us being young and learning a great deal from people like him.] You are a fine girl, we all like you. But Mr. Wiley, oh I am disappointed in that young man. He is a disappointment to me. He is close to Mr. Smith. Mr. Smith gets his information from Mr. Wiley. That's what he has a personnel man for. But why doesn't Mr. Wiley give him the whole story? Why doesn't he tell him, "Now Mr. Smith, Larry has a hard job, but he is trying to do his best?" No he just sat there and Larry had to defend himself. I do not complain, I can defend myself. I do not need defense, but I wonder why the personnel man does not tell all the facts.

LENTZ: You feel he didn't get all the information he should have?

LARRY: What do you think? Now take these two men here, remember them? That one man didn't stay because he didn't get his meals. He said, "Why should I stay here? I can go to the Royal and get the same pay and meals too." Well why did they hire that man? And then we had that fellow who was out on strike. He was on strike, mind you, and he knew when he came on that he would only work a few days till the strike ended. Now you are in Personnel, why don't you get on the phone and check up on these people? Why don't you check their references? You don't do that, do you?

LENTZ: Yes we do, Larry.

LARRY: Not before they come on, though.

LENTZ: Well the thing in your case is, the captains come up begging us for men, so we put them on the job and send letters out at the same time. Sometimes it is a day or so before we get the reply, you see.

LARRY: Why didn't Mr. Wiley tell Mr. Smith that? Why didn't he say, "Mr. Smith, Larry does the best he can, but the need of men is so great, we have to take anything we can get?" No, he didn't say anything.

Do you think that was right? Tell me your honest opinion, what do you think the personnel man should do in a place like this? I think Mr. Wiley and I should work together to figure these things out and if I do anything wrong, he should tell me about it and I should try to fix it up. I don't understand why Mr. Smith should call us together to put me on the carpet that way.

LENTZ: Larry, maybe he didn't mean to put anybody on the carpet. Maybe he just noticed that your turnover was running heavier than say the Zebra Room. Maybe he wondered what handicap the King Cole Room had that the Zebra Room didn't have and therefore wanted to give you a chance to say how we could help you better than we do. Do you think so?

LARRY: They kept saying, "How can we help you?" Why should they be so suspicious? What is there to be suspicious about? If they think something is wrong, why doesn't Mr. Wiley come down to see me about it?

I don't mind, Miss Lentz, I try to do my work just the same. I don't hold things against people. And I don't play favorites, although they seemed to think I did. I'm going to change those stations around here. That's definite. I'm going to rotate them. There will be a lot of hard feelings too, I know that, but my mind is made up.

LENTZ: Is that right? You're going to try that now.

LARRY: Yes, and you see, lots of the girls won't like it, either. That was Sophie's idea. Because 2 percent of the girls don't like the way things are, we have to change them for everybody. Isn't that favoritism? I try to go by the 98 percent. That Sophie—she's been a headache ever since she was transferred in here. She's always griping about something. I've tried to work with her and I'll go on trying, but she is a cross to bear, believe me. She's the one, she went to the union and complained about those stations. She tried to make trouble at that meeting yesterday, too. I called the meeting to tell them that Sam would be the boss of the night shift and she sat in the back of the room and snickered. She really did, she just sat there and snickered and tried to get the other girls' attention, until finally I had to say to her, "Sophie, if you can't stop that snickering I'm going to have to ask you to leave." She is a very difficult person to work with, Miss Lentz.

You know some people are like that. I try to get along with everybody. It is my job to get along with people. I have won many friends in my work here, although that isn't what I set out to do. But I have, I have won friends all over the city. Now if I get along with the public that well, why do they think I can't get along with my help? I like my girls. I like them too much, that's my trouble, I am too easy on them. But some, like that Sophie, they cannot be pleased. No matter what you give them, they want what the other fellow has. Eva too, she was like Sophie, she kept talking about her seniority rights. I said to her, "What seniority rights? You had seniority rights in the Zebra Room, but here you have your job. That's what your seniority means here, your job. How can I put you ahead of the girls who have been here for years? They have their stations and they have built up their trade over a period of years, why should I take that away from them to give it to you? Would that be right?" I can't see it, Miss Lentz, but if they want it that way, I'll change it.

LENTZ: Larry, you mentioned Sophie going to the union and I have been wondering how does the union fit into this picture? Do they get into your hair?

LARRY (*backing away and looking down at his fingers*): Oh no, no I don't complain about them. I have no complaints, I get along with him. (*After a minute or so he changed this.*) Well there you really have favoritism, Miss Lentz. If you want to know who has favoritism, you have it there. Mr. Thor came over here about those stations did you know?

LENTZ: No, I didn't know that.

LARRY: Well, he did. This Sophie went over to Mr. Thor and cried on his shoulder. You see how it is? He has a few who run to him when something irks them and then he listens to their side of the story. I said to him, "Why don't you hold a meeting and see how the rest feel? Go right ahead, call a meeting now, it's okay with me." But no, he doesn't do that. Now, I'll tell you how it is, we are ruled by our employees, Miss Lentz. That's how it is with the unions now. We don't run our business now, the employees run it. I could improve the efficiency of this room a lot. I see many things that should be improved, but with the policies of the management what they are today, I can't do it. I can't do a thing.

LENTZ: They have you stymied, do they? You say the policies of management—

LARRY: I try so hard to do a good job, Miss Lentz. I don't claim to be perfect, but I work hard to have a good room here. If they don't think I do a good job, why don't they put somebody else in here? If they don't like the way I do things, why don't they say what I do wrong? Why do they act so suspicious? What is there to be suspicious of? Everything I do is open and above-board, always. Anybody can come down here and see for themselves, how I run things. Mr. Wiley can come down here, anytime at all. I wish he would, I am disappointed in him, I thought he was going to do this hotel a lot of good. Well, we all make mistakes, don't we? I used to make mistakes, I know that, but I don't make them any more, Miss Lentz. I educated myself not to, I just forced myself to not make those mistakes any more. We all have to learn.

LENTZ: That's right, and it takes a big man to change, doesn't it? We all have to learn, I know I have to, I've got a lot to learn yet.

LARRY: You have come a long way since you came here. Everybody likes you, I wish you could stay here, I like to talk to you. But here, I've talked to you too long, I'm keeping you from your work.

LENTZ: No, it was a pleasure, Larry. I enjoy talking to you and learn a lot that way.

LARRY: Now those night girls, they may not all feel satisfied with things the way they are. We have a couple of gripers on that side. You'll understand that, won't you? You know, nobody can please everybody. There are always a few you can't please.

LENTZ: Sure, I know that. Some are pretty tough nuts to crack.

LARRY: I try to treat all my employees alike Miss Lentz. Some are harder to win around, but I try to develop each and every one. I work over them and try to win them around and most of the time I succeed but it may take a while. How did you get along with the day crew? What can you give me, what can I change to make them happier, you tell me?

LENTZ: I haven't any suggestions to make at this point, Larry. You have some fine people on your staff. I enjoyed talking to them.

LARRY: Aren't they good girls? We get along fine. Now why the night girls don't work together that way, I don't know. These day girls work things out together. If one doesn't feel well or if another one's mother is ill, they work that out between them. Isn't that right? Isn't that how you would do it? I'm pleased that they handle things that way, I'd much rather they did it themselves. Now the night crew—listen, remember that day you had to talk to Miss Dickson? Remember that?

LENTZ: Yes, that was a long time ago, wasn't it?

LARRY: (delighted to find this chink in the armor): Yes, but you had to speak firmly to her, didn't you? You treated her nice just so long and then she thought you were just a softie. You had to be firm with her, isn't that right? You had to let her know you knew what the score was. She has been fine ever since, hasn't she? Sure she has, I have seen that. You handled that very well, she has been just fine ever since, but you had to be firm that once. Now that's how it is with me. I have to speak to these girls firmly. Not to crack a whip or be sharp, but just to let them know that I know what is going on. This night shift is different from the day shift. They aren't used to pulling together, but they will come around too. You see, they will come around if I have time and if they will leave me alone. I ran this place for many years, Miss Lentz, and if I do say so myself, I had it running pretty well, too. If they would only leave me alone, I could get everybody pulling together. Now I've kept you long enough, I'm keeping you from your work. You don't want to sit around talking to an old man like me.

LENTZ: Sure I do, I enjoy it. I like to hear your philosophy, Larry.

LARRY: Well a person develops one in a place like this. I don't let things get me down like I did once. I don't let people upset me, you get that way. You just let it go in one ear and out the other. I'll just go on doing the best I can and trying to cooperate with Mr. Wiley and Mr. Kraus and everybody else around here. That's all any of us can do, isn't it?

LENTZ: That's right. Well good luck to you.

Appendix G

KING COLE: DISCUSSION OF A DEPARTMENTAL STUDY [1]

Present: Wiley, Larry, Sam (night manager), Kraus.

We went into Mr. Kraus's office and sat down. There seemed to be quite an air of tension in the room. Mr. Kraus was talking on the phone and when he finished, he began signing payroll checks.

> KRAUS (*turning to* WILEY): Well you go ahead with the meeting. I'll just listen while I sign these checks and say something when I hear what you are talking about.
>
> WILEY: Well before we start I would like to tell you, Larry, that we found your day crew seems to be quite a contented bunch. They like working there, seem to be working together and helping each other and cooperating and for the time being, at least, they seem to be pretty much satisfied with things as they are.
>
> I think we are here mostly to discuss the problems of the night crew. What we want to do is work together and as a result of this meeting, get stability there. It seems to me that Larry has a pretty good grasp of the problems there. I talked to him the early part of last week and it was pretty obvious to both of us that it is no-body's fault that the night crew of the King Cole has drifted away. I would say offhand there have been about ten night managers since I came here. Well we may look at that and find that there has been a lack of leadership. There have been a number of various

[1] June 11, 1946, 2:30 P.M. Reported by M. W.

opinions for each night manager had different ideas. Not only that, we have had times when there wasn't any night manager and Larry has had to work many long hours which has been too much for any one man. The whole room, then, seemed to drift away. This made Larry's job very difficult [*to* SAM] and it has made your job very difficult since you came, for the room has been very upset. It isn't anyone's fault. We lost the night managers for one reason or another. A couple got drunk on the job; one couldn't find a place to stay, and so forth. But the fact remains that the whole organization seems to have broken down because of this.

Now one of the problems has been that of stations. I have a chart of the way the night crew stations are today and the way the day crew stations are today. There is little similarity. [I passed the charts to Kraus and then to Larry. Kraus glanced at it for a second.]

LARRY (*looking at the chart*): Why that isn't right! (*in an almost surprised way*) The station division of both crews should be the same!

WILEY: I agree with you, Larry, I think you are right. And it seems to me that you have the day crew divided much better. It is my understanding that both crews' divisions were the same at one time, is that correct?

LARRY: Yes; that's right they used to be both the same. And we should have it that way now. (*He passed the charts to* SAM.)

SAM: Yes, I think they should both be like the day crew. But I have got to have more authority. I can't supervise that room unless I have some authority to do it. They just don't pay any attention to me.

WILEY: Yes, you hit on a very important point. The supervisor can't be responsible for the operation of his room unless he has authority to do something about it. The authority comes from two places; it comes from the top and it comes from the employees. You have to be given the authority and I think Larry has the right idea when he wants to turn the night crew over to you. It is quite natural that you answer to Larry and that he will work directly thru you. He will not go to the employees directly but will go to you and you will go to the employees. How does that sound, Larry?

LARRY: Yes, I always said that Sam should be in charge down there. I can't do it all. I would like to be there all the time but it is impossible. I can't work 16 hours a day, so Sam should be in charge.

SAM: Well they have to respect me. They have to know that I'm in charge.

WILEY: That's very good. Because as I said you get your authority from two places. One, Larry gives it to you, and two, you have to have followers in order to be a leader. You have to have the respect of the people who work under you. First thing, of course, is for Larry to announce that you do have the authority. You are in charge of the room, so everyone knows it.

LARRY: I would rather you did that, Mr. Wiley.

WILEY: I will be glad to help you follow up and support you.

KRAUS (interrupting): Now I think you should do that, Larry. You should tell them that you are turning over the night crew to Sam.

WILEY: Yes, I believe that's right. It seems to me that everyone has to know it and that since you are delegating authority, Larry, it is only proper that you make the announcement. That will place Sam in charge of the efficiency, supervision, human relations, and service of the night crew. This places much responsibility on you, Larry, for you must help Sam in all these aspects. You have to work through him at all times and you will have to work very closely with him to see that he gets the support and attains the standards that you want. And it places a lot of responsibility on you, Sam, because you have complete charge of the operation of the room while you are there and your responsibility is much broader than it has been in the past. It means that both of you will have a great deal of responsibility with the employees; and two, realizing that when people speak up they are trying to help you and the King Cole and themselves. And then finally after knowing how the employees feel and considering it in your decisions, there is the responsibility placed on you to lead the group all the time. They must feel that they have a leader. Unfortunately they haven't experienced that enough in the past because as I have said, there was so much turnover among night managers.

LARRY: I have always told them that I wanted them to cooperate. I have asked them to work together and I always want their ideas.

WILEY: Well I didn't mean that in any way as a criticism of

you, Larry. I was merely referring to the fact that since thru no fault of yours we have had so many night managers in that room, it has gotten out of hand as far as the night crew is concerned. Since it is out of hand, it is even a harder job to bring it back in line. As far as cooperation is concerned, I have observed that you can't ask for cooperation and expect to get it unless some of those things that we have been discussing are straightened out. You have to make cooperation easy and then the employees will fall right in line.

KRAUS: Now about that drinking down there. I know it hasn't been going on since you are there, Sam, I'm not saying it's your fault.

LARRY (*interrupting*): No, we haven't had any drinking for the last three or four days, have we? (*To* SAM.)

SAM: No.

KRAUS: Well I think you should watch that. We can't have that. We want a fine dining room and we just can't have waitresses drinking on the job.

SAM: Well they have got to work with me now, then. It can't be like it was the other night where we had a girl go home sick so I asked the swing girl to take the place of the girl who went home. Now there was no other station for her but she did a lot of hollering.

WILEY: Well it seems to me—

KRAUS: What girl?

SAM: Kate. [He must have been wrong, Kate is not a swing girl.]

KRAUS: Well I think she's one of the worst of them all. You should watch her.

WILEY: Well I think if it's your custom in the past to have the swing girl take over that she should understand that. But it seems to me that you should consider two things. First, if you are required to make a change, explain it to the girl.

SAM (*interrupting*): Well, seems to me I have to change those stations in a hurry sometimes. We have large parties come in and I have to move tables around. Now I can't take time to line things up as they should be.

WILEY: No, I didn't mean that. But generally speaking regardless of what the situation or who the supervisor is, it is only right in fairness to the employees to let them know why you have to do something out of the ordinary. Then as soon as possible, get the stations the way you think they should be. You can't go wrong if you always explain just how you see things. And I know that you do. Well, it seems to be getting late.

I'd like to suggest that we consider this a fresh start for the night crew, then, and try to forgive and forget anything that is past. We can consider this a new beginning and start from this point.

KRAUS: Well we all have to get to meetings at three o'clock so I guess we will have to break this up.

WILEY: Well let me see, then, if we have got this straight. We all agree that the stations should be the same for both night and day crews as far as that is concerned. This afternoon at the meeting, Larry, we will place the authority for supervising the night crew with Sam and we will discuss how they want their stations. It looks like we will have pretty much to put it to a vote. Is there anything wrong with that? (*They all agree that this is the fairest way of doing it and we adjourn.*)

INDEX

*This book has been set on the Linotype in 11
and 10 point Janson, leaded 2 points. Chapter
numbers and titles are in 18 point Arrighi
italic. The size of the type page is 25 by 42½
picas.*